THE FIERCE LIGHT

THE
FIERCE
LIGHT

The Battle of the Somme
July - November 1916

PROSE AND POETRY

**Selected and edited
by
Anne Powell**

Palladour Books
Aberporth
1996

ON REVISITING THE SOMME

SILENCE BEFITS ME HERE

Silence befits me here. I am proudly dumb,
Here where my friends are laid in their true rest,
Some in the pride of their full stature, some
In the first days of conscious manhood's zest:

My foot falls tenderly on this rare soil,
That is their dust. O France, were England's gage
The fruitful squiredoms of her patient toil,
Her noble and unparalleled heritage
Of the great globe, or all her sceptres sway
Wherever the eternal ocean runs
All, all were less than this great gift to-day,
She gives you in the dust of her dear sons.
Here I was with them. Silence fits me here,
I am too proud in them to praise or grieve;
Though they to me were friends and very dear,
I must to other battles turn, and leave
These now for ever in a sacred trust -
To God their spirits and to France their dust.

THE FIERCE LIGHT

If I were but a Journalist,
And had a heading every day
In double-column caps, I wist
I, too, could make it pay;

But still for me the shadow lies
Of tragedy. I cannot write
Of these so many Calvaries
As of a pageant fight;

For dead men look me through and through
With their blind eyes, and mutely cry
My name, as I were one they knew
In that red-rimmed July;

Others on new sensation bent
Will wander here, with some glib guide
Insufferably eloquent
Of secrets we would hide -

Hide in this battered crumbling line
Hide in these rude promiscuous graves,
Till one shall make our story shine
In the fierce light it craves.

Major John Ebenezer Stewart, M.C.
8th Battalion, Border Regiment

– 1st JULY 1916 –

FLIGHT-LIEUTENANT CECIL LEWIS, M.C.
Royal Flying Corps

Cecil Lewis joined No. 3 Squadron in the village of La Houssoye shortly after his eighteenth birthday. The Squadron had two flights of Parasols and one flight of Biplanes. Their main function was Artillery Observation (correcting a battery's shooting until it had accurately ranged the target), Photography, and Contact Patrol (aerial liaison between the front line and the battalion and brigade headquarters). Before daylight on 1st July Lewis was out on the first patrol with orders to watch the opening of the attack, co-ordinate the infantry flares, and remain over the lines for two and a half hours.

We climbed away on that cloudless summer morning towards the lines. There was a soft white haze over the ground that the sun's heat would quickly disperse. Soon we were in sight of the salient, and the devastating effect of the week's bombardment could be seen. Square miles of country were ripped and blasted to a pock-marked desolation. Trenches had been obliterated, flattened out, and still, as we watched, the gun fire continued, in a crescendo of intensity. Even in the air, at four thousand feet, above the roar of the engine, the drumming of firing and bursting shells throbbed in our ears...

Now the hurricane bombardment started. Half an hour to go! The whole salient, from Beaumont-Hamel down to the marshes of the Somme, covered to a depth of several hundred yards with the coverlet of a white wool - smoking shell bursts! It was the greatest bombardment of the war, the greatest in the history of the world. The clock hands crept on, the thrumming of the shells took on a higher note. It was now a continuous vibration, as if Wotan, in some paroxysm of rage, were using the hollow world as a drum and under his beat the crust of it was shaking. Nothing could live under that rain of splintering steel. A whole nation was behind it. The earth had been harnessed, the coal and ore mined, the flaming metal run; the workshops had shaped it with care and precision; our womenkind had made fuses, prepared deadly explosives; our engineers had designed machines to fire the product with a maximum of effect; and finally, here, all these vast credits of labour and capital were being blown to smithereens. It was the most effective way of destroying wealth that man had yet devised; but as a means of extermination (roughly one man for every hundred shells), it was primitive and inefficient.

Now the watch in the cockpit, synchronized before leaving the ground, showed a minute to the hour. We were over Thièpval and turned south to watch the mines. As we sailed down above it all, came the final moment. Zero!

At Boisselle the earth heaved and flashed, a tremendous and magnificent column rose up into the sky. There was an ear-splitting roar, drowning all the guns, flinging the machine sideways in the repercussing air. The earthy column rose, higher and higher to almost four thousand feet. There it hung, or seemed to hang, for a moment in the air, like the silhouette of some great cypress tree, then fell away in a widening cone of dust and debris. A moment later came the second mine. Again the roar, the upflung machine, the strange gaunt silhouette invading the sky. Then the dust cleared and we saw the two white eyes of the craters. The barrage had lifted to the second-line trenches, the infantry were over the top, the attack had begun...

– 1st JULY 1916 –

SECOND-LIEUTENANT EDWARD G.D. LIVEING
1st/12th Battalion London Regiment (The Rangers)

Edward Liveing's Battalion was part of 56th Division which had been given the task of carrying out a diversionary attack on the south-west side of the Gommecourt Salient on 1st July. Liveing commanded No. 5 Platoon, and with his men moved up on the evening of 30th June to be in position for zero hour the following morning opposite Nameless Farm.

It was just past 7.30 a.m. The third wave, of which my platoon formed a part, was due to start at 7.30 plus 45 seconds - at the same time as the second wave in my part of the line. The corporal got up, so I realised that the second wave was assembling on the top to go over. The ladders had been smashed or used as stretchers long ago. Scrambling out of a battered part of the trench, I arrived on top, looked down my line of men, swung my rifle forward as a signal, and started off at the prearranged walk.

A continuous hissing noise all around one, like a railway engine letting off steam, signified that the German machine-gunners had become aware of our advance. I nearly trod on a motionless form. It lay in a natural position, but the ashen face and fixed, fearful eyes told me that the man had just fallen. I did not recognise him then... To go back for a minute. The scene that met my eyes as I stood on the parapet of our trench for that one second is almost indescribable. Just in front the ground was pitted by innumerable shell-holes. More holes opened suddenly every now and then. Here and there a few bodies lay about. Farther away, before our front line and in No Man's Land, lay more. In the smoke one could distinguish the second line advancing. One man after another fell down in a seemingly natural manner, and the wave melted away. In the background, where ran the remains of the German lines and wire, there was a mass of smoke, the red of the shrapnel bursting amid it. Amongst it, I saw Captain H. and his men attempting to enter the German front line. The Boches had met them on the parapet with bombs. The whole scene reminded me of battle pictures, at which in earlier years I had gazed with much amazement. Only this scene, though it did not seem more real, was infinitely more terrible. Everything stood still for a second, as a panorama painted with three colours - the white of the smoke, the red of the shrapnel and blood, the green of the grass.

If I had felt nervous before, I did not feel so now, or at any rate not in anything like the same degree. As I advanced, I felt as if I was in a dream, but I had all my wits about me. We had been told to walk. Our boys, however, rushed forward with splendid impetuosity to help their comrades and smash the German resistance in the front line. What happened to our materials for blocking the German communication trench, when we got to our objective, I should not like to think. I kept up a fast walking pace and tried to keep the line together. This was impossible. When we had jumped clear of the remains of our front line trench, my platoon slowly disappeared through the line stretching out. For a long time, however, Sergeant S., Lance-Corporal M., Rifleman D [C.S. Dennison], whom I remember being just in front of me, raising his hand in the air and cheering, and myself kept together. Eventually Lance-Corporal M., was the only one of my platoon left near me, and I shouted out to him, "Let's try and keep together." It was not long, however, before we also parted company. One thing I remember very well about this time, and that was that a hare jumped up and rushed towards and past me through the dry, yellowish grass, its eyes bulging with fear.

We were dropping into a slight valley. The shell-holes were less here, but bodies lay all over the ground, and a terrible groaning arose from all sides. At one time we seemed to be advancing in little groups. I was at the head of one for a moment or two, only to realise shortly afterwards that I was alone.

I came up to the German wire. Here one could hear men shouting to one another and the wounded groaning above the explosions of shells and bombs and the rattle of machine-guns. I found myself with J., an officer of 'C' company, afterwards killed while charging a machine-gun in the open. We looked round to see what our fourth line was doing. My company's fourth line had no leader. Captain W., wounded twice, had fallen into a shell-hole, while Sergeant S. had been killed during the preliminary bombardment. Men were kneeling and firing. I started back to see if I could bring them up, but they were too far away. I made a cup of my mouth and shouted, as J. was shouting. We could not be heard. I turned round again and advanced to a gap in the German wire. There was a pile of our wounded here on the German parapet.

Suddenly I cursed. I had been scalded in the left hip. A shell, I thought, had blown up in a water-logged crump-hole and sprayed me with boiling water. Letting go of my rifle, I dropped forward full length on the ground. My hip began to smart unpleasantly, and I felt a curious warmth stealing down my left leg. I thought it was the boiling water that had scalded me. Certainly my breeches looked as if they were saturated with water. I did not know that they were saturated with blood.

So I lay, waiting with the thought that I might recover my strength (I could barely move) and try to crawl back. There was the greater possibility of death, but there was also the possibility of life. I looked around to see what was happening. In front lay some wounded; on either side of them stakes and shreds of barbed wire twisted into weird contortions by the explosions of our trench-mortar bombs. Beyond this nothing but smoke, interspersed with the red of bursting bombs and shrapnel.

From out of this ghastly chaos crawled a familiar figure. It was that of Sergeant K. bleeding from a wound in the chest. He came crawling towards me.

"Hello, K.," I shouted.

"Are you hit, sir?" he asked.

"Yes, old chap, I am," I replied.

"You had better try and crawl back," he suggested.

"I don't think I can move," I said.

"I'll take off your equipment for you."

He proceeded very gallantly to do this. I could not get to a kneeling position myself, and he had to get hold of me, and bring me to a kneeling position, before undoing my belt and shoulder-straps. We turned round and started crawling back together. I crawled very slowly at first. Little holes opened in the ground on either side of me, and I understood that I was under the fire of a machine-gun. In front bullets were hitting the turf and throwing it four or five feet into the air. Slowly but steadily I crawled on. Sergeant K. and I lost sight of one another. I think that he crawled off to the right and I to the left of a mass of barbed wire entanglements.

I was now confronted by a danger from our own side. I saw a row of several men kneeling on the ground and firing. It is probable that they were trying to pick off German machine-gunners, but it seemed very much as if they would "pot" a few of the returning wounded into the bargain...

I crawled through them. At last I got on my feet and stumbled blindly along.

I fell down into a sunken road with several other wounded, and crawled up over the bank on the other side. The Germans had a machine-gun on that road, and only a few of us got across. Some one faintly called my name behind me. Looking round, I thought I recognised a man of 'C' company. Only a few days later did it come home to me that he was my platoon observer. I had told him to stay with me whatever happened. He had carried out his orders much more faithfully that I had ever meant, for he had come to my assistance, wounded twice in the head himself. He hastened forward to me, but, as I looked round waiting, uncertain quite as to who he was, his rifle clattered on to the ground, and he crumpled up and fell motionless just behind me... Shortly afterwards I sighted the remains of our front line trench and fell into them.

At first I could not make certain as to my whereabouts. Coupled with the fact that my notions in general were becoming somewhat hazy, the trenches themselves were entirely unrecognisable. They were filled with earth, and about half their original depth. I decided, with that quick, almost semi-conscious intuition that comes to one in moments of peril, to proceed to the left (to one coming from the German lines). As I crawled through holes and over mounds I could hear the vicious spitting of machine-gun bullets. They seemed to skim just over my helmet. The trench, opening out a little, began to assume its old outline. I had reached the head of New Woman Street, though at the time I did not know what communication trench it was...

A signaller sat, calmly transmitting messages to Battalion Headquarters. A few bombers were walking along the continuation of the front line...

I asked one of the bombers to see what was wrong with my hip. He started to get out my iodine tube and field dressing. The iodine tube was smashed. I remembered that I had a second one, and we managed to get that out after some time. Shells were coming over so incessantly and close that the bomber advised that we should walk farther down the trench before commencing operations. This done, he opened my breeches and disclosed a small hole in the front of the left hip. It was bleeding fairly freely. He poured in the iodine, and put the bandage round in the best manner possible. We set off down the communication trench again, in company with several bombers, I holding the bandage to my wound. We scrambled up mounds and jumped over craters (rather a painful performance for one wounded in the leg); we halted at times in almost open places, when machine-gun bullets swept unpleasantly near...

After many escapes we reached the Reserve Line, where a military policeman stood at the head of Woman Street... He consigned me to the care of some excellent fellow.

Walking was now becoming exceedingly painful and we proceeded slowly. I choked the groans that would rise to my lips and felt a cold perspiration pouring freely from my face. It was easier to get along by taking hold of the sides of the trench with my hands than by being supported by my guide. A party of bombers or carriers of some description passed us. We stood on one side to let them go by. In those few seconds my wound became decidedly stiffer, and I wondered if I would ever reach the end of the trenches on foot. At length the communication trench passed through a belt of trees, and we found ourselves in Cross Street.

Here was a First Aid Post, and R.A.M.C. men were hard at work. I had known those trenches for a month past, and I had never thought that Cross Street could appear so homelike. Hardly a shell was falling and the immediate din of battle had subsided...

After about five or ten minutes an orderly slit up my breeches.

"The wound's in the front of the hip," I said.

"Yes, but there's a larger wound where the bullets come out, sir." I looked and saw a gaping hole two inches in diameter...

The orderly painted the iodine round both wounds and put on a larger bandage. At this moment R., an officer of 'D' company, came limping into Cross Street.

"Hello, Liveing," he exclaimed, "we had better try and get down to hospital together."

We started in a cavalcade to walk down the remaining trenches into the village...[Hébuterne].

R. led the way, with a man to help him, next came my servant, then two orderlies carrying a stretcher with a terribly wounded Scottish private on it; another orderly and myself brought up the rear - and a very slow one at that!

Loss of blood was beginning to tell, and my progress was getting slower every minute... Down the wide, brick-floored trench we went, past shattered trees and battered cottages, through the rank grass and luxuriant wild flowers, through the rich, unwarlike aroma of the orchard, till we emerged into the village "boulevard".

The orderly held me under the arms till I was put on a wheeled stretcher and hurried along, past the "boulevard pool" with its surrounding elms and willows, and, at the end of the "boulevard", up a street to the left. A short way up this street on the right stood the Advanced Dressing Station - a well-sandbagged house reached through the usual archway and courtyard. A dug-out, supplied with electric light and with an entrance of remarkable sand-bag construction, had been tunnelled out beneath the courtyard. This was being used for operations.

In front of the archway and in the road stood two "padrés" directing the continuous flow of stretchers and walking wounded. They appeared to be doing all the work of organisation, while the R.A.M.C. doctors and surgeons had their hands full with dressings and operations...

Under the superintendence of the R.C. padré, a man whose sympathy and kindness I shall never forget, my stretcher was lifted off the carrier and I was placed in the archway. The padré loosened my bandage and looked at the wound, when he drew in his breath and asked if I was in much pain.

"Not an enormous amount," I answered, but asked for something to drink.

"Are you quite sure it hasn't touched the stomach?" he questioned, looking shrewdly at me...

Shells, high explosive and shrapnel, were coming over every now and then. I kept my helmet well over my head. This also served as a shade from the sun, for it was now about ten o'clock and a sultry day. I was able to obtain a view of events round about fairly easily... Out in the road the R.A.M.C. were dressing and bandaging the ever-increasing flow of wounded. Amongst them a captive German R.A.M.C. man, in green uniform, with a Red Cross round his sleeve, was visible, hard at work. Everything seemed so different from the deadly strife a thousand or so yards away. There, foe was inflicting wounds on foe; here were our men attending to the German wounded and the Germans attending to ours. Both sides were working so hard now to save life. There was a human touch about that scene in the ruined village street which filled one with a sense of mingled sadness and pleasure. Here were both sides united in a common attempt to repair the ravages of war. Humanity had at last asserted itself...

– 1st JULY 1916 –

LIEUTENANT GEOFFREY DEARMER
1st/2nd Battalion (Royal Fusiliers) London Regiment

At 5 a.m. on 1st July Geoffrey Dearmer was with the Battalion in reserve trenches at Hébuterne ready for the attack on Gommecourt. The Battalion Headquarters was in dugouts in Yiddish Street. Battle police were in position at the ends of communication trenches and Prisoners of War guards were ready. All ranks were issued with hot pea soup.

At 7.30 a.m. the assault started. Lines advanced steadily and the enemy opened fire on the trenches but many men from the Battalion reached enemy trenches with comparatively small losses. By 9.30 a.m. the Battalion was engaged in vigorous grenade fighting in Gommecourt Park and was coming under heavy rifle and machine-gun fire. By mid-morning about 80 prisoners had been captured but the supply of bombs taken over in the initial assault was almost exhausted and the men were being forced back from the enemy front line. Another attack was launched but was repelled by a very intense barrage. The Battalion casualties for that day were 12 officers and 241 other ranks killed, wounded or missing.

The following day the Battalion Diary recorded:

"The enemy were seen in Ferret [trench] showing a white flag. With the General's permission M.O.'s of our Battalion and L.R.B. and about 50 men, went down Gommecourt Road with stretchers and got in about 45 wounded, the enemy also leaving their trenches for the same purpose. This truce lasted about an hour and was honourably kept by the enemy, who gave us ten minutes warning to get back to our trenches at its expiration and sent over shells behind us to help us to do so quickly! Some of the wounded lying near the German wire stated that the Germans had come to them in the night and given them coffee."

GOMMECOURT

The wind, which heralded the blackening night,
Swirled in grey mists the sulphur-laden smoke.
From sleep, in sparkling instancy of light,
Crouched batteries like grumbling tigers woke
And stretched their iron symmetry; they hurled
Skyward with roar and boom each pregnant shell
Rumbling on tracks unseen. Such tyrants reign

The sullen masters of a mangled world,
Grim-mothered in a womb of furnaced hell,
Wrought, forged, and hammered for the work of pain.

For six long days the common slayers played,
Till, fitfully, there boomed a heavier king,
Who, couched in leaves and branches deftly laid,
And hid in dappled colour of the spring,
Vaunted tornadoes. Far from that covered lair,
Like hidden snares the sinuous trenches lay
'Mid fields where nodding poppies show their pride.
The tall star-pointed streamers leap and flare,
And turn the night's immensity to day;
Or rockets whistle in their upward ride.

II

The moment comes when thrice-embittered fire
Proclaims the prelude to the great attack.
In ruined heaps, torn saps and tangled wire
And battered parapets loom gaunt and black:
The flashes fade, the steady rattle dies,
A breathless hush brings forth a troubled day,
And men of sinew, knit to charge and stand,
Rise up. But he of words and blinded eyes
Applauds the puppets of his ghastly play,
With easy rhetoric and ready hand.

Unlike those men who waited for the word,
Clean soldiers from a country of the sea;
These were no thong-lashed band or goaded herd
Tricked by the easy speech of tyranny.
All the long week they fought encircling Fate,
While chaos clutched the throat and shuddered past.
As phantoms haunt a child, and softly creep
Round cots, so Death stood sentry at the Gate
And beckoned waiting terror, till at last
He vanished at the hurrying touch of sleep.

The beauty of the Earth seemed doubly sweet
With the stored sacraments the Summer yields -
Grass-sunken kine, and softly-hissing wheat,

Blue-misted flax, and drowsy poppy fields.
But with the vanished day Remembrance came
Vivid with dreams, and sweet with magic song,
Soft haunting echoes of a distant sea
As from another world. A belt of flame
Held the swift past, and made each moment long
With the tense horror of mortality.

That easy lordling of the Universe
Who plotted days that stain the path of time,
For him was happy memory a curse,
And Man a scapegoat for a royal crime.
In lagging moments dearly sacrificed
Men sweated blood before eternity:
In cheerful agony, with jest and mirth,
They shared the bitter solitude of Christ
In a new Garden of Gethsemane,
Gethsemane walled in by crested earth.

They won the greater battle, when each soul
Lay naked to the needless wreck of Mars;
Yet, splendid in perfection, faced the goal
Beyond the sweeping army of the stars.
Necessity foretold that they must die
Mangled and helpless, crippled, maimed and blind,
And cursed with all the sacrilege of war -
To force a nation to retract a lie,
To prove the unchartered honour of Mankind,
To show how strong the silent passions are.

III

The daylight broke and brought the awaited cheer,
And suddenly the land is live with men.
In steady waves the infantry surge near;
The fire, a sweeping curtain, lifts again.
A battle-plane with humming engines swerves,
Gleams like a whirring dragon-fly, and dips,
Plunging cloud-shadowed in a breathless fall
To climb undaunted in far-reaching curves.
And, swaying in the clouds like anchored ships,
Swing grim balloons with eyes that fathom all.

But as the broad-winged battle-planes outsoared
The shell-rocked skies, blue fields of cotton flowers,
When bombs like bolts of thunder leapt and roared,
And mighty moments faded into hours,
The curtain fire redoubled yet again:
The grey defence reversed their swift defeat
And rallied strongly; whilst the attacking waves,
Snared in a trench and severed from the main,
Were driven fighting in a forced retreat
Across the land that gaped with shell-turned graves.

IV

The troubled day sped on in weariness
Till Night drugged Carnage in a drunken swoon.
Jet-black, with spangling stars athwart her dress
And pale in the shafted amber of the moon,
She moved triumphant as a young-eyed queen
In silent dignity: her shadowed face
Scarce veiled by gossamer clouds, that scurrying ran
Breathless in speed the high star-lanes between.
She passed unheeding 'neath the dome of space,
And scorned the petty tragedy of Man.

And one looked upward, and in wonder saw
The vast star-soldiered army of the sky.
Unheard, the needless blasphemy of War
Shrank at that primal splendour sweeping by.
The moon's gold-shadowed craters bathed the ground -
(Pale queen, she hunted in her pathless rise
Lithe blackened raiders that bomb-laden creep)
But now the earth-walled comfort wrapped him round,
And soon in lulled forgetfulness he lies
Where soldiers clasping arms like children sleep.

Sleep held him as a mother holds her child:
Sleep, the soft calm that levels hopes and fears,
Now stilled his brain and scarfed his eyelids wild,
And sped the transient misery of tears,
Until the dawn's sure prophets cleft the night
With opal shafts, and streamers tinged with flame,
Swift merging riot of the turbaned East.

distorted with terror and crying out something I could not in that infernal din understand. I could see nothing ahead of me through the barrage so, as there was no communication trench and the pieces of metal were whizzing round me and the fountains of earth spurting up in front, I turned back to my O.P. which was now being sprinkled with gas shells.

The sun rose higher and higher in the sky, the heat of that scorching summer day grew and grew, but though I was never able to get any coherent picture, the failure of our assault on Serre gradually became obvious. Those three or four hundred yards of rough ground that lay in front of our lines were thickly sprinkled with silver triangles, only a few of which still moved, while the German parapet was bare and still the pounding of our front trenches went on. Then darkness fell and the stories began to come in. They told of appalling casualties of whole battalions reduced to thirty or forty men and I have since read that no British army corps had ever before suffered such losses in a single day. The pick of our young men, the first to volunteer for the war, were dead and on our corps front not a yard of ground had been gained.

And this was not all. During the next few days terrible stories began to come in from the survivors of parties that had got through to the outskirts of Serre. After fifty-six hours spent in shell-holes, sleeping among and even pillowed on their dead comrades, without water, without food, having to defend themselves all the time, a few of the more determined had managed to creep or fight their way back through the German lines to tell their tale. I saw two of them and they looked like men who had been pulled out of a mine after being entombed for a week by an explosion..."

– 1st JULY 1916 –

LIEUTENANT-COLONEL FRANK CROZIER, D.S.O.
9th Battalion Royal Irish Rifles

At 6.45 a.m. the Battalion, part of the 36th (Ulster) Division, assembled on the Hamel-Albert Road, ready for the attack on Thièpval Wood. As part of the second wave, the men were to advance across the Ancre causeways through Thièpval Wood to cross No Man's Land and assault the enemy line. The trenches and strong points in Thièpval Wood were named after Highland places - Gordon Castle, Elgin Avenue, Speyside and Blair Atholl. The 9th Battalion's Commanding Officer, Lieutenant-Colonel Frank Crozier, later wrote an account of the day's fighting.

Suddenly the air is rent with deafening thunder; never has such man-made noise been heard before! The hour has struck! 7.30 a.m. has arrived. The first wave goes over, 'carrying the creeping barrage on its back'. We wait. Instantly the enemy replies, putting down a counter-barrage which misses us by inches. Thanks to the steep slope of Speyside we are immune. That half hour is the worst on record, for thoughts and forebodings; so we sing, but it is difficult to keep in tune or rhythm on account of the noise. At last *our* minute, *our own* minute arrives. I get up from the ground and whistle. The others rise. We move off, with steady pace. As we pass Gordon Castle we pick up coils of wire and iron posts. I feel sure in my innermost thoughts these things will never be carried all the way to the final objective; however, even if they get half way it will be a help. Then I glance to the right through a gap in the trees. I see the 10th Rifles plodding on and then my eyes are riveted on a sight I shall never see again. It is the 32nd Division at its best. I see rows upon rows of British soldiers lying dead, dying or wounded, in no man's land. Here and there I see an officer urging on his followers. Occasionally I can see the hands thrown up and then a body flops to the ground. The bursting shells and smoke make visibility poor, but I see enough to convince me Thièpval village is still held, for it is now 8 a.m. and by 7.45 a.m. it should have fallen to allow of our passage forward on its flank... My upper lip is stiff, my jaws are set. We proceed. Again I look south-ward from a different angle and perceive heaped up masses of British corpses suspended on the German wire in front of the Thièpval stronghold, while live men rush forward in orderly procession to swell the weight of numbers in the spider's web. Will the last available and previously detailed man soon appear to do his futile duty unto death on the altar of sacrifice? We march on - I lose sight of the 10th Rifles and the human corn-stalks, falling before the Reaper. My pace unconsciously quickens, for I am less heavily burdened than the men behind me, and at last I see the light of day through the telescopic-like avenue which has been cut for our approach. We are nearing the fringe of the wood and the old fire trench. Shells burst at the rate of six a minute on this trench junction, for we have been marching above Elgin Avenue and alongside it. My adjutant, [Major Hine] close behind me, tells me I am fifty yards in front of the head of the column. I slacken my pace and they close up to me. 'Now for it,' I say to Hine, 'it's like sitting back for an enormous fence.' My blood is up and I am literally seeing red. Still the shells burst at the head of Elgin, plomp, plomp - it is 'good-bye', I think, as there is no way round. 'This way to eternity' shouts a wag behind. Thirty yards ahead now, still a shell - plomp - a splinter flies past my shoulder, and embeds itself in the leg of a leading man behind. He falls and crawls out of the way, nothing must stop the forward march of the column... I cross the fire trench. The next shell and I should have absolutely synchronised. It does not arrive! 'What's up?' I think. Still once more too far ahead, I wait on the edge of the wood. They close up once more. I double out to see what's up on the right. Bernard, [Colonel, in command of the 10th Battalion Royal Irish Rifles], where is he? Machine-guns open fire on us from Thièpval village; their range is wrong: 'too high', I say to Hine. I survey the situation still; more machine-gun fire: they have lowered their sights: pit, pit, the bullets hit the dry earth all round. The shelling on to the wood edge has ceased. The men emerge. A miracle has happened. 'Now's the chance,' I think to myself, 'they must quicken pace and get diagonally across to the sunken road, disengaging from each other quickly, company by company.' I stand still and erect in the open, while each company passes. To each commander I give the amended order. Men are falling here and there, but the guns previously firing on the edge of the wood are quite silent. Imagine a timed exposure with your camera. The button is pressed, the shutter opens, another press and it again shuts. That is what happened to us. The German shelling ceased for five minutes, we hurried through the gap of mercy, and as Major Woods, bringing up the rear, was just clear of Elgin, the shelling started again. Most of the men were spared for a further few hours of strenuous life that day. Berry is badly wounded, and, with Gold, later finds himself in Germany...

The battalion is now formed up lying down on the road. They are enfiladed from Thièpval village while field guns open on them from the front. They can't stay here. Where is Colonel Bernard? I walk over to find out. I find a few men of the 10th, and attach them to the right of my line. I blow shrill whistle calls and signal the advance. They go on their last journey. 'Bunny', now a captain, comes up to me. He has lost his way. I set him on his path. Later he dies at the head of his company. And what of the dead and wounded? This spirited dash across no man's land, carried out as if on parade, has cost us some fifty dead and seventy disabled. The dead no longer count. War has no use for dead men. With luck they will be buried later; the wounded try to crawl back to our lines. Some are hit again in so doing, but the majority lie out all day, sun-baked, parched, uncared for, often delirious and at any rate in great pain. My immediate duty is to look after the situation and not bother about wounded men. I send a message to brigade and move to my battle headquarters in the wood. It is a deep dug-out which has been allocated to me for my use. It needs to be deep to keep out heavy stuff. The telephone lines are all cut by shell fire. A wrong thing has been done. I find the place full of dead and wounded men. It has been used as a refuge. None of the wounded can walk. There are no stretchers. Most are in agony. They have seen no doctor. Some have been there for days. They have simply been pushed down the steep thirty-feet-deep entrance out of further harm's way and left - perhaps forgotten. As I enter the dugout I am greeted with the most awful cries from these dreadfully wounded men. Their removal is a Herculean task, for it was never intended that the dying and the helpless should have to use the deep stairway. After a time, the last sufferer and the last corpse are removed. Meanwhile I mount the parapet to observe. The attack on the right has come to a standstill; the last detailed man has sacrificed himself on the German wire to the God of War. Thièpval village is masked with a wall of corpses

The adjutant of the 10th tells me Colonel Bernard is no more. The colonel and half his men walked into the barrage of death during the advance. All died behind him as he resolutely faced the edge of the wood in an impossible effort to walk through a wall of raining iron and lead, which had lifted for us that brief five minutes.

All at once there is a shout. Someone seizes a Lewis gun. 'The Germans are on us' goes round like wildfire. I see an advancing crowd of field grey. Fire is opened at six hundred yards range. The men behind the guns have been with Bernard in the shambles. Their nerves are utterly unstrung. The enemy fall like grass before the scythe... I look through my glasses. 'Good heavens,' I shout, 'those men are prisoners surrendering, and some of our own wounded men are escorting them! Cease fire, cease fire, for God's sake,' I command.

The fire ripples on for a time. The target is too good to lose... But I get the upper hand at last - all is now quiet - for a few moments. The tedium of the battle continues.

I hear a rumour about Riflemen retiring on the left and go out to 'stop the rot'. At the corner of Elgin I wait to head them off. Meanwhile I see a German soldier, unarmed, sitting at a newly made shell hole. I ask him if he speaks English. He does. He was once a waiter at Bude in Cornwall. He is fed up with the war, and glad to be where he is. I advise him to move away, or he will not be there long as his countrymen shell that place badly. He thanks me. I offer him a cigarette. His eyes light up. He does not smoke although he takes it. I ask him why. He points to his throat. 'Roach,' I call out, 'any water in your bottle? If so, give this fellow some.' He drinks the bottle dry and is profuse to Roach in his thanks. Might he stay with me he asks! 'You will be safer behind, old cock,' I say. No, he would like to stay! 'Take him to the dugout, Roach,' I say, 'give him some food and let him sleep - he tells me he hasn't slept for ten days on account of the shelling.' The old sailor and the ex-German waiter walk along together, comparing notes and talking of England. Suddenly there is a cloud of smoke, a deafening roar - exit Roach and the unknown German soldier, killed by a German shell.

At that moment a strong rabble of tired, hungry, and thirsty stragglers approach me from the east. I go out to meet them. 'Where are you going?' I ask. One says one thing, one another. They are marched to water reserve, given a drink and hunted back to fight. Another more formidable party cuts across to the south. They mean business. They are damned if they are going to stay, it's all up. A young sprinting subaltern heads them off. They push by him. He draws his revolver and threatens them. They take no notice. He fires. Down drops a British soldier at his feet. The effect is instantaneous. They turn back to the assistance of their comrades in distress. It is now late afternoon. Most of my officers are dead and wounded. I send for twelve more who have been held in reserve, to swell the corpse roll. Other reinforcements arrive only to be thrown into the melting pot for a similar result. The Germans launch an overwhelming counter-attack which proves successful. They win - to suffer later. At 10 p.m. the curtain rings down on hell. The cost? Enormous. I have seventy men left, all told, out of seven hundred.

– 1st JULY 1916 –

CAPTAIN ROWLAND FEILDING, D.S.O.
1st Battalion Coldstream Guards

Rowland Feilding was sent to an Entrenching Battalion at Bois des Tailles, near Bray-sur-Somme, to command the Coldstream Company, in April 1916. He described it as 'A kind of advanced Depot - a stepping-stone to the trenches, where the young officers and soldiers are near enough to the front line to get used to the smell of gunpowder and the noise of shells, before actually joining their battalions.' On 1st July, Feilding was in billets in Corbie, where the officers' mess was a room over an ironmonger's shop, 'with chairs, a big table, a piano and a stuffed heron.' That evening he wrote to his wife:

This has been a great day, as you will have learnt from the newspapers. The battle, for which we have for some months been preparing has begun, and thanks to a newly-made friend, Thornhill [a Major in the Royal Engineers], and his car, I have been able to see a lot of it.

The culmination of our bombardment - that is the infantry attack - took place this morning. It was originally planned for Thursday, but was postponed for forty-eight hours owing to the bad weather, which makes most of the roads, which in this part of France are not cobbled, impassable for heavy transport. When the weather is good the roads are good, and the reverse when it rains. The same rule no doubt applies to the roads on the German side.

The weather, yesterday, had become fine. To-day it was perfect. Between 6.30 and 7.30 a.m. our bombardment was intensified. To give you an idea of what it then became I quote Major Watkins, a Coldstream officer attached to the Staff of the XIII Corps, which is in front of us here. He told me that, on his Corps frontage alone (about 3,000 yards), 42,000 shells were sent over by our artillery in sixty-five minutes, or nearly 650 shells per minute. I hear we have 360 guns on this sector, including 8-inch, 12-inch, and 15-inch howitzers. At 7.30 the infantry went over.

Thornhill called for me between 9 and 9.30. We motored to Bronfay Farm, which is just behind Maricourt, opposite Mametz and Montauban. The battle was then in full swing, and the sight was inspiring and magnificent. From right to left, but particularly opposite the French, where the more rugged character of the country is especially adapted to spectacular effects, the whole horizon seemed to be on fire, the bursting shells blending with the smoke from the burning villages. As I have said before, this is essentially a district of long views. Never was there a field better suited for watching military operations, or for conducting them.

As we looked on, the shells from our heavier guns were screaming over our heads, but still, strange to say, the enemy were not replying behind our front line of the morning.

The wounded - those who could walk - were streaming back, some supported by others; crowds of them. Parties of German prisoners too - I counted over seventy in one group - were being marched under escort to the rear. They were pitiful objects to look upon; some with beards; all unshaven and dirty; some big, some small with spectacles; most with bare heads; a few wounded; all unkempt, dejected, abject, and dazed. Some looked up as they saw us. Most hung their heads and gazed at the ground...

We stayed half an hour or so at Bronfay; then we motored to other parts of the line, passing through Méaulte and Albert, where the statue on the Cathedral is beginning to look very shaky. Here we saw many more wounded, and more German prisoners... Then we came home, stopping at various points along the way to watch the progress of the battle. Our artillery was still busy, and I counted twenty English and French observation balloons up together. Not a single German balloon was to be seen. All had been driven from the sky, for the time being, by our wonderful airmen.

In the evening, once more, Thornhill came with his car, and we went towards the line. The scene had changed. In the morning the weather had been fine and clear. It was still fine, but, owing to the smoke and dust of the battle, there was now a thick haze. The cannonade had, for the time being, died away. With the exception of a little shelling far away to the right, all had become silent as the grave. One could only imagine our men hard at work in the trenches they had captured, converting them to their own use.

The German artillery scarcely replied to our bombardment of the past week, which must have been very exasperating to their infantry. They shelled our front-line trenches and did some damage, but, so far as this part of the line is concerned, they made no effort to silence the artillery or to block the roads. Even when the infantry attack commenced they failed to put up the usual "barrage". Probably, for the first time in the war, our supporting troops, helped by the undulations in the ground, were able to reach their positions without much difficulty.

It is said that the Germans were unprepared for an offensive in this locality; that the last place they expected to be attacked was opposite the point of contact between the French and British armies; - that, in consequence, they had no great concentration of artillery to meet our troops. If so they must be blind. Our preparations have been so immense that any photograph from the air must have revealed them. We have made new railways and new roads. The whole landscape has been altered, to say nothing of the fact that, for weeks past, every valley has been filled with troops, horses, guns, and transport.

We have been continually surprised at the way in which the enemy has allowed our transport to crowd over roads which are within easy reach of his artillery, and under direct observation from his balloons and even the ground observation posts.

I hope and believe our people have got the best of them this time, but do not expect to get much definite news for a few days yet. The wounded I have seen have mostly been hit by machine-guns. Judging from the numerous loaded ambulances I have passed, there must, I fear, be many casualties.

It has been a wonderful day, and my first experience of a battle as a sightseer. I feel rather a beast for having done it in this way, but shall continue to see all I can of it, nevertheless, for the sake of experience, which may be useful later...

– 1st JULY 1916 –

CAPTAIN CLAUDE QUALE LEWIS PENROSE, M.C., AND BAR

Attached 4th Field Survey Company, Royal Garrison Artillery

Claude Penrose had been in the Somme area since August 1915. During the early summer of 1916, when in command of a Survey Section, he was involved in establishing new Survey Posts just behind the front line. Headquarters was at the top of a ridge in a little dell west of Bray. On 1st July he went from Headquarters to the Péronne Post, opposite Mametz. His impressions of the early morning as the battle started were found in his papers after he died of wounds in August 1918; he also wrote a letter home on 10th July describing the day's events and later wrote a poem.

There was something suspended in the atmosphere, besides the great white mist wreath that hung like a halo round the hills as I came down from the Bray-Corbie road soon after dawn. The mist was there most mornings, hesitant, half-rising, then falling - a cloud rather, so that we saw clearly above it, and as clearly below, in the bottom of the valley, while in it we had a scope of 50 yards, if as much. But the other thing that could be discerned almost as clearly by all of us who knew what this day was to bring was the potential thunder, waiting to roll out, amid the uncanny stillness of the early morning - a stillness that could be felt, after the previous week's incessant bombardment, more keenly than the chill of the dawn, as we swung along out of the village and up, on to the Bronfay road. As we turned the corner the first gun spoke; then they started all round us, and something seemed to give way. A kind of quiet content took the place, from that moment, of the strained expectancy in the faces that we saw as we passed. One great roar drowned all lesser sounds. The engine's insistent throb sank to a distant purr; and, as we climbed the last bit of hill to the new railway loop, the 12-inch howitzers behind us, under the east slope of the valley, were firing at their maximum rate, their great low-pitched reports filling the air - stolid, determined beings that seemed to have minds of their own and a sense of direction, as I watched them, over my shoulder, feel up and up for their elevation, stop, fire, recoil, and recuperate majestically, immensely - dignified and relentless...

I stayed until 4 p.m. at the Péronne Post, with Norris [the signaller in charge]. The mist did not lift during the hour's bombardment before the assault, which took place at 7.30 a.m. But almost at the moment of the infantry advance it lifted rapidly, and we could observe the whole thing up to the sky-line, except on the right, towards Montauban, where smoke candles had been used to cover our infantry. They advanced steadily, with heavy shrapnel fire over them, at a walk; and, as they went on, left parties to deal with the dug-outs. In only one place did I see the Germans come out to meet us. There was some very pretty bayonet work there, but that only lasted a few minutes, and by 9 a.m. we were over the sky-line here, and had Montauban by about 10 a.m. The village to the west of this gave more trouble, but we had it by 1 p.m...

ON THE SOMME

Who heard the thunder of the great guns firing?
Who watched the line where the great shells roared?
Who drove the foemen back, and followed his retiring,
When we threw him out of Pommiers to the glory of the Lord?

Englishmen and Scotsmen, in the grey fog of morning
Watched the dim, black clouds that reeked, and strove to break the gloom;
And Irishmen that stood with them, impatient for the warning,
When the thundering around them would cease and give them room -

Room to move forward as the grey mist lifted,
Quietly and swiftly - the white steel bare;
Happy, swift, and quiet, as the fog still drifted,
They moved along the tortured slope and met the foeman there.

Stalwart men and wonderful, brave beyond believing -
Little time to mourn for friends that dropped without a word!
(Wait until the work is done, and then give way to grieving) -
So they hummed the latest rag-time to the glory of the Lord.

All across the No Man's Land, and through the ruined wiring,
Each officer that led them, with a walking-cane for sword,
Cared not a button though the foeman went on firing
While they dribbled over footballs to the glory of the Lord.

And when they brought their captives back, hungry and downhearted,
They called them "Fritz" and slapped their backs, and, all with one accord
They shared with them what food they'd left from when the long day
    started,
And gave them smokes and bully to the glory of the Lord.

– 2nd - 4th JULY 1916 –

SECOND-LIEUTENANT SIEGFRIED SASSOON, M.C.
1st Battalion Royal Welch Fusiliers

On 30th June, Siegfried Sassoon was told that he had been awarded the Military Cross for his part in a raiding party south of Fricourt on 25th May. On the opening day of the Battle of the Somme, in his 'fortunate role of privileged spectator', five hundred yards behind the front trenches, where Sandown Avenue joined Kingston Road Trench, he watched the battle as it developed round the fortress village of Fricourt. The following day he continued his diary comments from the same position.

A quiet night. Fine sunny morning. Nothing happening at present. Fricourt and Rose Trench to be attacked again to-day. Everything all right on rest of XV Corps front...

2.30 p.m. Adjutant just been up here, excited, optimistic and unshaven. Fricourt and Rose Trench have been occupied without resistance (there was no bombardment). Over two thousand prisoners taken by Seventh Division alone. First R.W.F. took over two hundred. Germans have gone back to their second line.

I am lying out in front of our trench in the long grass, basking in sunshine where yesterday morning one couldn't show a finger. The Germans are shelling our new front line. Fricourt is full of British soldiers seeking souvenirs. The place was a ruin before; now it is a dust-heap. Everywhere the news seems good: I only hope it will last.

A gunner Forward Observation Officer just been along with a Hun helmet; says the Huns in Fricourt were cut off and their trenches demolished. Many dead lying about...

Next thing is to hang on to the country we've taken. We move up to-night. Seventh Division has at any rate done all that was asked of it and reached the ground just short of Mametz Wood...

– 3rd JULY 1916 –

Siegfried Sassoon left his 'subterranean sanctuary', Kingston Road Trench at 6.45 a.m., and joined his Battalion at 71 North. They marched two miles to a concentration point between Mametz and Carnoy. In a wide hollow the four units of the Brigade 'piled arms, lay down on the grass, and took their boots off'. Many of the men had been without sleep for two nights and were able to rest in the sun during the day.

I think we move up this evening and probably attack Mametz Wood to-morrow...

Evening falls calm and hazy; an orange sunset, blurred at the last. At 8.45 I'm looking down from the hill, a tangle of long grass and thistles and some small white weed like tiny cow-parsley. The four battalions are in four groups. A murmur of voices comes up - one or two mouth-organs playing - a salvo of our field-guns on the right - and a few droning airplanes overhead. A little smoke drifting from tiny bivouac-fires. At the end of the hollow the road to Mametz (where some captured German guns came along two hours since). Beyond that the bare ground rising to the Bazentin ridge, with seams of our trench-lines and those taken from the enemy - grey-green and chalk-white stripes.

AT CARNOY

Down in the hollow there's the whole Brigade
Camped in four groups: through twilight falling slow
I hear a sound of mouth-organs, ill-played,
And murmur of voices, gruff, confused and low.
Crouched among thistle-tufts I've watched the glow
Of a blurred orange sunset flare and fade;
And I'm content. To-morrow we must go
To take some cursèd Wood... O world God made!

In the evening Sassoon and his Battalion received orders to dig a trench 'somewhere in front of Mametz'. They started off at 9.15 p.m. and, after a delay of over four hours passed through Mametz and went up a long communication-trench towards the front line.

4.30 a.m. Three very badly mangled corpses lying in it: A man, short, plump, with turned-up moustaches, lying face downward and half sideways with one arm flung up as if defending his head, and a bullet through his forehead. A doll-like figure. Another hunched and mangled, twisted and scorched with many days' dark growth on his face, teeth clenched and grinning lips. Came down across the open hillside looking across to Mametz Wood, and out at the end of Bright Alley. Found that the Royal Irish were being bombed and machine-gunned by Bosches in the wood, and had fifteen wounded. A still grey morning; red east; everyone very tired.

12.30 p.m. These dead are terrible and undignified carcases, stiff and contorted. There were thirty of our own laid in two ranks by the

Mametz-Carnoy road, some side by side on their backs with bloody clotted fingers mingled as if they were hand-shaking in the companionship of death. And the stench undefinable. And rags and shreds of blood-stained cloth, bloody boots riddled and torn. This morning the facts were: R.W.F. and Royal Irish were sent up to consolidate trenches close to the south-east end of Mametz Wood and to clear the wood outskirts. The Irish got there and found enemy machine-guns and bombers and snipers in the wood, which is of big old trees. Our A Company went forward to join them, but were sniped on the road, and got into a quarry where they lost four wounded and one killed. The Irish meanwhile had tried to bomb the Bosches in the wood, failed entirely, and suffered sixty casualties... Our guns then chucked a lot of heavy shrapnel over the wood and the Irish got away. The whole thing seems to have been caused by bad staff-work (of the Division). We were out eleven hours and got back to our field about 8.30 a.m. Mametz is as badly smashed as Fricourt. A few skeleton-sheds and one small white fragment of a church-tower, no more than fifteen feet high. Hun communication trenches quite decent. Eight-inch guns firing three hundred yards from our bivouac. Rumour has it that the Seventh Division are to be taken out of the show soon. Not for long, if they are! Great fun these last two days.

9.15 p.m. The Battalion just moving off for the attack on Quadrangle Trench, by Mametz Wood... The attack-scheme was sprung on us very much at the last moment.

C Company can muster only twenty-six men, so we are carrying R.E. stuff. B and D attack. A are in reserve. We attack from Bottom Wood on a six-hundred-yard front...

We struggled up to Mametz and on to Bottom Wood in awful mud. I sat with C Company in a reserve trench till we were sent for (about 2.30 a.m.) to reinforce. This order was cancelled before we got there, but I went on to see what was happening (and got cursed considerably by the Colonel for doing so!). It was beginning to be daylight. I crossed from Bottom Wood, by the way they had attacked, and found our D Company had got there all right, but things seemed in rather a muddle, especially on the right, where B did no good - got lost or machine-gunned - and A had gone up and saved the situation. The companies advanced at 12.45 a.m. after a short bombardment by our guns. They had to cross five hundred yards of open ground and occupy Quadrangle Trench (a half-finished work the Germans were said to be holding lightly). There seems to have been a working-party there digging, but they cleared off without showing fight (except for a little bombing). Our attack was quite unexpected.

When I got there, morning was just getting grey; the trench taken had some wire in front, but was quite shallow and roughly dug. On the right loomed Mametz Wood - in front open country, a Bosche trench about five hundred yards away. Our men were firing a good deal at Bosches they couldn't see, and were rather excited, mostly.

The enemy were bombing up a communication-trench from the wood. The Royal Irish had attacked on our right and failed to get into the enemy trenches (Strip Trench and Wood Trench). We got a bombing-post established on our right where the Quadrangle Trench came to a sudden end. The Germans had fled, leaving their packs, rifles, bombs etc on the edge of the trench...

The Germans had left a lot of shovels, but we were making no use of them. Two tough-looking privates were disputing the ownership of a pair of field glasses, so I pulled out my pistol and urged them, with ferocious objurgations, to chuck all that fooling and dig. I seem to be getting pretty handy with my pistol, I thought, for the conditions in Quadrangle Trench were giving me a sort of angry impetus. In some places it was only a foot deep, and already men were lying wounded and killed by sniping. There were high-booted German bodies, too, and in the blear beginning of daylight they seemed as much the victims of a catastrophe as the men who had attacked them. As I stepped over one of the Germans an impulse made me lift him up from the miserable ditch. Propped against the bank, his blond face was undisfigured, except by the mud which I wiped from his eyes and mouth with my coat sleeve. He'd evidently been killed while digging, for his tunic was knotted loosely about his shoulders. He didn't look to be more than eighteen. Hoisting him a little higher, I thought what a gentle face he had, and remembered that this was the first time I'd ever touched one of our enemies with my hands. Perhaps I had some dim sense of the futility which had put an end to this good-looking youth. Anyhow I hadn't expected the Battle of the Somme to be quite like this...

We began digging the trench deeper, but the men were rather beat. After daylight the enemy sniped a lot from the wood, and we had five men killed and several wounded... I went across from our bombing-post to where Wood Trench ended, as there was a Bosche sniper: the others fired at the parapet, so they didn't see me coming. When I got there I chucked four Mills bombs into their trench and to my surprise fifty or sixty (I counted eighty-five packs left on the firestep) ran away like hell into Mametz Wood. Our Lewis-gun was on them all the way and I think they suffered... We had got the Quadrangle Trench well held by mid-day - no counter-attacks, only a little bombing (and the damned snipers playing hell).

Quadrangle Trench was then the most advanced position held by the XV Corps. The Fourteenth R.W.F. relieved us at 9.30 p.m. and we started back for Heilly (about twelve miles). Coming through Mametz we were heavily shelled. The total casualties of First R.W.F. for the last seven days have been a hundred and thirty, and two officers (only fourteen dead of this lot). We have been very lucky: gained our objective in two attacks (the night one a very chancy affair)...

We took a long time getting back, owing to congestion of artillery in Fricourt; we reached the hill above Bécordel at 1.45. Slept for an hour in the long wet grass, with guns booming and flashing all round in the valley below, and in the glimmer of a misty dawn - cold, with clear stars overhead - the Battalion fell in and marched on to Heilly, which we reached in hot weather about 7.45, all very tired and sleepy. We are in a camp on a sort of marsh by the river Ancre. Not very nice...

A NIGHT ATTACK

The rank stench of those bodies haunts me still,
And I remember things I'd best forget.
For now we've marched to a green, trenchless land
Twelve miles from battering guns: along the grass
Brown lines of tents are hives for snoring men;
Wide, radiant water sways the floating sky
Below dark, shivering trees. And living-clean
Comes back with thoughts of home and hours of sleep.

To-night I smell the battle; miles away
Gun-thunder leaps and thuds along the ridge;
The spouting shells dig pits in fields of death,
And wounded men are moaning in the woods.
If any friend be there whom I have loved,
God speed him safe to England with a gash.

It's sundown in the camp; some youngster laughs,
Lifting his mug and drinking health to all
Who come unscathed from that unpitying waste.
(Terror and ruin lurk behind his gaze.)
Another sits with tranquil, musing face,
Puffing his pipe and dreaming of the girl

Whose last scrawled letter lies upon his knee.
The sunlight falls, low-ruddy from the west,
Upon their heads; last week they might have died;
And now they stretch their limbs in tired content.

One says "The bloody Bosche has got the knock;
And soon they'll crumple up and chuck their games.
We've got the beggars on the run at last!"
    Then I remembered someone that I'd seen
Dead in a squalid, miserable ditch,
Heedless of toiling feet that trod him down.
He was a Prussian with a decent face,
Young, fresh, and pleasant, so I dare to say.
No doubt he loathed the war and longed for peace,
And cursed our souls because we'd killed his friends.

One night he yawned along a half-dug trench
Midnight; and then the British guns began
With heavy shrapnel bursting low, and "hows"
Whistling to cut the wire with blinding din.
    He didn't move; the digging still went on;
Men stooped and shovelled; someone gave a grunt,
And moaned and died with agony in the sludge.
Then the long hiss of shells lifted and stopped.

He stared into the gloom; a rocket curved,
And rifles rattled angrily on the left
Down by the wood, and there was noise of bombs.
    Then the damned English loomed in scrambling haste
Out of the dark and struggled through the wire,
And there were shouts and curses; someone screamed
And men began to blunder down the trench
Without their rifles. It was time to go:
He grabbed his coat; stood up, gulping some bread;
Then clutched his head and fell.
                            I found him there
In the gray morning when the place was held.
His face was in the mud; one arm flung out
As when he crumpled up; his sturdy legs
Were bent beneath his trunk; heels to the sky.

– 4th - 10th JULY 1916 –

CAPTAIN ROWLAND FEILDING, D.S.O.
1st Battalion Coldstream Guards

Captain Rowland Feilding wrote to his wife from billets in Corbie over the next few days.

In the afternoon, with three of my officers, I visited the battlefield of three days ago. We lorry-jumped to Bray. From there we struck off on foot along the road towards Mametz, one of the villages captured by our troops. The fighting was still continuing in front, but in the ruined village itself all was quiet. Our heavy guns were firing over our heads as we walked, but beyond an occasional shrapnel burst in the distance, the German artillery was quiescent, and we were able to explore the surface in safety.

After proceeding three and a half miles we reached what last Saturday was the British front line. It was very battered, and scarcely recognizable as a fire-trench. Then we crossed No Man's Land, where we found infantry at work, salving equipment, and collecting the dead. Of the latter I counted a hundred in one group - a pitiful sight!

Then we came to what had been the German wire entanglements. Here our guns had certainly done their work well. The wire was completely demolished. Not one square yard had escaped the shells. Then we came to the German fire-trench. It is difficult to understand how any living creature could have survived such bombardment. The trench was entirely wrecked, and so flattened that it could have given little if any cover at the end...

Fifty yards beyond the German fire-trench was their Support trench, and about the same distance further on, their Reserve trench. Both had suffered severely. The ground is strewn with unexploded shells of ours, mostly of heavy calibre.

I went into some of the dug-outs, but, as I had neither electric torch nor matches, it was not possible to see much. They are of varying depths, some being quite 20 feet below the surface, and are well made, the sides and roofs being strongly supported by timber. I saw only one that had more than one entrance, and it was on fire.

After exploring these remains of the German trenches we went on into Mametz village where living man was represented by the Salvage folk and a few infantry making their way up to the new front line.

Scarcely a wall stands, and of the trees nothing remains but mangled twisted stumps. The ruins present an appalling and most gruesome picture of the havoc of war, seen fresh, which no pen or picture can describe. You must see it, and smell it, and hear the sounds, to understand. It brings a sort of sickening feeling to me even now, though I consider myself hardened to such sights.

To give an idea of the long period of time through which the line at this point has remained stationary, I may say that in No Man's Land I saw two skeletons, one in German uniform, and the other in the long since discarded red infantry breeches of the French.

– 5th JULY 1916 –

About midday yesterday a thunderstorm burst out, and for a couple of hours there was torrential rain, so that the roads became like rivers. Thornhill and I motored to Bronfay Farm, and from there struck out on foot to our old front line. This brought us to the right of where I had been the day before.

The experience was practically a repetition of what I have described to you; the sordid scenes the same. The scaling ladders used by our troops to climb out of the trenches at the moment of assault were still in position - most suggestive to the imagination! The dead in many cases still lay where they had fallen. Less than a mile along the valley a furious fight was going on around Fricourt and Fricourt Wood. On our right the French were hard at it, and continued so throughout the night. For the time, I have seen enough of battlefields. I am "fed up" as a sightseer.

On 6th July Rowland Feilding rejoined the Entrenching Battalion in the Bois des Tailles. Two days later he visited Fricourt, which the British had occupied on 2nd July. The Church and all the houses were ruins; only fragments of walls remained. It rained heavily almost continuously for over twelve hours.

– 8th JULY 1916 –

As you enter the village from this side you pass the cemetery. The tombstones - practically all - have been shattered and scattered broadcast. Scarcely a grave could be recognised by its nearest and dearest, save through its position. In one case, near the roadside, a shell has fallen upon one of those elaborate and rather pretentious family vaults so much in vogue in France, pulverizing the great black granite slab which covered it, and exposing the coffin shelves below....

The wounded were being carried back in streams, all covered from head to foot with the mud in which they had been fighting, slimy and glistening like seals. It looks more and more as if Hell cannot be much worse than what our infantry is going through at the present moment.

I mentioned to a machine-gun officer, whom I met, that I might be going on leave in a day or two, and should like a souvenir from Fricourt. Said he, "I think I can help you then," and took me to a place his men had just discovered. I have seen many dug-outs, but this beat them all. It might almost be described as an underground house, where instead of going upstairs you went down, by one flight after another, to the different stories. There were three floors, the deepest being 60 feet or more from the door by which I entered. The entrance hall - so to speak - was the brick cellar of a former house. There were two entrances, one of which, however, could only be recognized from the inside, since the doorway had been blown in. The other door, by which we entered, had been partly closed by a shell, a hole being left just big enough to crawl through on hands and knees.

The German occupants had evidently abandoned the place in a hurry, in the fear - entirely justified - that they might be buried alive if they stayed there. They had left everything behind. The floors were littered with every kind of thing, from heavy trench mortar bombs to grenades the size of an egg, and from steel helmets to underclothing. Many rifles hung from the wooden walls of the first flight of stairs. The nooks and corners of the rooms were occupied by sleeping-bunks, and from one of these I picked up the French Alphabet de Mademoiselle Lili, par "un papa", delightfully illustrated, which I will send home to the children...

One meets nowadays on the roads many wagons returning from the direction of the line, loaded with "swab" equipment. The troops of the new army wear pieces of cloth of different colours to distinguish their Divisions and Brigades. A battalion - I think of Royal Fusiliers - which I saw marching up, fresh and clean and full of life and vigour, a day or two before July 1st, had pieces of pink flannel over their haversacks, displayed in such a way as to be recognizable in battle by our aeroplanes.

A few days later I passed a wagonload of salved equipment returning from the line. It was interleaved with the same pink flannel, now no longer fluttering gaily, but sodden and bedraggled, and caked with sticky clay.

– 10th JULY 1916, Bois des Tailles. –

Yesterday I went and explored the line of trenches captured this week between Mametz and Fricourt. It is one of the most mined sections of the whole of our front. For a length of 800 yards a practically continuous line of huge craters, some 50 feet deep at least, occupies the full width of No Man's Land from the British to the German parapet. Most of these contain water, which in some cases is red with blood, even to-day, a week after the battle.

The contrast between the two front trenches is remarkable. Though the line has remained stationary so long, ours gives the impression of a temporary halting-place; the German of a permanent defence. The effect of the suicidal German practice of having deep dug-outs in their front line is illustrated here, for most contain dead, who never could have fought, but must have been killed like rats in their holes. The havoc of our bombardment is wonderful, and greatly in excess of that done to our own trenches by the enemy artillery.

Many French dead - skeletons now - still lie unburied in No Man's Land, dating from the period before our troops took over this part of the line. I saw some even between the German fire and support trenches, which, one would have thought, the enemy would have buried for the sake of their own comfort, if for no other reason...

– 10th - 11th JULY 1916 –

PRIVATE DAVID JONES

15th (1st London Welsh) Battalion Royal Welch Fusiliers

During the bitter fighting for Mametz Wood the 38th (Welsh) Division was principally involved. There had been a number of unsuccessful attempts to dislodge the German defenders, and a further assault was planned for the early morning of 10th July. Private David Jones was with the 15th Battalion Royal Welch Fusiliers; they were in position in Bunny Trench, Mametz Wood at 2.15 a.m. and two hours later were in attack formation between Queen's Nullah and White Trench. Jones was wounded in the leg during the fighting.

You stumble on a bunch of six with Sergeant Quilter getting
them out again to the proper interval, and when the chemical
thick air dispels you see briefly and with great clearness what
kind of a show this is.

The gentle slopes are green to remind you
of South English places, only far wider and flatter spread and
grooved and harrowed criss-cross whitely and the disturbed
subsoil heaped up albescent.

Across upon this undulated board of verdure chequered
bright
when you look to left and right
small, drab, bundled pawns severally make effort
moved in tenuous line
and if you looked behind - the next wave came slowly, as successive surfs creep in to dissipate on flat shore;
and to your front, stretched long laterally,
and receded deeply,
the dark wood.

And now the gradient runs more flatly toward the separate
scared saplings, where they make fringe for the interior thicket
and you take notice.
    There between the thinning uprights
at the margin
straggle tangled oak and flayed sheeny beech-bole, and fragile
birch whose silver queenery is draggled and ungraced

and June shoots lopt
and fresh stalks bled
      runs the Jerry trench.
And cork-screw stapled trip-wire
to snare among the briars
and iron warp with bramble weft
with meadow-sweet and lady-smock
for a fair camouflage.

Mr. Jenkins half-inclined his head to them - he walked just
barely in advance of his platoon and immediately to the left of
Private Ball.

  He makes the conventional sign
and there is the deeply inward effort of spent men who would
make response for him,
and take it at the double.
He sinks on one knee
and now on the other,
his upper body tilts in rigid inclination
this way and back;
weighted lanyard runs out to full tether,
      swings like a pendulum
      and the clock run down.
Lurched over, jerked iron saucer over tilted brow,
clampt unkindly over lip and chin
nor no ventaille to this darkening
    and masked face lifts to grope the air
and so disconsolate;
enfeebled fingering at a paltry strap -
buckle holds,
holds him blind against the morning.
  Then stretch still where weeds pattern the chalk predella
- where it rises to his wire[17] - and Sergeant T. Quilter takes
over.

* * * * *

Now you looked about you for what next to do, or you fired
blindly among the trees and ventured a little further inward;
but already, diagonally to your front, they were coming back
in ones and twos.

You wished you could see people you knew better than the
'C' Company man on your right or the bloke from 'A' on your
left, there were certainly a few of No. 8, but not a soul of
your own - which ever way.

No mess-mates at call in cool interior aisles, where the
light came muted, filtered from high up traceries, varied a re-
fracted lozenge-play on pale cheeks turned; on the bowels of
Sergeant Quilter,
and across feet that hasted
and awkward for anxiety,
             and behind your hurrying
you could hear his tripod's clank[21] nearer than just now.
But where four spreading beeches stood in line and the ground
shelved away about splayed-out roots to afford them cover
Dawes and Diamond Phelps
and the man from Rotherhithe
with five more from 'D', and two H.Q. details, and two from
some other unit altogether.

And next to Diamond, and newly dead the lance-jack from
No. 5, and three besides, distinguished only in their variant
mutilation.

* * * * *

And to Private Ball it came as if a rigid beam of great weight
flailed about his calves, caught from behind by ballista-baulk
let fly or aft-beam slewed to clout gunnel-walker
below below below.
When golden vanities make about,[40]
             you've got no legs to stand on.
He thought it disproportionate in its violence considering
the fragility of us.
The warm fluid percolates between his toes and his left boot
fills, as when you tread in a puddle - he crawled away in the
opposite direction.

It's difficult with the weight of the rifle.
Leave it - under the oak.
Leave it for a salvage-bloke
let it lie bruised for a monument
dispense the authenticated fragments to the faithful.

* * * * *

Slung so, it swings its full weight. With you going blindly on
all paws, it slews its whole length, to hang at your bowed neck
like the Mariner's white oblation.

    You drag past the four bright stones at the turn of Wood
Support.

It is not to be broken on the brown stone under the gracious
tree.

    It is not to be hidden under your failing body.

    Slung so, it troubles your painful crawling like a fugitive's
irons.

The trees are very high in the wan signal-beam, for whose slow
gyration their wounded boughs seem as malignant limbs,
manoeuvring for advantage.

    The trees of the wood beware each other
                and under each a man sitting;
their seemly faces as carved in a sardonyx stone; as undiademed
princes turn their gracious profiles in a hidden seal, so did
these appear, under the changing light.

* * * * *

At the gate of the wood you try a last adjustment, but slung
so, it's an impediment, it's of detriment to your hopes, you
had best be rid of it - the sagging webbing and all and what's
left of your two fifty - but it were wise to hold on to your
mask.

You're clumsy in your feebleness, you implicate your tin-hat
rim with the slack sling of it.

    Let it lie for the dews to rust it, or ought you to decently
cover the working parts.

    Its dark barrel, where you leave it under the oak, reflects
the solemn star that rises urgently from Cliff Trench.

    It's a beautiful doll for us
it's the Last Reputable Arm.

    But leave it - under the oak.
leave it for a Cook's tourist to the Devastated Areas and crawl
as far as you can and wait for the bearers.[45]

See Appendix A for explanatory notes.

– 10th - 11th JULY 1916 –

CAPTAIN LLEWELYN WYN GRIFFITH

15th (1st London Welsh) Battalion Royal Welch Fusiliers

Llewelyn Wyn Griffith was a Staff Captain at Brigade Headquarters, a dug-out on the high ground at Pommiers Redoubt, when the attack on Mametz Wood opened at dawn on 10th July. At 7 a.m. he received a message from Brigadier-General H.J. Evans, saying that the Brigade Major had been wounded and Griffith was to join him in the Wood at once. Two of Griffith's brothers were in the 15th Battalion at the time; one serving as a Bombardier and the other, Watcyn, a Private, was a runner.

I passed through two barrages before I reached the Wood, one aimed at the body, and the other at the mind. The enemy was shelling the approach from the South with some determination, but I was fortunate enough to escape injury and to pass on to an ordeal ever greater. Men of my old battalion were lying dead on the ground in great profusion. They wore a yellow badge on their sleeves, and without this distinguishing mark, it would have been impossible to recognize the remains of many of them. I felt that I had run away.

Before the Division had attempted to capture Mametz Wood, it was known that the under-growth in it was so dense that it was all but impossible to move through it. Through the middle of the Wood a narrow ride ran to a communication trench leading to the German main Second Line of defence in front of Bazentin, a strong trench system permitting of a quick reinforcement of the garrison of the Wood. With equal facility, the Wood could be evacuated by the enemy and shelled, as it was not part of the trench system.

My first acquaintance with the stubborn nature of the undergrowth came when I attempted to leave the main ride to escape a heavy shelling. I could not push a way through it, and I had to return to the ride. Years of neglect had turned the Wood into a formidable barrier, a mile deep. Heavy shelling of the Southern end had beaten down some of the young growth, but it had also thrown trees and large branches into a barricade. Equipment, ammunition, rolls of barbed wire, tins of food, gas-helmets and rifles were lying about everywhere. There were more corpses than men, but there were worse sights than corpses. Limbs and mutilated trunks, here and there a detached head, forming splashes of red against the green leaves, and, as in advertisement of the horror of our way of life and death, and of our crucifixion of

45

youth, one tree held in its branches a leg, with its torn flesh hanging down over a spray of leaf.

Each bursting shell reverberated in a roll of thunder echoing through the Wood, and the acid fumes lingered between the trees. The sun was shining strongly overhead, unseen by us, but felt in its effort to pierce through the curtain of leaves. After passing through that charnel house at the southern end, with its sickly air of corruption, the smell of fresh earth and of crushed bark grew into complete domination, as clean to the senses as the other was foul...

I reached a cross-ride in the Wood where four lanes broadened into a confused patch of destruction. Fallen trees, shell holes, a hurriedly dug trench beginning and ending in an uncertain manner, abandoned rifles, broken branches with their sagging leaves, an unopened box of ammunition, sandbags half-filled with bombs, a derelict machine-gun propping up the head of an immobile figure in uniform, with a belt of ammunition drooping from the breech into a pile of red-stained earth - this is the livery of War. Shells were falling, over and short, near and wide, to show that somewhere over the hill a gunner was playing the part of blind fate for all who walked past this well-marked spot. Here, in the struggle between bursting iron and growing timber, iron had triumphed and trampled over an uneven circle some forty yards in diameter. Against the surrounding wall of thick greenery, the earth showed red and fresh, lit by the clean sunlight, and the splintered tree-trunks shone with a damp whiteness, but the green curtains beyond could conceal nothing of greater horror than the disorder revealed in this clearing...

Near the edge I saw a group of officers. The Brigadier was talking to one of his battalion commanders, and Taylor, the Signals officer, was arguing with the Intelligence officer about the position on the map of two German machine-guns. The map itself was a sign of the shrinking of our world into a small compass: a sheet of foolscap paper bearing nothing but a large scale plan of Mametz Wood, with capital letters to identify its many corners, was chart enough for our adventure this day.

'What has happened to the Brigadier?' I asked Taylor. 'Why is his arm in a sling?'

'Shrapnel,' he answered. 'He got hit as he was coming up to the Wood, but he got the doctor to dress it for him. He says it doesn't hurt him, but I expect it will before the day is over.'

'Did you see the Brigade Major... was he badly hit?'

'Shrapnel in the leg - his gammy leg. The stretcher-bearers took him away, cursing everybody and damning his luck. Seems to me he doesn't know luck when he sees it. You'll have to get down to it now.'

'Yes. Tell me what has happened so far.'

'You never saw such a mess. Nobody knows where anybody is, the other brigades are still here - what's left of them - all mixed up.'

'Are your lines holding? Are you through to anybody?'

'Devil a soul,' answered Taylor. 'As soon as I mend a line the Boche breaks it. You can't keep a line up with that barrage across the bottom of the Wood. There's an artillery F.O.O. just behind you, in that shell hole; I don't know what the devil he's doing up here - he can't see twenty yards in front of him, and all his lines are gone. He might as well be in Cardiff.'

As soon as the battalion commander had gone I joined the Brigadier.

'Is this the Brigade Headquarters?' I asked.

'It is,' he replied. 'It's an unhealthy place, but we've got to be somewhere where we can be found by night as well as by day. Get your notebook and take down the position of affairs at the moment. We have been sent here to take over the line and to make secure against counter-attacks. There are four battalions of our brigade, and what is left of four other battalions. We are holding an irregular line about three hundred yards from the end of the Wood, bending back towards the West. The units are very mixed up, and I've just come back from trying to give them their boundaries. They are all straightening themselves out and digging in, but the undergrowth is so dense that it will be some hours before they are in their proper places.'

'Are we supposed to attack and clear the Wood?'

'No. Orders last night were to take over the line. I've told the battalion commanders to reconnoitre and to push out where they can. We don't know whether the enemy is holding the far end in any great strength.'

'If we have to attack later on, how do you propose to do it?'

'By surprise,' answered the General. 'With the bayonet only. That's the only way to get through the Wood. If our artillery will keep quiet, we can do it. Here's my map - make a summary of what I've told you. It took me hours to get round our line.'

Runners came from the battalions giving news of progress in consolidation, and reporting that the enemy was in considerable strength on the Northern edge, with plenty of machine-guns. I sat down on a fallen tree-trunk and made a report of the situation, read it over to the General, and went in search of a runner to take it to the Division. Taylor was standing by a large shell hole, talking to his signallers.

'How can I get this to the Division?' I asked.

'Give it to me: that's my job. I've got a telephone down at Queen's

Nullah, and if a runner can get out of the Wood and through the barrage, the message gets through.'

'Are the runners getting through?'

'Some don't, and some of those that do don't get back... Don't give me any messages that are not absolutely essential and urgent. I'm getting short of men - seven down already this morning. I don't know what it will be like when the Boche wakes up. He's got us taped here. Look at those cross-rides - did you ever see such a butcher's shop?'

At this moment a signaller orderly came up to deliver a message. I opened it, glanced through it, and took it to the General. His face hardened as he read it. The Divisional Commander informed us that the enemy's trenches in front of Bazentin were being shelled, and that it was quite impossible that he had any strong force in Mametz Wood. The brigade was to attack and occupy the Northern and Western edges of the Wood at the earliest possible moment. Indeed, the Corps Commander strongly impressed the importance of clearing the Wood without delay.

While we were digesting this order, and drafting new orders to the battalions, a Staff Officer came up to join us. His red and black arm-band showed that he came from Army Headquarters, and he spoke with all the prestige native to a traveller from distant lands who had penetrated to within a few hundred yards of the enemy. He brought orders that we were to carry out an attack upon the two edges of the Wood. The Brigadier listened to him with the patience of an older man coldly assessing the enthusiasm of youth. When the Staff Officer had finished, the General spoke.

'I've just had orders from the Division to attack and clear the rest of the Wood, and to do it at once. The defence is incomplete, the units are disorganized, and I did not propose to attack until we were in a better position. My patrols report that the Northern edge is strongly held. I haven't a fresh battalion, and no one can say what is the strength of any unit.'

'What do you propose to do?' asked the Staff Officer.

'My intention is to take the remainder of the Wood by surprise, with the bayonet if possible; no artillery bombardment to tell him that we are coming. I want a bombardment of the main German second line when we have taken our objective, to break up any counter-attack. Do you know anything about the artillery programme?'

'No, I do not. Are you in communication with the Division or with any of the artillery groups?'

'No, except by runner, and that takes a long time. I'm issuing orders to the battalions to get ready to advance quietly at three o'clock, and

I'm sending a copy of the order to the Division; if you are going back will you get in touch with them as soon as possible and tell them that I don't want a barrage?'

The Staff Officer left us, and we worked at the orders for the battalions. The enemy was shelling the Wood, searching it, as the gunners say, and there were intermittent bursts of machine-gun fire, with an occasional uneven and untidy rush of rifle fire. On our right a few bombs burst in a flat, cracking thud. At a quarter to three, while we were waiting for the hour, a sudden storm of shells passed over our heads, bursting in the Wood some two hundred yards ahead of us.

'Good God,' said the General. 'That's our artillery putting a barrage right on top of our battalion! How can we stop this? Send a runner down at once... send two or three by different routes... write the message down.'

Three men went off with the message, each by a different way, with orders to get to Queen's Nullah somehow or other. Our barrage had roused the enemy, and from every direction shells were falling in the Wood; behind us a devilish storm of noise showed that a heavy price must be paid for every attempt to leave the Wood.

The Brigadier sat on a tree-trunk, head on hand, to all appearances neither seeing nor hearing the shells.

'This is the end of everything... sheer stupidity. I wonder if there is an order that never reached me... but that Staff Officer ought to have known the artillery programme for the day. And if there is another order, they ought not to have put down that barrage until they got my acknowledgement. How can we attack after our own barrage has ploughed its way through us? What good can a barrage do in a wood like this?'

At twenty past three our own artillery was still pouring shells into the wood. None of the runners had returned. Taylor sent three more to try to rescue us from this double fire, but ten minutes later we were left with no worse burden than the enemy's shelling. Reports came through from the battalions that we had suffered severely. As the afternoon drew out into the evening, we nibbled away here and there with fluctuating fortune, but at the approach of night the enemy reinforced his line and kept us from the edge while he pounded away with his artillery.

It was nearing dusk when Taylor came up to me.

'I want to have a word with you,' he said, drawing me away. 'I've got bad news for you...'

'What's happened to my young brother... is he hit?'

'You know the last message you sent out to try to stop the barrage...

well, he was one of the runners that took it. He hasn't come back... He
got his message through all right, and on his way back through the
barrage he was hit. His mate was wounded by the shell that killed your
brother... he told another runner to tell us.'

'My God... he's lying out there now, Taylor!'

'No, old man... he's gone.'

'Yes... yes, he's gone.'

'I'm sorry... I had to send him, you know.'

'Yes, of course... you had to. I can't leave this place... I suppose
there's no doubt about his being killed?'

'None - he's out of it all now.'

So I had sent him to his death, bearing a message from my own
hand, in an endeavour to save other men's brothers; three thoughts that
followed one another in unending sequence, a wheel revolving within
my brain, expanding until it touched the boundaries of knowing and
feeling. They did not gain in truth from repetition, nor did they reach
the understanding. The swirl of mist refused to move.

Within the unclouded portion of my being a host of small things
took their place on the stage, drawing their share of attention, and
passing on. More orders to draft, situation reports to send out,
demands for more bombs, enemy trench-mortars to be shelled into
silence, machine-guns wanted by everybody. The General put his hand
on my shoulder. It began to grow dark. An order came from the
Division to say that we would be relieved that night by a brigade from
another Division, and that on completion of the relief we were to
return to our bivouacs. More orders to the battalions. The wheel was
still revolving, while the procession of mere events moved without a
break.

I walked towards the large shell hole that served as a shelter for the
signallers, carrying in my hand a sheaf of messages for delivery. From
the background of bursting shells came a whistle, deepening into a
menace, and I flung myself on my face. I remembered a momentary
flash of regret that I was still two yards from the protection of that
shell hole. A black noise covered everything. When my eyes opened I
was lying on my back, further away from the hole. I got up on my
hands and knees and crawled to the signallers, still clutching the
crumpled messages, and spoke to them. There was no answer. The rim
of another large shell hole nearly touched their shelter, and the three
signallers were huddled together, dead, killed by the concussion, for
there was no mark of a wound.

The wheel came to rest, and I do not remember much of what
happened afterwards...

THE SONG IS THEIRS

Mametz Wood, 1916

A knave in borrowed clothes this Spring across the sea,
trust it not... look there is murder here
grey behind a thorn, snare in the willow's curve
and rusty barb in the ragwort's yellow ranks.

My flesh is quick tonight : I had forgotten fear.
Love stripped me naked.

Hark to the drumbeats... this Drummer
hath he report I fled his parade?
Make room for me, this odour calls me
sharp to kill all fragrance.

    I have said Farewell my love.

This man, is he dead?
I had forgotten death cold hunger fury
torment and toil, leaden drag of limb
fumes of the pit grey lids and red-rimmed eyes
Fear set this face to stone
     Make room for me
     I have dallied enough.

Remembering now that I have left love
tenderness, kind touch of flesh far
in another land far in another time,
Remembering now all beauty gone
as a dream goes
     Turn back delight
     Reach not to me
This land a pockmarked harridan
brownskinned furrowed with debauchery
flaunting a raddled face greystreaked
gaunt, each empty eye a crater
where a lust burnt through

This Summer morn a mockery

Remembering this also
I have known mountains gold under the sun

I have trodden scree to bare a fern
mounted crest to meet dawn over sea
and this I know
I shall not die before her eyes
a man. A memory a legend that was life.
No more, no more.

Limbs strangely bent to mock the hurry of a start
a hand pointing the way... turn not,
evil athwart the path.
They blacken in the sun, scatter of a storm now past.

A sentinel walks unseen before this wood,
flame where his footsteps fall and cloud.
He sleeps not. The acres of the sky
burn bright and a lark publishes freedom
in a land of slaves, but lo!
what butchery within this wood,
rending of flesh and red limbs crucified
on a tree?
              Is there no end to murdering of man
be he Christ or ploughman? No.
Is death a joy to hold?
These words betray.

Eyes countering mine smoulder and shine not,
say they this of me?
I am dead to all I knew before.
Is there no end to this vast continent of day?
No end but night.

Ride the great stallions of dismay
along the veins of other men?
Silence that moaning boy
let him not cry again in the dark
he hath no hurt but fear.
And in this glade hearken
answer stand to your names.

They answer not,
Their names are dead as they.

This tree stained red
the leaves were green
now pale as we,
rust not of steel
upon this green

We have borne enough:
Let them be buried in their market-place.

– 13th JULY 1916 –

LIEUTENANT CYRIL WILLIAM WINTERBOTHAM
'C' Company 1st/5th Battalion Gloucestershire Regiment

The Battalion was in trenches at Hébuterne from 4th to 8th July and 13th to 16th July; during this time Cyril Winterbotham wrote the poem 'The Cross of Wood'. Between 13th and 16th the Battalion was ordered to raid enemy trenches but the two attempts were driven back by rifle fire and bombs; on 14th the Hébuterne trenches came under heavy enemy bombardment.

THE CROSS OF WOOD

God be with you and us who go our way
And leave you dead upon the ground you won;
For you at last the long fatigue is done,
The hard march ended, you have rest to-day.

You were our friends, with you we watched the dawn
Gleam through the rain of the long winter night,
With you we laboured till the morning light
Broke on the village, shell-destroyed and torn.

Not now for you the glorious return
To steep Strand valleys, to the Severn leas
By Tewkesbury and Gloucester, or the trees
Of Cheltenham under high Cotswold stern.

For you no medals such as others wear -
A cross of bronze for those approved brave -
To you is given, above a shallow grave,
The Wooden Cross that marks you resting there.

Rest you content, more honourable far
Than all the Orders is the Cross of Wood,
The symbol of self-sacrifice that stood
Bearing the God whose brethren you are.

– 14th JULY 1916 –

RIFLEMAN GILES EYRE

2nd Battalion Kings Royal Rifle Corps

Giles Eyre was a member of a bombing party, lent to the Leicestershire Battalions of the 110th Brigade. They were to lead the attack on Bazentin-le-Petit Wood with orders to open the way to the railway track crossing the wood. The bombardment of the German front line commenced at 2 a.m. on 14th July.

This terrific bombardment had extended along the whole line from Pozières, over the Bazentin ridges and beyond. My mind could not grasp the magnitude of the effort, or the countless tons of lethal steel that were being flung, like a monster hosepipe vomiting a stream of water, at the hapless enemy. Minute after minute the noise increased until our ear-drums hammered like mad, and the quivering air, laden with the acrid tang of explosives, became difficult to breathe. My heart was thumping heavily, rapidly. My pulses beat quicker and even our own trenches shook and quivered and rocked about at the shock of this tremendous burst of fire. One's being shrunk back appalled at this display of ferocious destructive might. I could sense the thoughts of those around me as if this wave of blasting sound had destroyed the material world and bestowed on me telepathic powers. Most of the men were gripped by unplumbed horror, and yet at the same time uplifted to the extent that space and time ceased to have any meaning. We were living in a world where flames, pandemonium and death held undisputed sway and our living bodies were as nothing. It is impossible to clothe the scene in adequate terms...

The tumult increased constantly as more and heavier guns came into action, and we stood there on that trench parapet dazed and hypnotized by the spectacle of that raging, all-devouring storm of shells all around us...

At length we felt a touch, and turning round found our Officer gesturing at us to get down. We stepped down in the trench. He shouted at us, as the din rendered ordinary speech impossible, and pointed at his wrist-watch.

"It is nearly four! The bombardment will stop at four and we will get over. Get ready to move!"

The moment was at hand. I gave a last look at my arms, jerked a round up the breech of my rifle, pulled tight the straps of my bombing apron, made quite sure that the pins of my bombs would pull out easily and pinned my respirator on my chest at the ready. The others were similarly engaged. One last pull at my water-bottle, my mouth felt hot and dry, a flicker of steel as we fixed our bayonets and we stood ready. The men in the trench were scrambling on the fire-steps, a few of the Leicesters came up behind us carrying loose Mills bombs in canvas buckets and the Lewis-gun team lined up. Everyone tense with excitement waited for the fateful minute that would send us tearing out into the open and towards our fate.

The guns with a last soul-blasting sound increased their rate of fire and hurled a final, awful thundering blast of shell at the heaps of heaving earth in front of us and then, as if hurled into oblivion by some unknown force, suddenly ceased.

The instant of profound silence was more impressive than all the noise our ears had been subjected to. It was gripping, staggering, awesome. I heard the piping of a lark and then the shrill blasting of whistles here and there as with a roaring cheer the lines of the attacking infantry crossed the parapets and swarmed towards the wrecked German line.

At the same time, with another terrific surge of sound, the guns, having lengthened their ranges, hurled their massed loads of death into and beyond the wood, with rending crashes.

I found myself moving at a loping run beside my two chums, dodging round shell-holes and the usual muck and rubbish of no-man's-land, and all about me in the growing light lines of men moving forward with their bayoneted rifles at the high port. We moved forward in perfect safety for the first fifty yards or so and then a sputtering tac-tac-tac began to break out from the German line. By some super-human miracle its survivors were getting some machine-guns into action.

"Come on, Eyre!" yelled O'Donnell, "move faster, let's get into them before they start properly!" and with a wild shout we forged forward with a rush.

The growing light showed things plainer. Here and there men stumbled and fell as the machine-guns took their toll, but on the whole the attack reached the trench with very slight loss and no hold up.

Trench? There was none. Only a few holes and a flattened, humped and hummocky ditch. A few tattered, bloody and dusty horrors sprang up, hands held high. Half-buried bundles in grey uniforms sprawled about here and there. We jumped in a sort of shallow ditch filled with dead bodies and a wrecked machine-gun and lay down getting our breath back. The trench had been won without a struggle.

"Come on, men, forward," yelled our Sub., waving his stick. Out of the corner of my eye I could see the line of Leicester men rise again and vault over towards the next trench by the road and the wood beyond.

As we rose again, however, we realized that the Hun defence was coming into action. A wave of intense machine-gun fire broke out and bullets began to drone. At the same moment German shrapnel started bursting over our heads unpleasantly.

Once more with a high shrill cheer the straggling wave of men hurled itself forward, to be met by a blast of fire. Unfortunates were pitching forward at every step, and flopping down like empty sacks, writhing, twisting and moaning. The ground here was a mass of holes and dead men, sand-bags and scattered, blasted bushes and wood.

"Down," cried Rodwell as a blaze of machine-gun fire plopped in front of us, sending up spurts of earth in all directions, together with the buzzing wh-a-ng of ricochetting slugs.

"Oh, my Gawd!" cried a voice behind me in stricken, dazed tones, and one of the men carrying a Mills box crumpled and fell, bumping into me and pitching heavily down, his helmet spinning off, tinkling and rattling.

"Christ! move on," I yelled frenziedly.

Crash! Crash! O'Donnell slung a couple of bombs, rose and ran forward. We scotched him up quickly and then, hurling another flight of grenades, we slithered down within a few yards of the trench, with a machine-gun spluttering and roaring close in front. Trr-trr-trr spoke the Lewis behind us as, with a last rush, we flung ourselves over the obstacle. Blam! snapped a pistol-shot close to me, and then I found myself standing over a writhing German on the ground. I had pinned him with my bayonet! Crashes and shots, shouts and scurry all round me. The Subaltern yelling like mad - a confused splatter of machine-guns, rifle-shots, running men, cries, groans, the slam of shrapnel howling and whistling, faint cheers - and the road in front of me. We have gained the position and the wood is before us.

We re-group ourselves pantingly. The Subaltern is still with us. The Lance-Corporal has disappeared. Two men and the Lewis gun get in beside us. No trace of the party with the bombs. Probably somewhere behind us. Groups of men are lining the trench and more are crowding in all the time. Lewis guns and German machine-guns are plopping and spluttering everywhere. Farther to our left the Huns have put down an artillery screen, and their shells are screeching and bursting. Here they are treating us to a heavy dose of shrapnel. Wounded Huns and some of our boys are moaning and staggering in near us. There is a tang and sour reek of all battle smells about us. Dead men, hideously mangled, are now being revealed to our eyes by the rising sun, lighting the ground in its rays and chasing the shadows.

The wood looms menacingly before us, just a clump of interlaced foliage and broken, scarred stumps, with the enemy lurking within it. A slight pause to regain our scattered wits and then, glancing round, the officer waves us onward.

We inch forward warily and get ready to make another rush.

"Over by that shell-hole," yells Rodwell, pointing to the spot about twenty yards ahead. We gather ourselves together and then make a dash for it.

Tac-tac-tac-tack! splutters a gun at us as we run. It misses us and down we go into the shell-hole - just the three of us and the Subaltern. The Lewis gunners have hung back and are firing over our heads, to keep the Huns down.

The Hun gun is slap in front of us, somewhere in the bushes at the edge of the trees, another twenty yards onward.

"Sling some grenades and rush it," cries the officer as the Lewis ceases fire. "Our gunners are about to follow us!"

"Over she goes, boys!" yells Rodwell and, half standing, hurls a grenade. We follow suit, and as they burst we yell like devils out of hell and rush. Crashing through the bushes we just catch sight of a couple of scuttling grey figures and reach the gun. It's lying over lop-sided, a Boche, covered in blood, twitching and swaying drunkenly over it. Another flat on his back in the complete abandon of death with knees drawn up and arms outflung. We poke about with our bayonets. A caved-in dug-out entrance, hidden by leaves and fallen branches, a limb of a tree blocking our path forwards and a pain-laden voice: "Englishman, mercy!"

I look by the gun. A young German with white, scared face and holding one hand up feebly is half lying, half leaning by the dug-out, with Rodwell standing over him with his bayonet.

"All right, Fritz," I hear him. "Get up and beat back there, quick!" The scared boy gets up feebly, blood dripping from shoulder and useless arm, and with a wild glance scrambles away in the direction of our lines.

"Come on, men, get forward, don't stop!" orders the officer.

The Lewis-gun team, three men now, crashes through. Sounds of battle all over the place. The dull thud, thud of grenades, the rat-tat-tat of machine-guns and the sharp crack of scattered rifle-shots come to us from all sides. The Leicesters are attacking the line of the wood on our left, but seem to be hung up, for all of a sudden a wave of rapid fire breaks out from them. We move forward again now, but very carefully, and plunge into the tangle of trees and scrub. We inch on, grenades in hands, crawling on hands and knees, stopping at every few paces. Rodwell is on my left and Don on my right-hand side, the Subaltern just behind me, and farther back the Lewis gun, its men alert and ready to cover us with a blast of fire. Crash! A German stick-grenade bursts just beyond us.

"There are the swine!" yells out O'Donnell, and heaves over a bomb.

The Lewis opens fire quickly and we make another rush, only to crash against a barrier of barbed wire stretched and tangled between the trees.

"To the left," yells the Sub., and we swerve round rapidly as another burst of fire crashes out from in front of us. Somehow we get over the wire, our clothes tearing and the barbs scratching and pulling at our bodies and equipment, and we run slap-bang into another gun just behind. Germans jump up and come at us. For a moment there is a flurry of figures, half-seen, hazy faces loom in front of me. I push forward my rifle and let go, working the bolt automatically, and then, as I empty my magazine, slash forward with my bayonet. I glimpse O'Donnell flailing about with clubbed rifle, I hear the short, sharp bark of the Subaltern's pistol and suddenly trip over the gun and fall headlong over a struggling and kicking German, who tries to make a grab at me. Oh, my God, as I go down I hear the stutter of another gun close by, and a rushing, whizzing sound of bullets, and then some more shattering crashes and Rodwell's high cry: "That's for you, you bastards!"

Short, sharp bursts of fire and a crowd of the Leicesters break through.

I pick myself up. The Boche is moving slowly, snorting and wheezing feebly. He is done for all right. We are in a small glade with broken trees and a barricade of branches and bays before us. The splutter of machine-guns all about us. This wood is stiff with them! O'Donnell is in rags, blackened and grimed and in an excited state, gesturing wildly. "Come on after them, we are near that bloody railway line!" he yells, brandishing his rifle. The Lewis gun has come up, and the Leicesters are moving on our left and behind us. The noise is terrific, a blend of crashes, bursts and occasionally falling branches and huge bits of trees. We are now drunk with it all and have become utterly reckless. With cries and whoops we dash on again, breaking through wire and obstacles. There's more open space here and we can see the railway line winding like a snake through the trees with a line of sandbags and tree branches flung down just beyond, from which the Boche is firing away. The ground is absolutely a confusion of pits, holes, ditches, broken gear and God knows how many dead men.

But by now we are only concerned with getting to that railway line, and are deaf and blind to all else.

"Have you any more bombs, Eyre?" howls Don. "I have run out of mine!"

"No!" I hoot back. "I've only one!"

"Where is the carrying party?" asks the Subaltern, glancing back. But those fellows have either got wiped out or lost all touch with us. "Here you are, use these!" cries Rodwell, flourishing German stick-bombs in his hands.

Plenty of these are lying about, so we grab them, stick them on our equipment belts by their hooks and prepare to make our last plunge forward.

Bang! Bang! Bang! Our artillery slams again beyond the railway line, and with a last rush we forge ahead, running and zigzagging like mad under a terrific hail of machine-gun-fire, scramble on to the twisted and broken rails and sleepers and start slinging grenades as fast as we can over the barricade. We have reached our objective! The Leicesters begin to arrive in small groups and line the barricade, firing over and through the interstices and gaps. Lewis guns begin to chatter, gradually the Boche fire dies down, and we look about us.

"Where's the officer?" cried Rodwell.

A minute ago he was near me; now, as I look back, I see him waving from the ground a few yards away.

"Looks as if he is hit," I cry, and dash back to him.

"It's quite all right," he says as I come up. "Get back to your post. I am hit in the knee."

"All right, sir, you are in the open," I reply, grabbing him by the arm. "Get up with us, there's more shelter." And, leaning on me, I get him up next to Don, rip his putties and trousers and smack a bandage on. He has a slug in the leg, does not bleed much.

"Thank you," he gasps. "I'll be all right. How are things going on?"

"All right, as far as we can judge," I reply. "The enemy has retired back!"

"There will be another battalion coming through to us now," he goes on, "and then you men will be able to get back."

Things have quietened down for the minute here. Farther on our fellows are working through the wood. I carefully raise my head over the parapet of the barricade. A welter of tumbled bags and shell-holes, a bit of a clearing and more thick woods beyond. Crowds of dead Germans, some wounded moaning in the open, between our line and the wood, waving arms feebly. We can't help them, though, until the attack goes farther, and the enemy is flung back.

"Well, I wish the next lot would hurry up," says Rodwell wearily. "It's been a tough job all right!"

Bang! Whan-ngg! Crash! Crash! Crump! a perfect tornado of high explosive and shrapnel shells falls hissing and bursting round our breast-work. Geysers of earth hurtle skyward, tree branches and leaves shower down, crashing and bumping. A curtain of black smoke momentarily hides the sun.

Tac-tac-tac-tack! A heavy bout of Boche machine-gun fire lashes out madly at us from the wood, its bunches of bullets hiss, whizz and plop all over the place.

We cower down as best as we can to dodge the deluge of fire the enemy is hurling at us.

"Down under cover!" yells hoarsely an officer's voice farther down. "Get ready and load your magazines!" There's a rattle of rifle-bolts, men become tense with expectation.

"By all that's holy," grates out O'Donnell pantingly, "Fritz is going to counter-attack us!"

Another wave of heavy gun-fire falls like a curtain behind us, crashing down amongst the trees and into the road beyond, trying to bar the way to the advancing lines of British infantry, and then the counter-attack burst on us like a thunderbolt.

The Boche machine-guns blaze away furiously for some instants and then, from the depths of the wood, there emerges a surging mob of big, hefty-looking Huns, yelling like the souls of the damned and rushing forward with fixed bayonets.

"Stand-to! Rapid fire!" the commands hurtle down our line, and we jump up, pumping lead into the assaulting Boches. The Lewis guns are blazing away madly. We work our bolts frantically. The Germans go down in heaps in that confined space, but the assault reaches our barricade.

We are chucking bombs frantically. Men are going down. Huns appear, scrambling over the obstacle and jumping in amongst us. Now it becomes a hand-to-hand mêlée. Faces and huge grey uniforms appear before me through the eddies of smoke. I strike out and lunge. Ti-ng goes my steel helmet, I reel, stumble and fall amongst a heap of writhing figures. For an awful instant that seems a lifetime I look up with wide, terrified eyes at a gigantic, steel-helmeted, red-faced Hun plunging at me with a bayonet. The thought flashes through my numbed brain: "This is the end," and I await the stroke that will send me to oblivion with terror-sickened soul, when there is a flurry, a figure hurls itself like a battering-ram at the Hun. A terrible yell goes up and my assailant disappears in a shower of blood and crashes down against the sand-bags, tearing at his stomach, with heels drumming and kicking at me. There's a wild scramble all round. I jump up, grab my rifle and lay about me blindly, madly. Men fall, rise, come at me, melt away. A pistol snaps in my face, I hear a gasp beside me and down goes the khaki-clad figure of my saviour. Some more confused struggling, O'Donnell's voice hooting like a banshee, a rush of khaki figures, which suddenly appear from nowhere, roaring and stabbing at the Huns. I find myself on top of the barricade, yelling inanely, amid a roar of Lewis-gun fire, smoke, explosions, while the survivors of the counter-attack run off, falling and stumbling to the shelter of the trees, leaving a trail of dead and mangled, moaning figures behind them in the open.

The air is trembling with the burst of British shells falling amongst the trees screening the Huns. A roaring cheer goes up behind me. We've beaten the counter-attack! But at what a cost! Our position is heaped with mounds of slain and quivering, wailing wounded. I come back to reality and stagger about, looking for my chums.

New troops are constantly coming up in groups and sections, jumping over us and plunging beyond into the wood, from whence comes a clatter and stutter of machine-guns and the dull thuds of bomb explosions. Everything seems unreal - just like a dream. Streams of prisoners are being collected and sent off under escorts. Big, hefty-looking Prussian Guards, Jaegers, men from the Lehr Regiment, quite a hotch-potch of various units mixed together. The Boche must have scraped together all the men he could lay hands on and flung them recklessly into action in a desperate attempt to hold up our advance. Most of them, although grimed and blackened by battle, bloodshot of eye, tattered and torn, look well set up, nothing like the figures of fun of the comic papers. They have fought hard and well, and the tale that they must be driven into action at the pistol point is just moonshine.

O'Donnell sidles up, the light of battle still glinting in his eye, his bayonet all spattered and streaked with blood, steel helmet at the back of his head and his clothing tattered, and rent and covered with chalk, mud and brick dust.

"By the powers, Eyre," he gasps, "it's been a tearing, raging time." And then, looking round: "Where's Rod?"

I come to with a start. The last glimpse I had of Rodwell was in the flurry of the attack. We begin looking round. Shells are still bursting fitfully, but the Boche curtain of fire has ended. Having failed with the counter-attack it looks as if they are content to concentrate on the defence. A furious cannonade has broken away on our left flank on the ridge covering Martinpuich, and also on the right, where they are attacking Bazentin from the other side. No trace of Rodwell amongst the men lining the barricade and busy putting themselves to rights. The cries of the wounded rising on all sides are pitiful and heartrending; this slaughter-house is beyond description. The Leicesters have been cut to ribbons and the survivors of our attacking waves now lining the railway are but a pitiful reminder of that unfortunate battalion. Stretcher-bearers are busily tending the wounded, who, when possible, are scrambling back as fast as they can into the conquered woodland behind us, and to safety and care beyond.

And then we find Rodwell lying amongst a confused pile of dead men, mostly Huns, at the point where I had been overwhelmed and flung down.

"Oh, pitiful Mother of Sorrows!" cries O'Donnell in a cracked, stricken voice, running forward and dropping down. "Here he is!"

Suddenly I recollect that furious, lunging figure that had crashed out of nowhere at the crucial moment when the Boche was about to stick me. It had been my poor, brave pal who had snatched me from the very maw of death - and had paid the price for me!

We two, stricken with sudden, searing sorrow, bent over him. He was still alive, breathing stertorously, with eyes closed. An awful bloody wound on the side of his face just below his left temple gaped, blackened and scorched, and blood was seeping and spurting out every time he breathed.

Tenderly I wiped his forehead with hastily damped rag, while O'Donnell, shaking like a leaf, fumbled for his first-aid bundle, kept in the special pocket on the front hem of his tunic. At our touch poor old Rod's eyelids fluttered and his eyes opened, and he gazed up at us with dawning recognition, struggled to speak, spluttering painfully and expelling blood.

"All right, Rod, boy," I cried encouragingly, "keep quiet and we'll have you out of here in a jiffy!"

"Don't move me!" he gasped with an effort, his voice choked with the blood welling into his mouth. "I - am - done for! Ow! Give me water!" And he rolled his head helplessly in pain.

O'Donnell lifted his head gently, while I unfastened my water-bottle and put it to his lips. He swallowed greedily for an instant and then, feebly: "Lay my head down - everything - is - spinning!" he muttered thickly. "Good-bye, Don - Eyre - It - had to be - I always knew it. Oh, God! My head!"

"Pull yourself together, Rod," I cried wildly. "We'll bandage you and get you away; you'll be all right." But as I gazed at his poor shattered face I knew all would be in vain. Our poor old chum had been shot at point-blank range by a pistol. The bullet must have ploughed through his left cheek-bone, for as O'Donnell and I essayed to apply the field dressing we saw with horror that it had broken the cheek-bone, made a horrible cavity of red, mangled flesh, with gouts of blood seeping up, and had carried away part of his ear. Only his vitality had kept him alive at all. He spoke painfully once more: "Look after - yourselves - boys - and try to bury me - decently -!" A tremor shook him, his head lolled back - his eyes rolled. He muttered incoherently: "Slaughter - the Old Corps -" and suddenly stiffened and then went limp, while we two grief-stricken, heedless of the war, of battle, the burst of shells, or the wails of the stricken men around us, watched the great soul of our pal wing its way free to soar to realms beyond our ken. I stood thus petrified, grasping the hand of the pal that had saved me from oblivion and in so doing had forfeited his own life, full of purpose and promise. O'Donnell was mute, filled with the sense of our loss, and we two, who had learned to look on death unmoved, bowed down and wept, while round us the din of conflict waxed louder as the Boche began to plaster shells again on the railway line.

"Come on, Don," I cried at length, realizing our position. "Empty his pockets. We can do no more."

"By Christ!" he answered in a low, fierce voice. "We can't leave him to be trampled and heaved about like an old sack. Come on, Eyre, let's try to cover him up."

We lifted the poor body and painfully we carried him to a shell-hole below and close to the barricade of bags and wood and there we laid him, painfully scooping earth and debris over him, until at last we covered his poor remains up, and then we stuck a rifle over the improvised grave with a hastily scribbled line on a bit of white bandage O'Donnell produced, and wrote on, with indelible pencil: "Rfn. Rodwell, D.C.M. - 2nd K.R.R.C. - lies here - Ave!" And then, our task over, we busied ourselves aiding the pitiful, broken wreckage of men we could get at.

– 15th JULY 1916 –

CAPTAIN GRAHAM SETON HUTCHISON, D.S.O., M.C.

33rd Battalion Machine-Gun Corps

Graham Seton Hutchison, commanding a machine gun company, waited in a valley about 800 yards west of High Wood. His company was in support behind the Glasgow Highlanders, who with the 16th King's Royal Rifle Corps were to lead the assault on the wood. By 8.30 a.m. on 15th July the men were in position lying in the long grass. Graham Seton Hutchison was awarded the Military Cross for his part in the action.

My eyes swept the valley - long lines of men, officers at their head in the half-crouching attitude which modern tactics dictate, resembling suppliants rather than the vanguard of a great offensive, were moving forward over three miles of front. As the attackers rose, white bursts of shrapnel appeared among the trees and thinly across the ridge towards Martinpuich.

For a moment the scene remained as if an Aldershot manoeuvre. Two, three, possibly four seconds later an inferno of rifle and machine-gun fire broke from the edge of High Wood, from high up in its trees, and from all along the ridge to the village. The line staggered. Men fell forward limply and quietly. The hiss and crack of bullets filled the air and skimmed the long grasses. The Highlanders and Riflemen increased their pace to a jog-trot. Those in reserve clove to the ground more closely.

I, looking across the valley to my left flank, could see the men of the 1st Queen's passing up the slope to Martinpuich. Suddenly they wavered and a few of the foremost attempted to cross some obstacles in the grass. They were awkwardly lifting their legs over a low wire entanglement. Some two hundred men, their Commander at their head, had been brought to a standstill at this point. A scythe seemed to cut their feet from under them, and the line crumpled and fell, stricken by machine-gun fire. Those in support wavered, then turned to fly. There was no shred of cover and they fell in their tracks as rabbits fall at a shooting battue.

Up the slope before me, the line of attack had been thinned now to a few men, who from time to time raised themselves and bounded forwards with leaps and rushes. I could see men in the trees taking deliberate aim down upon those who still continued to fight, or who in their scores lay dead and wounded on the hill-side.

My orders were to move forward in close support of the advancing waves of Infantry. I called to my Company, and section by section in rushes we were prepared to move forward. As we rose to our feet a hail of machine-gun bullets picked here an individual man, there two or three, and swept past us. I raised a rifle to the trees and took deliberate aim, observing my target crash through the foliage into the undergrowth beneath. On my right, an officer commanding a section had perished and all his men, with the exception of one who came running towards me, the whole of the front of his face shot away. On my left two other sections had been killed almost to a man, and I could see the tripods of the guns with legs waving in the air, and ammunition boxes scattered among the dead.

With my runner, a young Scot, I crept forward among the dead and wounded who wailed piteously, and came to one of my guns mounted for action, its team lying dead beside it. I seized the rear leg of the tripod and dragged the gun some yards back to where a little cover enabled me to load the belt through the feed-block. To the south of the wood Germans could be seen, silhouetted against the skyline, moving forward. I fired at them and watched them fall, chuckling with joy at the technical efficiency of the machine. Then I turned the gun, and, as with a hose in a garden, sprayed the tree-tops with lead.

The attack of the Rifles and Highlanders had failed; and of my own Company but a few remained. My watch showed that by now it was scarcely ten o'clock. I hurriedly wrote a message reporting the position and that of the attack for the Colonel of the 2nd Worcestershires, a gallant soldier and good friend, who was in a sunken road with his battalion in reserve three hundred yards to the rear. I gave this to my runner.

"Keep low," I said, "and go like blazes," for the waving grass was being whipped by bullets, and it scarcely seemed possible that life could remain for more than a few minutes.

A new horror was added to the scene of carnage. From the valley between Pozières and Martinpuich a German field battery had been brought into action, enfilading the position. I could see the gunners distinctly. At almost point-blank range they had commenced to direct shell-fire among the wounded. The shells bit through the turf, scattering the white chalk, and, throwing aloft limbs, clothing, and fragments of flesh. Anger, and the intensity of the fire, consumed my spirit, and, not caring for the consequences, I rose and turned my machine-gun upon the battery, laughing loudly as I saw the loaders fall.

I crept forward among the Highlanders and Riflemen, spurring them to action, giving bullet for bullet, directing fire upon the machine-gun nests, whose red flashes and wisps of steam made them conspicuous targets. The shell-fire increased from both flanks, and the smooth sward became pitted and hideous, but as each shell engraved itself upon the soil, a new scoop of cover was made for the safety of a rifleman.

A Highlander, terror in his eyes, lay on his back spewing blood, the chest of his tunic stained red. I tore open the buttons and shirt. It was a clean bullet wound, and I gave words of encouragement to the man, dragging him to a shell cavity, so that in a more upright position he could regain strength after the swamping of his lungs, and then creep back to safety.

The dismal action was continued throughout the morning, German fire being directed upon any movement on the hill-side. Towards noon, as my eyes searched the valley for reinforcements or for some other sign of action by those directing the battle, I descried a squadron of Indian Cavalry, dark faces under glistening helmets, galloping across the valley towards the slope. No troops could have presented a more inspiring sight than these natives of India with lance and sword, tearing in mad cavalcade on to the skyline. A few disappeared over it: they never came back. The remainder became the target of every gun and rifle. Turning their horses' heads, with shrill cries, these masters of horsemanship galloped through a hell of fire, lifting their mounts lightly over yawning shell-holes; turning and twisting through the barrage of great shells: the ranks thinned, not a man escaped...

I realized the utter futility of any further attempt to advance, and bent my energies to extricating such men as remained alive and unwounded from the battleground, now the point of concentration of gun and machine-gun fire, upon which it was suicide to remain. During the advance I had noted a small chalk quarry, screened by a low hedge. My runner rejoined me with another youngster, and together we dismantled the machine-gun and, after passing the word among those few who survived, for withdrawal, with my sergeant who laid strong hands on the ammunition boxes, we commenced the retirement to this position of better advantage.

Half-way down the slope a shell burst almost at our feet, tearing the tripod from my hands and throwing me face down-wards. I rose immediately through the smoke. The lad, still clasping the gun to his side, both legs shattered and a stream of blood pouring from under his helmet, lay unconscious. We carried the broken body into the quarry. Tenderly we stripped the wounded lad's jacket, and cut away the blood-stained trouser-ends and puttees, removing the boots. We bound the broken legs with first-aid dressings and made tight tourniquets above the knees to prevent further loss of blood. The lad had served with me since the formation of the Company and had always been interesting. He was a dreamer and used to sit on the edge of my dugout at La Bassée and tell me of his dreams. The lad was half-way to Heaven; and though he had purged his soul for a celestial life, he was as good a gunner as ever I experienced.

"It's a miracle if 'e lives," said the sergeant. "Those legs are pulp: they'll 'ave to come off." Many minutes passed, then the lad shuddered a little and opened his eyes. He winced, as in his recovering consciousness he sought to move, and the pang of pain shot through his body. Tears flooded his eyes as he realized his impotence.

"Hutchy," he whispered, one of those rare occasions in soldiering days in which a man addressed me by the familiar name by which I was known by the rank and file, "is it bad?"

I bent my ear to the strained words. "A smack in the legs, that's all, kid. Just stick it," I replied. "Then we'll be able to get you down the line."

The wounded man smiled around him at the familiar faces, then closed his eyes.

There was nothing to do but wait.

Once I gazed across the edge of the quarry. Great shells plunged continuously upon the slope before me, the ceaseless rattle of musketry reverberated against the hill-side, and echoed among the ruins of Bazentin. Martinpuich and the wood were wreathed in smoke, shrouded in columns of dust. The stench of blood and gas pervaded the hot atmosphere: it sickened the throat and caught the lungs tightly.

Death had cut swiftly with his scythe, and now his foul breath fanned the nostrils with the nauseating reek of blood, he winked his eye from aloft with each burst of shrapnel, and his harsh laugh chattered from the mouths of a score of machine-guns.

Half an hour passed, then the wounded lad re-opened his eyes. The brightness in them had departed.

"Give me some water," he panted. I pressed his emptying bottle to the lips, placing my arm around his shoulders. I was all too familiar with the look, in which the brightness of vitality was disappearing with the pallor which robbed the skin of its warm texture.

I pressed my forefinger to the pulse: its beats were slow.

Around the quarry the turmoil heightened in its fury. The ground heaved and shuddered: great tufts of earth were hurled through the air. The descending metal bore down upon the dead and wounded, grinding battered bodies to pulp, or throwing disembered limbs high in the air.

The lad's face paled, his lips blue, and a troubled look came for a moment into his eyes; then they brightened, an expression of ecstasy lighting the face. "Look...look...the Cross," he whispered. I glanced across the lip of the quarry, and the eyes of others crouching beside me followed my own. As it were suspended between Martinpuich and High Wood there appeared to be a brilliant light with wide wings shaped like some giant aeroplane. It hovered above the scene of carnage. A shiver passed through the wounded man's body. For a moment he clung tightly to me, then the whole body relaxed. I glanced down quickly. Death looked from the eyes of a machine-gunner, but a smile lay on the blood-flecked lips.

The fall of shells had suddenly ceased on our immediate front. As the area previously had been a maelstrom of explosives, so now, except for wisps of smoke hovering above the shell-holes, and bitter cries of the few wounded who still miraculously had survived the bombardment and now whimpered piteously for aid, or screamed in delirium and with hysteria, all was calm. The light still persisted.

My remaining N.C.O., a realist always, spoke. "A new stunt by the Staff...Good one this time...Better than Cavalry."

But on our immediate front all for a moment was quiet, and after surveying the landscape I said grimly, "We're going on now, Sergeant."

"That's good, sir: been in this 'ole long enough for the good of our 'ealth."

"Tighten up your belts, lads," I ordered. "We're going to advance in short bounds. After the first rush, take cover beside a casualty. Fill up with his ammunition and iron rations. I'll give you a few minutes for that... then on. We are going for the wood. Between each rush take good cover... are you ready?... right, come on!"

Forty-one men, remnants of three regiments, rushed over the lip of the quarry and ran swiftly forward through the long dried grass. Not a shot greeted us. I, disciplined warrior, every sense alert, threw myself beside the equipment which still clung intact to the torso of a Highlander, stripped almost naked and splashed with the blood which had poured from the distorted figure. I snatched the clips of ammunition, thrusting them into my pouches, and ransacked the haversack for rations. The water-bottle had been pierced and drained. With the aid of elbows and toes I wriggled forward to another figure lying face down to the ground, unslung the water-bottle, hot in the blazing sun, and added it to my equipment. I glanced round me: some men were ready, crouching like cats, heads sunk in cover behind the dead or in shell-pits, others completing their task. I raised my head slowly and viewed the wood. The storm of battle, shrapnel, machine-gun and rifle fire, still raged on either flank, while German heavy shells crashed in Pozières and Montauban.

The tree-tops of the Bois de Foureaux, once safe harbour for pigeons, giving shade to peasant lovers, now the High Wood of battle, murder and of sudden death, hung as crazy scarecrows, their broken branches waving in mockery. They assumed fantastic human form, buffoons on stilts, the leaves, at the twig ends, a feathery motley with which to crown man's vengeance upon Nature at the zenith of her summer glory. From a birch hung the limp body of a too daring sniper, the beheaded trunk like a flour sack caught in the fork of a branch, while blood had poured down the silver surface of its trunk, whereon it had silted, black and obscene. I offered a prayer and a curse, brief, the gasp of an overwrought soul, for my little band of followers.

Then I rose. With a swift rush we swept forward, the softness of bodies yielding to our step. A wounded man called to me, his plaintive wail tearing the heart. I damned the source of my compassion, and set myself to the purpose of the moment, then again dropped for cover and rest. No shot was fired. A third rush. The party on its narrow front in a thin irregular line was within forty yards of the wood's edge. I whispered the words to left and to right, "Fix bayonets." Once more my lads rose from the blood-soaked fields in a mad rush.

If there had been any martyr in my soul it had turned beast in the Pantheon of this modern Ephesus. I was murderer, breath coming in short gasps, teeth set, hands clenched round my rifle, nerves and sinews tense with life. "An eye for an eye, a tooth for tooth." Four German soldiers raised their arms in surrender. I could hear the breath of the Sergeant coming in deep snarls beside me. I crashed through the undergrowth, rifle and bayonet levelled to the charge, my great strength and weight gathered behind the thrust. A man, bearded and begrimed with battle, crumpled before my bayonet. The Sergeant pierced another as a knife goes through butter. A soldier, his arm broken, cowered back against a machine-gun, hands raised, face blanched with terror. With a cry he turned to run. I thrust with my bayonet at the full extent of a strong arm. The man stumbled and fell back, his weight dragging the rifle from the hand of his slayer.

I glanced about me, a stick-bomb in hand. The three Germans lay awry and huddled at my feet, and my men were now extended in a narrow trench a few yards within the wood. Other Germans stood to a flank, making overtures of surrender, and then came forward. Someone threw a bomb, then others. The Germans fell spattered with blood, lacerated and hideous. The bloodthirsty battle fury in me died down as I wiped the sweat from my eyes. I looked to the skies: the light which the lad had made me see had gone. Hypnotism, hallucination, self-deception, insanity? I wonder.

I dropped for cover as a German stick-bomb sped through the tree stumps. German shells were falling anew in the valley to the rear. Behind Bazentin the sun was sinking in a blood-red sky, a fitting epitaph to its day.

Quickly the trench was reversed, and the German machine-gun manned and placed in position to ward off any counter-attack. I wrote a short message, giving my position, and handed it to a lad, whom I chose as a runner to Brigade Headquarters.

Something was astir in the minds of the General Staff behind. A shrapnel barrage descended on the farther edge of the wood. My men and I were isolated, marooned in this distant corner of the "No Man's Land" of battle. Perhaps our advance had been seen by the watchers from the road in Bazentin. Dusk fell. Again and again I tapped out a brief message from my flash lamp to the trees and ruins in rear. "SOS" I spelt, "SOS." My party, cold in the night air with the dampness of sweat which had soaked their bodies, ate their frugal rations, greedily drank from the abandoned water-bottles of the enemy, and waited in vigilant watch. After two hours the familiar jangle of equipment was heard. Men were moving up the valley towards the wood. Relief. Soon I was among Welch Fusiliers of the 19th Brigade, on the left Battalions of the 98th Brigade, and others from Manchester, men fresh from divisional reserve. They had orders to send back any of my Brigade...

Forty-one men who had witnessed a miracle went back in file across the valley littered with dead. Released now from the strain of vigilance which had held death at bay, we stumbled with fatigue in the paling light. Stretcher bearers moved, turning over the fallen to discover if any yet lived, lifting the wounded, giving succour to those whose vitality had so ebbed that they could never withstand the renewed agony of the long journey down the road already dubbed "The Valley of Death." We reached Bazentin, in which high explosive still fitfully burst with loud detonation and which reeked of the sickly sweetness of gas. The Brigade Staff Captain, wounded a few minutes later, stood on the road. He peered at me. "Who are you?" he asked.

"Hutchison," I replied.

"Had a rough time?" he queried. "Have you come from High Wood? Was it you who sent through the runner?"

"Yes," I replied. "Glad the kid got through."

"All right, take your party down to Brigade Headquarters - bottom of the hill on the left. Rum issue!" he called to the men; and to me he added, "The General wants to see you. Well done!"

We passed on down the valley. I was back again, a return to the dugout at which orders for the attack had been issued but twenty-four hours earlier. Eleven only of the forty-one men now with me belonged to my Company: the others, stragglers from three regiments, the flotsam of a lost generation, survivors of disaster, and living witnesses of revelation.

I passed down the timbered stairway to the Brigadier's Headquarters. I stooped, entering the dugout, and momentarily was blinded by the flickering lights which threw weird shadows against the chalk-hewn white of the walls. The General with two staff officers was studying a map. He looked up quickly as I - ghastly figure of the modern gladiator - saved from the jaws of death, unshaven, heavy-eyed, begrimed, bloodstained, stood before him. I saluted. "Captain Hutchison," I said hoarsely.

The Brigadier tipped his peaked hat on his head and glanced at me with those vivid blue eyes, which in sharp contrast to the red hair seemed so brilliant, magnetic, and inspiring in a Commander. Deep lines shadowed his keen face, but the set mouth curved a trifle and the eyes were beacons of welcome.

"Sit down, Hutchison," invited the General, pouring out a stiff whiskey. "Drink that."

The strong spirit smote the back of my throat, and I gulped it gratefully.

"Relief all right?" questioned the General.

I nodded my assent.

"You've done very well... very well. I did not think it possible to reach High Wood. How many men were with you?"

"Forty-one, sir. They are all back now."

I stared at the table for a moment, fingering an unlighted cigarette nervously. The General thrust a candle towards me. I still remained silent, staring at the light, then put my cigarette to it and inhaled a whiff of smoke.

"What was the light over High Wood, sir?" I said, intently watching the General, who looked perplexed. "Like an aeroplane... just before we went forward... that was at 5 p.m... stopped the shells... not a shot was fired when we attacked. We got into High Wood without the loss of a man."

A look of astonishment crossed the General's face. "You are tired out, Hutchison," he exclaimed. "You will remember everything in the morning." He refilled my glass. "You had better sleep now. The Staff

Captain has arranged for that, and you will find your men in the dugouts just outside."

I gulped the spirit and withdrew unsteadily, my senses doped with fatigue, and then lay down to sleep.

– 15th - 17th JULY 1916 –

SECOND-LIEUTENANT CHARLES CARRINGTON, M.C.

1st/5th Battalion Royal Warwickshire Regiment

Charles Carrington and his Company, having failed in their attack on the cross-roads behind Ovillers, sheltered in an old German trench in the vicinity of La Boisselle and Ovillers. The Germans returned to attack the trench with bombs and after a fierce confrontation were beaten back. Sergeant Adams and Lance-Corporal Houghton were awarded the Military Medal as a result of their actions in this attack. Carrington wrote his account under the pseudonym 'Charles Edmonds'.

As it was getting light I happened to be on the right, where Griffin's party was struggling with a huge traverse. A man beyond me said excitedly:

"There's someone coming along the trench. I can hear 'em talking."

"Hurrah," I said, "this'll be the 17th." So I jumped on to the traverse and shouted, "Hullo there! Who the devil are you? Are you the 17th?"

Somebody along the trench stopped, and I heard whispering.

"Who are you?" I shouted again, with less confidence.

There was a sound as of someone scuttling up the trench.

"Why, it must have been the jolly old Boches."

We had sent the A company men back to their own trench and organised our own men with sentries on the flanks and a reserve platoon in the dugout, and were feeling safe and happy, when again I heard something going on on the right.

"Stand to," there was a shout; "they're coming!"

My servant and another man who had been hanging about beyond the sentry-post came flying round the traverse.

"Allemans," they said; "they're coming!"

This was a very different matter from running about in noise and darkness. I suddenly thought of Prussian Guardsmen, burly and brutal, and bursting bombs, and hand-to-hand struggles with cold steel. My first impulse was to tell Bickersteth [The Company Commander]. It was his responsibility now.

'Thud!' went a loud noise along the trench, and the air shook and whined with flying fragments.

I felt myself turning pale.

I found I was walking slowly away from the danger-point. "I must go and tell Bickersteth," I excused myself. I passed the word down the dugout. Then I pulled myself together and got up to the front somehow. The men too were very panicky. Poor devils, they hadn't had a good sleep or a square meal for three days.

'Thud' went a bomb three bays up the trench. I licked my lips and felt for my revolver.

'Thud' went a bomb two bays away.

I was standing at our extreme right flank where we had posted a sentry two bays beyond the half-finished bomb-stop.

"Come along, let's get back to the bomb-stop," said I not very bravely. Just then round the traverse from the dugout came Serjeant Adams, an old volunteer of many years' service in England. He was smoking a pipe and had a thin smile on his face.

"What's that, sir," he said pleasantly, "go back? No, sir, let's go forward," and he tucked his rifle under his arm and strolled along the trench alone - still smiling. A bomb burst in the bay beyond him. He climbed the traverse and took a snapshot with his rifle at some person beyond. A group of men stood wavering, and then I went and took my place beside him on the traverse.

Thirty or forty yards away I saw a hand and a grey sleeve come up out of the trench and throw a cylinder on the end of a wooden rod. It turned over and over in the air and seemed to take hours to approach. It fell just at the foot of the traverse where we stood, and burst with a shattering shock.

"The next one will get us," I thought.

Serjeant Adams pulled a bomb out of his pocket and threw it. I did the same, and immediately felt better. A young Lance-Corporal Houghton, did the same. The next German bomb fell short. Then someone threw without remembering to pull the pin, and in a moment the bomb was caught up and thrown back at us by the enemy.

I snapped off my revolver once or twice at glimpses of the enemy. a little of last night's feeling was returning. Adams and Houghton were moving forward now, and I was watching them over the traverse, when I had the impression that someone was throwing stones. Suddenly I saw lying in the middle of the trench a small black object, about the shape and size of a large duck's egg. There was a red band round it and a tube fixed in one end of it. What could this be?

I guessed it must be some new sort of bomb.

It was lying less than a yard from my foot; I was right in a corner of the trench. What was I to do? In an instant of time I thought: Had I the nerve to pick it up and throw it away? Should I step over it and run? Or stay where I was? There was no room to lie down. But too late.

The bomb burst with a roar at my feet. My eyes and nose were full of dust and pungent fumes. Not knowing if I was wounded or not, I found myself stumbling down the trench with a group of groaning men. One of them was swearing and shouting in a high-pitched voice and bleeding in the leg. All the nerve was blasted out of us.

I fetched up almost in tears, shaken out of my senses, at Bickersteth's feet. My clothes were a little torn and my hand was bleeding, but that was all.

Bickersteth was very cool. He was watching the fight through a periscope and organising relays of bomb carriers.

"You must get these men together, Edmonds," he was saying, "and make a counter-attack."

"I'm damned if I will," said I; "I'm done for," and I lay and panted.

He looked at me and saw I was useles. I hadn't an ounce of grit left in me.

It was Wells who rallied the survivors and went up again to find my revolver, 'shamefully cast away in the presence of the enemy,' and Serjeant Adams still holding his own.

"Come along, Edmonds," said Bickersteth, and in a minute or two I felt better and went up. We got the Lewis-gun out and the whole party moved forward. Houghton was throwing well. We rushed a bay, and Houghton, who was leading, found himself face to face with a German unter-offizier, the length of the next bay between them. He threw a lucky bomb which burst right in the German's face. Their leader fallen, the heart went out of the enemy's attack. At the same moment there were two diversions. An 8-inch shell, one of those which had been falling occasionally on our right, suddenly landed right in the bay behind the German bomber, and his supporters fled. So ended their attack. But as we moved forward a sniper fired almost from behind us. I felt the bullet crack in my ear, and Corporal Matthews, who was walking beside me, preoccupied and intent, fell dead in the twinkling of an eye. I was looking straight at him as the bullet struck him and was profoundly affected by the remembrance of his face, though at the time I hardly thought of it. He was alive, and then he was dead, and there was nothing human left in him. He fell with a neat round hole in his forehead and the back of his head blown out.

Other big shells followed the first, so we decided not to hold that part of the trench. We propped up the dead Boche as a warning to his friends against the furthest traverse, and set to work on a better bomb-stop behind, just where Corporal Matthews was hit.

It was now clear that we must set a definite limit to our fortress and make a strong bomb-stop on this most dangerous flank. The casual shelling seemed to have settled down into a regular slow bombardment of our extreme right with 8-inch shells, which fell at two-minute intervals just where we had killed the German N.C.O. Bickersteth decided to abandon the right-hand bay, even though it had a good dug-out, and to concentrate on the three bays below my earliest limit. Where I had set Griffin to work on a bomb-stop, he set about a larger and sounder plan. We must level one traverse flat and have a field of fire longer than the range of the German stick-bomb. He organised the work and left me in charge. We started to dig away the ten-foot cube of clay constituting the traverse by which Corporal Matthews had been shot. Almost as we approached and cut into it with pickaxes, the same sniper fired again from the village on our left, and a man called Pratt dropped like a stone just where the corporal had fallen. He, too, had a small round hole in his temple and the back of his skull blown away.

No one seemed very anxious to take his place on the bomb-stop. The body was moved down the trench and we stood around cutting gingerly into the pile of earth. I myself stood opposite the parapet gap through which the sniper fired and took care not to expose myself too much. We seemed to do very little good.

"Aw, give me that pick! Let me get at it!" suddenly roared one man, and he sprang up the traverse all exposed, striking giant blows that loosened the top of the mound where no one had dared to work. It was Jimmy Mills, and his time was short: for fifteen seconds, perhaps, he panted and drove his pick mightily, loosening the stiff clay, before the sniper fired again. Mills flung wide his pick and collapsed with a loud cry, inarticulate with rage and pain. The bullet had struck him in the left hip and pierced his bowels from side to side, emerging from the right.

"That's a third man dead," thought I. There were now two men dying on the trench floor, Pratt beating with helpless hands on the earth, the blood gushing from his nostrils, and now Mills, the old soldier, conscious and groaning, his trousers soaked with blood, thrilled with agony by every touch, by every movement. The other men, wounded earlier in the counter-attack, had been taken down into the dugout. These two more I brought to die in comfort in the deep safe firebay above it. Pratt was beyond hope. Hit in the same place as Corporal Matthews, his head was shattered: spatterings of brain lay in the pool of blood under him; but, though he had never been conscious since the shot was fired, he refused to die. An old Corporal looked after him, held his body and arms, which writhed and fought feebly as he lay. It was over two hours before he died, hours of July sunshine in a crowded space where perhaps a dozen men sat in a ditch ten yards long and five feet wide, reeking with the smell of blood, while all the time, above the soothing voice of the corporal, a gurgling and a moaning came from his lips, now high and liquid, now low and dry...

Old Mills, tough, bronzed, ginger-moustached and forty-one years old, lay beside this text 'that taught the rustic moralist to die'. No stretcher-bearers had come on with my wild adventure last night, but the old soldiers thought it best to leave him roughly bandaged until the inward wounds should close. Then he might have a chance. He was little, but hardened by fourteen years' soldiering and two previous wars. His work had not been in vain. The men at the traverse would be fully occupied in digging away the soil which he had loosened, till dusk, when someone could climb on top again.

The day wore on. No more Germans came, but squalls of shrapnel swept the valley behind us, and bombs thudded in the rear where we thought A company should be. I got some sleep in the afternoon. There was no bunk empty, but I flung myself on a stretcher by the side of Lee, my fellow-explorer of last night, and rested democratically.

That evening I began to understand our predicament. We had no good map, but Bickersteth made our situation clear. The village of Ovillers had been twice attacked from in front and twice successfully defended by the Prussian Guard. Further to the south at La Boisselle the British had advanced and driven the Germans back, which made it possible to take Ovillers in the flank. We had done more than this. We had advanced and placed ourselves in a trench behind the German stronghold, cutting if off from support and almost surrounding it; but at the same time we had now isolated ourselves, with Germans in front of us and behind us, the garrison of Ovillers in front, and those who were trying to relieve it behind. Consequently we were exposed to fire from almost any direction. On the other hand, to look for help we must turn back across the 1,000 yards of rough grass, impassable by day, which we had rushed across by night. This was actually looking for help in the direction of Germany. Bickersteth surprised me with the news that the heavy gun which persistently dropped shells near our right flank was an English gun, ignorantly trying to protect us, not a German gun ignorantly trying to destroy us. We had to be thankful for this protective fire, though the shell-splinters fell unpleasantly close. Since I had advanced too far in the night attack I had run into our own artillery fire, and the gunners still did not know exactly where we were.

We had little more cause for worry that day. The long silence came to Pratt at last; Mills, game and grumbling, got a little maudlin and was less in pain. We all began to suffer from thirst. Our water bottles, of course, had been filled at starting; but fighting is dry work. It was a muggy day and fear parches the throat. Most of us managed to hoard a few drops of water in case the ration-parties should not reach us early in the night. Work went on well at the bomb-stop, but the thousand cubic feet of clay were not easy to move. Before dark the Lewis-gun mounted on the next traverse could see at least the head and shoulders of a man two bays away. But now I found that the gun team had dispersed and only Bailey and Robinson, two good gunners, were with us. Bailey, who eventually became a serjeant, was a pale, square-jawed boy, whose firm mouth had impressed me as he stood to his gun during the attack... 'Granny' Robinson, was a thin, spectacled young man, a very devoted husband with the manners of a gentleman. He was a Salvationist and the only 'pious' soldier I ever met. Two of the best men in the trench, these two manned the gun in turn...

– 15th JULY 1916 –

CAPTAIN ROBERT GRAVES
2nd Battalion Royal Welch Fusiliers

The 2nd Battalion Royal Welch Fusiliers arrived at Longeau, near Amiens, from the Béthune sector on 10th July. On 15th the Battalion left bivouacs east of the village of Méaulte and marched through Fricourt to the south east corner of Mametz Wood near the front line. The Battalion was part of the 19th Brigade which was the reserve brigade for the Thirty-third Division.

We were in fighting kit and the nights were wet and cold. I went into the wood to find German overcoats to use as blankets. Mametz Wood was full of dead of the Prussian Guards Reserve, big men, and of Royal Welch and South Wales Borderers of the new-army battalions, little men. There was not a single tree in the wood unbroken. I got my greatcoats and came away as quickly as I could, climbing over the wreckage of green branches. Going and coming, by the only possible route, I had to pass by the corpse of a German with his back propped against a tree. He had a green face, spectacles, close shaven hair; black blood was dripping from the nose and beard. He had been there for some days and was bloated and stinking. There had been bayonet fighting in the wood. There was a man of the South Wales Borderers and one of the Lehr Regiment who had succeeded in bayoneting each other simultaneously...

A DEAD BOCHE

To you who'd read my songs of War
    And only hear of blood and fame,
I'll say (you've heard it said before)
    'War's Hell!' and if you doubt the same,
To-day I found in Mametz Wood
A certain cure for lust of blood:

Where, propped against a shattered trunk,
    In a great mess of things unclean,
Sat a dead Boche; he scowled and stunk
    With clothes and face a sodden green,
Big-bellied, spectacled, crop-haired,
Dribbling black blood from nose and beard.

– 16th JULY 1916 –

CAPTAIN GERALD BRENAN, M.C.
VIIIth Corps Cyclists Battalion

By mid-July Gerald Brenan had become an Assistant Provost Marshal which involved patrolling the roads and sleeping in a cellar at Sailly. Two days after the attack on Bazentin Ridge Brenan and his batman, Dartnell, went through the devastated battlefield, to take a few tins of pâté to Ralph Partridge, who was serving in the 6th Battalion Royal Warwickshire Regiment.

After passing through Albert, gaunt and shattered from the shelling it had received, we left our cycles with a sentry and continued on foot. As we crossed the old front line we seemed to be leaving a windswept yet solid shore for a treacherous, chaotic region recently abandoned by the tide. The further we went the more desperate and confused the landscape became - shattered woods and villages, shattered trenches, abandoned equipment and then unburied bodies. But it was also thickly populated: there was a continuous heavy traffic of mule-drawn limbers and wagons choking the roads and tracks and all round us batteries of guns were firing from the open without any attempt at camouflage and soldiers were camping by companies and battalions round their stacked rifles in great open bivouacs. The whole country swarmed with khaki figures, some on carrying parties, others cooking or brewing tea in black dixies, others lying on the ground or sitting up to clean their rifles or rewind their putties. Others again were foraging for firewood or souvenirs or squatting to relieve themselves. After a little we came to a large wood which the map told me was Mametz Wood. Its trees were torn and shattered, its leaves had turned brown and there was a shell-hole every three yards. This was a place where something almost unheard of in this war had taken place - fierce hand-to-hand fighting in the open with bombs and bayonets. What seemed extraordinary was that all the dead bodies there lay just as they had fallen in their original places as though they were being kept as an exhibit for a war museum. Germans in their field-grey uniforms, British in their khaki lying side by side, their faces and their hands a pale waxy green, the colour of a rare marble. Heads covered with flat mushroom helmets next to heads in domed steel helmets that came down behind the ears. Some of these figures still sat with their backs against a tree and two of them - this had to be seen to be believed - stood locked together by their bayonets which had pierced one another's bodies and sustained in that position by the tree trunk against which they had fallen. I felt I was visiting a room in Madame Tussaud's Chamber of Horrors, for I could not imagine any of those bodies having ever been alive. Yet the effect in its morbid way was beautiful.

On beyond, in the direction of Bazentin-le-Grand, the fighting had also been very heavy. Both sides had dug themselves in with entrenching tools and round one hastily scraped-up gun emplacement, which commanded a drive through the trees, the khaki bodies lay in heaps. We kept on across the battlefield - corpses of men, dead horses and mules, rifles, hand-grenades, gas-masks, those gimcrack spiked helmets worn by the Boche on parade, water-bottles, scattered like the debris on a beach after a winter storm - till we came to Trones Wood which, though greatly battered, had kept its green leaves. Here we were close to the front line and machine-gun bullets began to whistle over us, so, as I could not get any news of Ralph's battalion, we turned back...

– 18th - 20th JULY 1916 –

CAPTAIN ROBERT GRAVES

'D' Company 2nd Battalion Royal Welch Fusiliers

The Battalion, in Divisional Reserve in Mametz Wood, continued to come under heavy shell-fire and suffered casualties every day. On 18th July, the Battalion moved to a shallow road-side trench in the front line. The Germans were in a trench-system about five hundred yards away. The following day the Battalion Head Quarters was established in a deep dug-out in the village of Bazentin-le-Petit.

We had never seen artillery so thick. On the 18th we moved up to a position just to the north of Bazentin-le-Petit to relieve the Tyneside Irish. I was with D Company. The guide who was taking us up was hysterical and had forgotten the way; we put him under arrest and found it ourselves. As we went up through the ruins of the village we were shelled. We were accustomed to that, but they were gas shells. The standing order with regard to gas shells was not to put on one's respirator but hurry on. Up to that week there had been no gas shells except lachrymatory ones; these were the first of the real kind, so we lost about half a dozen men. When at last we arrived at the trenches, which were scooped at a roadside and only about three feet deep, the company we were relieving hurried out without any of the usual formalities; they had been badly shaken. I asked their officer where the Germans were. He said he didn't know, but pointed vaguely towards Martinpuich, a mile to our front. Then I asked him where and what were the troops on our left. He didn't know. I cursed him and he went off. We got into touch with C Company behind us on the right and with the Fourth Suffolks not far off on the left. We began deepening the trenches and locating the Germans; they were in a trench-system about five hundred yards away but keeping fairly quiet.

The next day there was very heavy shelling at noon; shells were bracketing along our trench about five yards short and five yards over, but never quite getting it. We were having dinner and three times running my cup of tea was spilt by the concussion and filled with dirt. I was in a cheerful mood and only laughed. I had just had a parcel of kippers from home; they were far more important than the bombardment...

Before the shelling had started a tame magpie had come into the trench; it had apparently belonged to the Germans who had been driven out of the village by the Gordon Highlanders a day or two before. It was looking very draggled. 'That's one for sorrow,' I said. The men swore that it spoke something in German as it came in, but I did not hear it. I was feeling tired and was off duty, so without waiting for the bombardment to stop I went to sleep in the trench. I decided that I would just as soon be killed asleep as awake. There were no dug-outs, of course. I always found it easy now to sleep through bombardments. I was conscious of the noise in my sleep, but I let it go by. Yet if anybody came to wake me for my watch or shouted 'Stand-to!' I was alert in a second. I had learned to go to sleep sitting down, standing up, marching, lying on a stone floor, or in any other position, at a moment's notice at any time of day or night. But now I had a dreadful nightmare; it was as though somebody was handling me secretly, choosing the place to drive a knife into me. Finally, he gripped me in the small of the back. I woke up with a start, shouting, and punched the small of my back where the hand was. I found that I had killed a mouse that had been frightened by the bombardment and run down my neck.

BAZENTIN, 1916

(A Reminiscence - Robert and David)

R. That was a curious night two years ago,
   Relieving those tired Dockers at Bazentin.
   Remember climbing up between the ruins?
   The guide that lost his head when the gas-shells came,
   Lurching about this way and that, half-witted,
   Till we were forced to find the way ourselves?

D. Yes, twilight torn with flashes, faces muffled,
   In stinking masks, and eyes all sore and crying
   With lachrymatory stuff, and four men gassed.

R. Yet we got up there safely, found the trenches
   Untraversed shallow ditches, along a road
   With dead men sprawled about, some ours, some theirs -

D. Ours mostly, and those Dockers doing nothing,
   Tired out, poor devils; much too tired to dig,
   Or to do anything but just hold the ground:
   No touch on either flank, no touch in front,

Everything in the air. I cursed, I tell you.
Out went the Dockers, quick as we filed in,
And soon we'd settled down and put things straight,
Posted the guns, dug in, got out patrols,
And sent to right and left to restore touch.

R. There was a sunken road out on the right,
With rifle-pits half dug; at every pit
A dead man had his head thrust in for shelter.

D. Dawn found us happy enough; a funny day -
The strangest I remember in all those weeks.
German five-nines were bracketting down our trenches
Morning and afternoon.

R.   Why, yes; at dinner,
Three times my cup was shaken out of my hand
And filled with dirt: I had to pour out fresh.

D. That was the mug you took from the Boche gun.
Remember that field gun, with the team killed
By a lucky shot just as the German gunners
Were limbering up? We found the gunner's treasures
In a box behind, his lump of fine white chalk
Carefully carved, and painted with a message
Of love to his dear wife, and Allied flags,
A list of German victories, and an eagle.
Then his clean washing, and his souvenirs -
British shell-heads, French bullets, lumps of shrapnel,
Nothing much more. I never thought it lucky
To take that sort of stuff.

R.   Then a tame magpie -
German, we guessed - came hopping into the trench,
Picking up scraps of food. That's 'One for sorrow'
I said to little Owen.

D.   Not much mistaken
In the event, when only three days later
They threw us at High Wood and (mind, we got there!)
Smashed up the best battalion in the whole corps.
But, Robert, quite the queerest thing that day

Happened in the late afternoon. Worn out,
I snatched two hours of sleep; the Boche bombardment
Roared on, but I commended my soul to God,
And slept half through it; but as I lay there snoring
A mouse, in terror of all these wild alarms,
Crept down my neck for shelter, and woke me up
In a great sweat. Blindly I gave one punch
And slew the rascal at the small of my back.
That was a strange day!

R.   Yes, and a merry one.

That afternoon the company got an order through from the brigade to build two cruciform strong-points at such-and-such a map reference. Moodie, the company commander, and I looked at our map and laughed. Moodie sent back a message that he would be glad to do so, but would require an artillery bombardment and strong reinforcements because the points selected, half way to Martinpuich, were occupied in force by the enemy. The colonel came up and verified this. He said that we should build the strong-point about three hundred yards forward and two hundred yards apart. So one platoon stayed behind in the trench and the other went out and started digging. A cruciform strong-point consisted of two trenches, each some thirty yards long, crossing at right angles to each other; it was wired all round, so that it looked in diagram, like a hot-cross bun. The defenders could bring fire to bear against an attack from any direction. We were to hold each of these points with a Lewis gun and a platoon of men.

It was a bright moonlight night. My way to the strong-point on the right took me along the Bazentin-High Wood road. A German sergeant-major, wearing a pack and full equipment, was lying on his back in the middle of the road, his arms stretched out wide. He was a short, powerful man with a full black beard. He looked sinister in the moonlight; I needed a charm to get myself past him. The simplest way, I found was to cross myself. Evidently a brigade of the Seventh Division had captured the road and the Germans had been shelling it heavily. It was a sunken road and the defenders had begun to scrape fire-positions in the north bank, facing the Germans. The work had apparently been interrupted by a counter-attack. They had done no more than scrape hollows in the lower part of the bank. To a number of these little hollows wounded men had crawled, put their heads and shoulders inside and died there. They looked as if they had tried to hide from the black beard. They were Gordon Highlanders.

I was visiting the strong-point on the right. The trench had now been dug two or three feet down and a party of Engineers had arrived with coils of barbed wire for the entanglement. I found that work had stoppped. The whisper went round: 'Get your rifles ready. Here comes Fritz.' I lay down flat to see better, and about seventy yards away in the moonlight I could make out massed figures. I immediately sent a man back to the company to find Moodie and ask him for a Lewis gun and a flare-pistol. I restrained the men, who were itching to fire, telling them to wait until they came closer. I said: 'They probably don't know we're here and we'll get more of them if we let them come right up close. They may even surrender.' The Germans were wandering about irresolutely and we wondered what the game was. There had been a number of German surrenders at night recently, and this might be one on a big scale. Then Moodie came running with a Lewis gun, the flare-pistol, and a few more men with rifle-grenades. He decided to give the enemy a chance. He sent up a flare and fired a Lewis gun over their heads. A tall officer came running towards us with his hands up in surrender. He was surprised to find that we were not Germans. He said that he belonged to the Public Schools Battalion in our own brigade. Moodie asked him what the hell he was doing. He said that he was in command of a patrol. He was sent back for a few more of his men, to make sure it was not a trick. The patrol was half a company of men wandering about aimlessly between the lines, their rifles slung over their shoulders, and, it seemed, without the faintest idea where they were or what information they were supposed to bring back...

The evening of the next day, July 19th, we were told that we would be attacking High Wood... I attended the meeting of company commanders; the colonel told us the plan. He said: 'Look here, you fellows, we're in reserve for this attack. The Cameronians are going up to the wood first, then the Fifth Scottish Rifles; that's at 5 a.m. The Public Schools Battalion are in support if anything goes wrong. I don't know if we shall be called on; if we are, it will mean that the Jocks have legged it. As usual,' he added. This was an appeal to prejudice. 'The Public Schools Battalion is, well, what we know, so if we are called for, that means it will be the end of us.' He said this with a laugh and we all laughed... He told us that if we did get orders to reinforce, we were to shake out in artillery formation; once in the wood we were to hang on like death. Then he said good-bye and good luck and we rejoined our companies...

The Jocks did get into the wood and the Royal Welch were not called on to reinforce until eleven o'clock in the morning. The

Germans put down a barrage along the ridge where we were lying, and we lost about a third of the battalion before our show started. I was one of the casualties.

It was heavy stuff, six and eight-inch. There was so much of it that we decided to move back fifty yards; it was when I was running that an eight-inch shell burst about three paces behind me...... One piece of shell went through my left thigh, high up near the groin; I must have been at the full stretch of my stride to have escaped emasculation. The wound over the eye was nothing; it was a little chip of marble, possibly from one of the Bazentin cemetery head stones. This and a finger wound, which split the bone, possibly came from another shell which burst in front of me. The main wound was made by a piece of shell that went in two inches below the point of my right shoulder, and came out through my chest two inches above my right nipple, in a line between it and the base of my neck.

My memory of what happened then is vague. Apparently Dr. Dunn came up through the barrage with a stretcher-party, dressed my wound, and got me down to the old German dressing-station at the north end of Mametz Wood. I just remember being put on the stretcher and winking at the stretcher-bearer sergeant who was looking at me and saying: 'Old Gravy's got it, all right.' The dressing-station was overworked that day; I was laid in a corner on a stretcher and remained unconscious for more than twenty-four hours.

It was about ten o'clock on the 20th that I was hit. Late that night the colonel came to the dressing-station; he saw me lying in the corner and was told that I was done for. The next morning the 21st, when they were clearing away the dead, I was found to be still breathing; so they put me on an ambulance for Heilly, the nearest field-hospital. The pain of being jolted down the Happy Valley, with a shell-hole at every three or four yards of the roads, woke me for awhile. I remember screaming. But once back on the better roads I became unconscious again. That morning the colonel wrote the usual formal letters of condolence to the next-of-kin of the six or seven officers who had been killed...

Later he made out the official casualty list and reported me died of wounds. It was a long casualty list, because only eighty men were left in the battalion...

– 19th - 20th JULY 1916 –

PRIVATE FRANK RICHARDS, D.C.M., M.M.
2nd Battalion Royal Welch Fusiliers

The Battalion arrived on the Somme from the Arras sector on 15th July. Three days later Frank Richards was with 'A' Company in a shallow trench which ran from the cemetery on the east front of Bazentin-le-Petit; High Wood was about seven hundred yards in front of them. They were shelled heavily by the enemy artillery.

By the afternoon they had a nasty barrage extending right down to the valley we had left. In our part of the trench the shells were falling either in front or behind us; but the other end of the Company was not so lucky, the shells bursting right on the parapet, blowing trenches and men to pieces. The whole of a Lewis-gun team was killed. In the cemetery the shells were throwing corpses and coffins clean out of the graves, and some of our killed were now lying alongside of them. We could only sit tight and grin and bear it. One shell burst just outside the trench not far from me, and a man had one side of his face cut clean away by a piece of shell. He was also hit low down but was still conscious. His two pals were deliberating whether they would put him out of his misery or not; fortunately they were spared that, as he died before they had made up their minds. One of our old stretcher-bearers went mad and started to undress himself. He was uttering horrible screams, and we had to fight with him and overpower him before he could be got to the Aid Post. He had been going queer for the last month or two.

Duffy was hit low down on the right side: it was a bad wound and I knew his case was hopeless; but he was still conscious. I asked the Company Commander if I could help to carry him down to the Aid Post. "Certainly," he replied. We had gone halfway to the Aid Post, four of us carrying the stretcher, one at each handle, when as I lifted my right foot in its stride a shell splinter buried itself in the ground beneath it. Although Duffy was dying on the stretcher he noticed it as he hung his head over the side and said: "Hard lines, Dick! If a youngster had been in your place he would have had a beautiful Blighty wound through the foot. We old ones aren't lucky enough to stop one that way. We generally stop one the way I have done." We told him to shut up, saying that he had every chance to get over it. He replied simply: "You know better than that, Dick." We arrived at the Aid Post and I should have liked to stay with him for a little while, but I had to get back to the Company. As I shook him by the hand he wished me the best of luck, and about two hours later I had news that he had died where I left him. No man could wish for a better pal, and I never scrounged much around the Company, when in the line, after he was gone.

We were relieved that evening and went back to Mametz Wood, and during the night we got wind that the Brigade were going to attack High Wood. A message came through that the Battalion would send one visual signaller to Brigade Headquarters who would report himself there at 2 a.m. on the morning of the 20th. I was detailed off for this and as I made my way there was wondering what the idea was. Eight of us and the Brigade Signalling Corporal were detailed off to form a transmitting station between High Wood and Brigade Headquarters which was situated on the fringe of Mametz Wood. No telephones would be carried and our station would receive messages by flag from the signallers with the attacking force; which we would transmit to Brigade by heliograph or flag. The position that we had to take up was by a large mill about six hundred yards this side of High Wood. The mill was built on some rising ground which made it a very prominent landmark. We had a good view of everything from here, but we also found that when we were exchanging messages with the wood, the enemy would have an equally good view of us, especially when we were flag-wagging. An old soldier of the Cameronians who was now a Brigade signaller, an old soldier of the Royal Welch who was now a Brigade runner, and the corporal, were the only ones I knew of our station. I was wondering how the other five would conduct themselves if we were heavily shelled.

The Cameronian and I fixed our heliograph and telescope up, and at 8 a.m. we were in communication with Brigade. Shortly after this the enemy began shelling us and by 10 a.m. they had put up one of the worst barrages that I was ever under. Twelve-inch, eight-inch, five-point-nines and whizzbang shells were bursting around us continually and this lasted during the whole of the day. North, south, east and west it was raining shells, and we seemed to be the dead centre of it all. The barrage of the previous day was a flea-bite to this one. The ground shook and rocked and we were continually having to reset the heliograph. When receiving a message the smoke of the bursting shells and the earth and dust that was being thrown up constantly obscured our vision, and we could only receive a word now and then.

The five men I didn't know were sheltering in a large shell hole by the side of the mill; they were absolutely useless and terror-stricken. We were not able to see our attacking troops who were to advance up a valley to the right of us at dawn, to enter the wood on our right front, but during the afternoon I saw some of our men moving about on the outskirts, and a flag commenced to call us up. I asked one of the men in the shell hole to come and write the message down, but not one of them would budge. The corporal and the Cameronian were busy receiving a message from Brigade at the time. I cursed them until I was blue, but it made no difference. The Brigade runner who was not a signaller then volunteered to write the message down and stood behind me in the doorway of the mill whilst I read it. The message said that the whole of High Wood had been captured. About an hour later I was receiving another message from the wood, the runner again writing it down, standing behind me in the doorway of the mill. When I was about halfway through it, he gave a shout; I turned round and found him groaning on the ground. A shell splinter which must have passed high up between my legs had hit him in the thigh. It was a nasty wound but he stopped groaning after a bit and said: "Carry on with the message, Dick, I can bandage this myself." I shouted to the Cameronian to come and finish writing the message down. We only received about another six words when the signaller in the wood who was sending the message, and the other with him who was evidently calling it out, both fell; that message was never completed. The message as far as we got with it stated that the enemy were counter-attacking. It was the last visual message that arrived from the wood: every message after this came by runner.

The enemy now turned a machine-gun on the mill, our flag-wagging had attracted their attention. On the right front of the mill a battalion of Manchesters of another division were in some shallow trenches; they had heavy casualties during the day, a number of shells bursting right among them. One of their captains ran across to us and asked if it was possible to get a message back to his Brigade Headquarters, as his men were being blown to pieces. We told him we were very sorry but we were under orders only to deal with messages connected with our own Brigade. As we were speaking, some large shells exploded right on the parapet of the trench he had left, knocking in a big stretch of it. He then rushed back there to look after the survivors. He was a very brave and humane man. But even if we had been able to send his message I don't suppose our Brigade Headquarters, being in a different division, would have known where his Brigade Headquarters was situated; and even if they had, and transmitted it on, his Brigadier would have taken no notice of it, for sure.

A number of lightly wounded men from the wood passed by us on their way to the dressing-station which was in the valley below. We inquired how things were going. Most of them said that half the Brigade had been wiped out before they entered the wood, and that old Jerrie was counter-attacking when they left. Many of these men were killed on their way to the dressing-station. I saw one of our old signallers limping along; he had stopped one through the ankle... We received a message that no more visual signalling would be carried out, and that we would be employed as runners between Brigade and High Wood. Down in the valley below us a company of Argyles were occupying some shell holes and shallow trenches: they seemed to be just outside the barrage. I had to pass them when I was taking back a message to Brigade Headquarters, about a hundred yards beyond. I had just reached Brigade when it seemed that every German artillery gun had lengthened its range and was firing direct on the Argyles. This lasted about fifteen minutes, and then the shelling slackened. I waited awhile before making my way back, and when I did pass by the Argyles' position I could only see heads, arms, legs and mangled bodies...

The Brigade, which was still hanging on to three parts of the wood, was relieved at 10 p.m., three-quarters of them being casualties. The Public Schools Battalion was practically annihilated, and the Royal Welch were not much better off. We had lost ten of our eighteen signallers. Half the Brigade had been knocked over before they ever entered the wood...

– 21st JULY 1916 –

SECOND-LIEUTENANT SIEGFRIED SASSOON, M.C.
1st Battalion Royal Welch Fusiliers

On the evening of 20th July Siegfried Sassoon moved from a reserve position at Transport Lines near Méaulte to a hill south-west of Dernancourt. The Seventh Division were being relieved after a week of fighting.

8.30 a.m... We waited at the crossroads for the Battalion from 11.30 to 5.30. I walked about most of the night, saw to moving tents up the hill, which had to be done at the last moment. The road where I sat was a moonlit picture (I sat among some oats and watched the procession of the Seventh Division). Guns and limbers, men sitting stiffly on tired horses - transport - cookers - they rolled and jolted past in the moonshine. Then, like flitting ghosts, last began to come the foot-weary infantry - stumbling - limping - straggling back after eight days in hell - more or less. They came silently - sometimes a petrol- (water-) tin would sound as it rattled chiming against the bayonet at the side. Then moonshine and dawn mingled their silver and rose and lilac, and a lark went up from the green corn. The kite-balloon, too, on the hill, began to sway huge and bulbous - upward - another was seen far off against the rosy east. All night the distant waves of gunfire had crashed and rumbled, soft and terrific with broad flashes, like waves of some immense tumult of waters, rolling along the horizon. As dawn broke, and I came down the hill again, I heard the clear skirl of the Second Gordons piping into their bivouac - a brave note, shrill as the lark, but the Jocks were a weary crowd as they hobbled in. Before dawn a horse neighed twice, high and shrill and scared. And then I began to see the barley-tops swaying lightly against the paling sky. And the hills began to gloom in the dusk, stretching away and upward, and the huge trees along the river stood out dark and distinct and solemn. The camp-fires burned low. The east was beginning to be chinked with red flames and feathers of scarlet. A train groaned along the line, sending up vast columns of whitish fiery vapour - a red light shone from behind.

And now I've heard that Robert [Graves] died of wounds yesterday, in an attack on High Wood. And I've got to go on as if there were nothing wrong...

TO HIS DEAD BODY

When roaring gloom surged inward and you cried,
Groping for friendly hands, and clutched, and died,
Like racing smoke, swift from your lolling head
Phantoms of thought and memory thinned and fled.

Yet, though my dreams that throng the darkened stair
Can bring me no report of how you fare,
Safe quit of wars, I speed you on your way
Up lonely, glimmering fields to find new day,
Slow-rising, saintless, confident and kind -
Dear, red-faced father God who lit your mind.

– 22nd JULY 1916 –

SECOND-LIEUTENANT FORD MADOX HUEFFER
9th Battalion Welch Regiment

Ford Madox Hueffer, was forty-three when he arrived on the Somme on 16th July. He was attached to the battalion's first line of transport in Bécourt Wood at the bottom of Sausage Valley. On 21st July the Battalion was bivouacked at the south end of Mametz Wood. The following day, from billets in Albert, Hueffer wrote 'The Iron Music'.

THE IRON MUSIC

The French guns roll continuously
And our guns, heavy, slow;
Along the Ancre, sinuously,
The transport wagons go,
And the dust is on the thistles
And the larks sing up on high...
But I see the Golden Valley
Down by Tintern on the Wye.

For it's just nine weeks last Sunday
Since we took the Chepstow train,
And I'm wondering if one day
We shall do the like again;
For the four-point-two's come screaming
Thro' the sausages on high;
So there's little use in dreaming
How we walked above the Wye.

Dust and corpses in the thistles
Where the gas-shells burst like snow,
And the shrapnel screams and whistles
On the Bécourt Road below,
And the High Wood bursts and bristles
Where the mine-clouds foul the sky...
But I'm with you up at Wyndcroft,
Over Tintern on the Wye.

– 22nd JULY 1916 –

LIEUTENANT EWART ALAN MACKINTOSH, M.C.
5th Battalion Seaforth Highlanders

In May 1916 Alan Mackintosh won the M.C. 'for conspicuous gallantry' in a raid on German trenches west of Arras. The Battalion arrived at Méricourt from the Arras sector on 21st July and within a few days was in reserve trenches south of Mametz Wood. Alan Mackintosh composed a poem 'Peace upon Earth' on the road to Fricourt and 'Before the Summer' from Corbie.

PEACE UPON EARTH

Under the sky of battle, under the arch of the guns,
Where in a mad red torrent the river of fighting runs,
Where the shout of a strong man sounds no more than a broken groan,
And the heart of a man rejoicing stands up in its strength alone,
There in the hour of trial; and when the battle is spent,
And we sit drinking together, laughing and well content,
Deep in my heart I am hearing a little still voice that sings,
"Well, but what will you do when there comes an end of these
    things?"

Laughter, hard drinking and fighting, quarrels of friend and friend,
The eyes of the men that trust us, of all these there is an end.
No more in the raving barrage in one swift clamorous breath
We shall jest and curse together on the razor-edge of death.
Old days, old ways, old comrades, for ever and ever good-bye!
We shall walk no more in the twisted ways of the trenches, you and I,
For the nations have heard the tidings, they have sworn that wars
    shall cease,
And it's all one damned long Sunday walk down the straight, flat road
    of peace.

Yes, we shall be raptured again by the frock-coat's singular charm,
That goes so well with children and a loving wife on your arm,
Treading a road that is paved with family dinners and teas,
A sensible dull suburban road planted with decorous trees,
Till we come at last to the heaven our peaceable saints have trod,
Like the sort of church that our fathers built and called it a house
    of God,

And a God like a super-bishop in an apron and nice top-hat -
O God, you are God of battles. Forbid that we come to that!

God, you are God of soldiers, merry and rough and kind,
Give to your sons an earth and a heaven more to our mind,
Meat and drink for the body, laughter and song for the soul,
And fighting and clean quick death to end and complete the whole.

Never a hope of heaven, never a fear of hell,
Only the knowledge that you are a soldier, and all is well,
And whether the end be death or a merrier life be given,
We shall have died in the pride of our youth - and that will be
    heaven.

BEFORE THE SUMMER

When our men are marching lightly up and down,
When the pipes are playing through the little town,
I see a thin line swaying through wind and mud and rain
And the broken regiments come back to rest again.

Now the pipes are playing, now the drums are beat,
Now the strong battalions are marching up the street,
But the pipes will not be playing and the bayonets will not shine,
When the regiments I dream of come stumbling down the line.

Between the battered trenches their silent dead will lie
Quiet with grave eyes staring at the summer sky.
There is a mist upon them so that I cannot see
The faces of my friends that walk the little town with me.

Lest we see a worse thing than it is to die,
Live ourselves and see our friends cold beneath the sky,
God grant we too be lying there in wind and mud and rain
Before the broken regiments come stumbling back again.

– 22nd - 23rd JULY 1916 –

LIEUTENANT ADRIAN CONSETT STEPHEN, M.C.
Trench Mortar Battery, Royal Field Artillery

On the night of July 22nd - 23rd the First Australian Division attacked Pozières; Adrian Stephen spent the whole night at his Observation Post watching his fellow country-men fight for the heavily fortified village.

As zero time became due, three or four guns opened out - there are always a few early guns - for it is impossible for 50 watches to synchronize, but after a second or two all the Batteries get into their stride, and the whole world becomes merely noise - noise! Though armed with a megaphone it was useless to attempt to shout orders to the four guns. I had to place the megaphone against the ear of each N.C.O. and speak very slowly and deeply. If he attempted to speak back, it was like two people screaming at each other in a ship's gale. I enjoyed myself. Even the prematures from the field guns behind (that wounded one of our men), and that sent their shrapnel singing overhead like spray, only added the necessary touch of danger. The roar of the guns, with their irregular pound-pound-pounding that sounded like hammer blows, filled one with a sense of immense power - and that in itself is an intoxication. Further south the bombardment was equally intense. The light in the sky was no more a jerky and intermittent flame; it was a continuously flickering blaze of yellow and red - like a coloured cinematograph.

The night itself - Nature's night I mean - was clean and fine; stars and a few clouds and the trench rockets and the flash of guns lit up the scene fitfully, shining on chalk heaps and the white curled back lips of the trenches like the moon on a rough sea. As time went on the bombardment slackened and finally settled into a sullen, steady rhythm. I had leisure to wander about and repeatedly walked down to the road, where fresh troops were beginning to stream up to the firing line. The wounded were coming back too - trolley loads of them were being pushed down the little railway. As they glided past I would ask, "How are things going?" "Orlright." "Have you got the village?" "Yer bet." And sometimes I could see by the movements of their inevitable "fags", that those who *could* were waving. All night long and far into the morning those trolleys streamed down. Bad cases were carried on stretchers. Soon after dawn more new troops swung up the valley road.

I sat and watched them, trying to pick out a face I knew. Most of the men had their sleeves rolled up, and one of our sergeants after surveying them critically announced: "Well, anyhow they *mean* it." The men marching to Pozières, and the loads of wounded streaming back from it, not ten yards between them, made a contrast. The battle seemed to consist of a passing circle of men through that inferno, some of them staying there for ever, some coming out broken, but few - I never saw any - coming back as they had gone. Of course the slightly wounded walked back, cutting - one must confess - rather a comic figure. Their bandages, and their torn bloody clothes made them appear like old time buccaneers. For a cigarette, they would stop and yarn, spinning harrowing tales - generally incorrect - of the progress of events. At about 10.30 a.m. I went to bed. When I got up at 4 p.m. the same stream of fresh men and wounded continued. Our guns were fairly quiet, though some 60 pounders on the left were firing steadily; for three days they only stopped firing for half an hour. The gun pits were made of biscuit boxes. After each round the gun would heave back on its haunches, as though taking a breath while smoke dribbled out of the long barrel (I saw one of their prematures wipe out 8 Australians). But Pozières itself was now a furnace; dense smoke, yellow and white and black, poured out of it; the Boche bombardment sounded like the crackling of tin; it seemed impossible that men without trenches could exist in such a cauldron - yet they did. But even on those whom it did not wound, Pozières will leave its mark... The line we *do* hold consists of scattered shell holes, manned probably by two of our men and one dead Boche and when, to cap everything, one distinctly *sees* some of our own men running about in front of all those points of view, one's state of mind is chaotic. The only safe thing to do is to "cock her up" and fire well behind the lines...

Our own Infantry were attacking certain trenches to the left of Pozières, and we could see their position from the O.P. The O.P. is an old German machine gun dug-out, and our own dead were strewn (I could have counted 50) in front of it. The machine gunner had died hard, but the view from the O.P. was rather far away and the approach to it rather unsavoury. The trenches leading to it were the graves of dozens of Germans; feet stuck out from the sides, and sometimes a thin transparent hand would claw at you as you passed. But this was as nothing compared to the road from the O.P. to Pozières... the machine guns were unpleasant, but not so unpleasant as the sights one passed. Corpses, both English and German, but chiefly English, were strewn on the road-side. The faces and hands were black like niggers, some had the tops of their skulls knocked off and hanging like the lid of a box while all were swollen so that the uniform fitted like a glove. Oh, the glamour and the glory of war! How safely the papers talk of "sleeping the last sleep," &c., and even Brooke with his "some corner of a foreign field is England" - "C'est la guerre," is the answer I suppose - as if *that* answered for *anything*...

August
1916

– 1st AUGUST 1916 –

LIEUTENANT EWART ALAN MACKINTOSH, M.C.
5th Battalion Seaforth Highlanders

The Battalion was in front-line trenches near High Wood on 1st August. The men came under heavy bombardment and Alan Mackintosh was wounded and gassed. He was sent home to recuperate.

TO THE 51st DIVISION: HIGH WOOD,
JULY - AUGUST 1916

Oh gay were we in spirit
In the hours of the night
When we lay in rest by Albert
And waited for the fight;
Gay and gallant were we
On the day that we set forth,
But broken, broken, broken
Is the valour of the North.

The wild warpipes were calling,
Our hearts were blithe and free
When we went up the valley
To the death we could not see.
Clear lay the wood before us
In the clear summer weather
But broken, broken, broken
Are the sons of the heather.

In the cold of the morning,
In the burning of the day,
The thin lines stumbled forward,
The dead and dying lay.
By the unseen death that caught us
By the bullets' raging hail
Broken, broken, broken
Is the pride of the Gael.

HIGH WOOD TO WATERLOT FARM

Tune - "Chalk Farm to Camberwell Green"

There is a wood at the top of a hill,
　If it's not shifted it's standing there still;
There is a farm a short distance away,
But I'd not advise you to go there by day,
For the snipers abound, and the shells are not rare,
And a man's only chance is to run like a hare,
So take my advice if you're chancing your arm
From High Wood to Waterlot Farm.

Chorus -　*High Wood to Waterlot Farm,*
　　　　　All on a summer's day,
　　　　　Up you get to the top of the trench
　　　　　Though you're sniped at all the way.
　　　　　If you've got a smoke helmet there
　　　　　You'd best put it on if you could,
　　　　　For the wood down by Waterlot Farm
　　　　　Is a bloody high wood

– 2nd - 8th AUGUST 1916 –

LIEUTENANT RAYMOND ASQUITH
3rd Battalion Grenadier Guards

Raymond Asquith, the eldest son of the Prime Minister, H.H. Asquith arrived from the Ypres Salient at the front line at Hébuterne during the first few days of August. Billets were at Bertrancourt and at the Bois du Warnimont. On the evening of 2nd August he went with his men to dig out a trench which had been blown in during the recent fighting; he described the following few days and nights in letters to his wife, Katherine.

It was a tiresome job, very little room to work and every now and then the Germans sent over a trench mortar bomb - to my mind the most alarming things in this war. It is a thing about the size and shape of a very big rum jar, has a range of 400 yards or so and goes very high and very slow. At night you see it slowly elbowing through the stars with a trail of sparks behind it, and the probability is that the trench is too full for you to get as far away as you would wish. Then it falls and fizzes for a little in the ground and then the most ear-splitting explosion you can ever hope to hear.

This night I was up at the forward end of this trench, rather engrossed in directing the men's work, when suddenly I found myself surrounded by a mob of terrified figures from the battalion which was holding that part of the line (we were only working on it) who gibbered and crouched and held their hands over their eyes and generally conducted themselves as if the end of the world was at hand. It was very alarming; they had seen one of these damned rum jars coming and I hadn't. Sure enough in about 5 seconds the thing went off - luckily just the other side of our parapet. The sky was black with smoke and dirt, and the people butted into one in the fog screaming, but much more frightened than hurt.

The explosion was as painful as a sound can be. In the moment immediately preceding it I made up my mind I was dead, and in the moment immediately following I said to myself "I suppose this is shell shock at last, now I shall get home." But it wasn't. The cracking of one's ear drums is painful and the extraordinary tension in the air and pressure on one's head and a smell which I can only describe as the smell of infinite force. And then one found after all that one was not much the worse. I felt a piece of the thing hit me on the leg, but alas it only made a small blood blister. I picked another fragment out of the shoulder of my jacket - it had cut through the khaki but not through my shirt, and there was quite a big dent in my steel helmet. A most disappointing result...

We got back for breakfast about 6 a.m. and I went to bed at 7 in my bivouac. One feels greatly tired after these nights of digging and a march of 6 miles or so each way. And as soon as one gets to bed the heat and noise begin, so that really one gets very little sleep. Then yesterday we went up again and did much the same thing...

If it weren't for the heat and the weariness and lack of shade and sleep parts of it have been quite pleasant. Our rest and bathe e.g. en route, and a lovely chateau near the bathing place with the ruins of an abbey and cloisters in the grounds, which some of us went to see. And the first part of our wait for the motor lorries wasn't so bad. We lay out in a cool field and the drums played and the men sang choruses and about 20 French children sprang up out of the ground and began dancing with extraordinary skill and brio to the popular tunes...

8th August. I am not favourably impressed by what I have seen of the 'K'[Kitchener] armies in this part of the line. I daresay they go ahead all right in an attack, but they are horribly nervous under the ordinary conditions of trench warfare...

We went on night after night marching 5 or 6 miles up to some rather bad trenches which we had to improve. We used to start about 7.30 p.m. after an early dinner and march over flat open country under the setting sun for about 4 miles to a point where we entered the hindmost of the vast maze of communication trenches which heads up to and around the front line. Usually as we approached this point we were spotted by a German balloon or aeroplane which dropped lights to signal to the guns which began loosing off in a desultory kind of way about 5 minutes afterwards, usually just after we had reached cover when it was pleasant enough to hear the shells whistling overhead on to the road behind us.

Then we wandered for ages through the widening trenches constantly losing our temper and our way till we got to a dump where we picked up tools and sandbags etc., and then advanced to the scene of operations. We would get there usually about 10.30 p.m., sometimes an hour or so later and work for 4 hours under rather adverse circumstances, bodies of engineers constantly forcing their way past us carrying long boards, pit props, dug-out frames, and swearing horribly. The trenches we dug in ran out to what had been our front line but it is now (since the crumping it has had during the last month) only a series of isolated posts held or not held as the case may be by nervous and incompetent groups of the new Army.

The first night I found I had nothing at all between me and the Germans except a few dead men whom I found while reconnoitering, so I had to send out a covering party of my own as well as digging. I had to borrow some bombs from the battalion which ought to be there and they got into serious trouble for not covering us and for the remaining nights they took measures to do so. Luckily we were not molested by the enemy except for a few trench mortar shells and rifle grenades. But it was disagreeable, tiring and rather nervous work, as we couldn't possibly have held the line we were in if we had been attacked, and should have had some difficulty in falling back upon any other.

Then about 2.30 a.m. we would deposit our tools and march back, arriving in camp about 5. We breakfasted on an oil sheet on a high curve of the downs, eating our bacon under the rising sun, dog tired but listening at ease to the noise of the harmless guns, which never ceases in these parts...

Yesterday we marched about 5 miles to a camp in a wood further back. I got a good night's rest on a stretcher in a tent and this morning we have done nothing but a little bayonet fighting...

– 5th - 9th AUGUST 1916 –

SECOND-LIEUTENANT MAX PLOWMAN
'C' Company 10th Battalion West Yorkshire Regiment

From bivouacs at Bellevue Farm, south-east of Albert, the Battalion marched to Pommiers Redoubt, on the road between Montauban and Mametz, on 4th August. The following day the men marched to trenches on the right of Bazentin-le-Grand and the left of Longueval; they were relieved on 9th August and returned to Pommiers Redoubt.

Hardy [a fellow officer] and I are off to Pommiers Redoubt, Mametz, where we are to report that the battalion will arrive this evening. We descend the long hill leading to Fricourt, dodging about the stream of traffic that stirs the dust of the road to a thick haze. Near the bottom of the hill we come upon the old front line of July 1st. The country here is stricken waste: the trees that formed an avenue to the road are now torn and broken stumps, some still holding unexploded shells in their shattered trunks, others looped about with useless telegraph-wire. The earth on both sides of the road is churned up into a crumbling mass, and so tossed and scarred is the ground that the actual line of the front trenches is hardly distinguishable. On the far side, in the face of a steep rise, we see the remains of what were deep German dug-outs; but everything needs pointing out, for the general impression is of a wilderness without verdure or growth of any kind. To our right we notice a ruined cemetery. It looks as if it might have heard the Last Trump. Graves are opened and monuments of stone and beaded wire lie smashed and piled in heaps.

Now, as we near Mametz, we come upon guns hidden under the banks of the roadside and camouflaged above by netting. The road through Mametz is still under enemy observation; so we turn sharply to the right to go round the back of the rising ground that faces us. All that remains of the village of Fricourt is a pile of bricks; there appear to be just about enough to build one house; and Mametz Wood is nothing more than a small collection of thin tree-trunks standing as if a forest fire had just swept over them. On the right of the sunken road we have now taken is a mound of sinking freshly-turned earth. It marks the grave of the Devons who died in the capture of Montauban. A little farther on we come upon all that remains of a German field cemetery: two or three painted triangular wooden crosses; the other graves will now go unmarked for ever. Here we leave the road and begin to climb over the forsaken trenches. Barbed wire, bombs, bully-beef tins, broken rifles, rounds of ammunition, unexploded shells, mess-tins, bits of leather and webbing equipment, British and German battered steel helmets, iron stakes, and all the refuse of a battlefield, still litter the mazy ground. I come across a skull, white and clean as if it had lain in the desert.

We can only move slowly over this confusion of forsaken trenches running in every direction, but at last we are clear of them and mount the hill which is our objective. It broadens out to a wide plateau. Little holes are cut in the ground just big enough to shelter one or two men and presumably give them cover from observation. The large old German dug-outs are not at first visible. We report at one of them and return along the hot road by the way we came.

GOING INTO THE LINE

At 3.15, No. 11 Platoon, 100 yards in rear of
No. 10, will move from Pommiers Redoubt.

      So soon!
At 3.15. And would return here... when?
It didn't say. Who would return? P'raps all,
P'raps none. Then it had come at last!
It had come at last! his own stupendous hour,
Long waited, dreaded, almost hoped-for too,
When all else seemed the foolery of power;
It had come at last! and suddenly the world
Was sharply cut in two. On one side lay
A golden, dreamy, peaceful afternoon,
And on the other, men gone mad with fear,
A hell of noise and darkness, a Last Day
Daily enacted. Now good-bye to one
And to the other... well, acceptance: that
At least he'd give; many had gone with joy:
He loathed it from his very inmost soul.

The golden world! It lay just over there,
Peacefully dreaming. In its clear bright depths
Friends moved - he saw them going here and there,
Like thistledown above an August meadow:
Gently as in a gentle dream they moved,

Unagonized, unwrought, nor sad, nor proud,
Faces he loved to agony - and none
Could see, or know, or bid him well-adieu.
Blasphemous irony! To think how oft
On such a day a friend would hold his hand
Saying good-bye, though they would meet next day,
And now... He breathed his whole soul out,
Bidding it span the unbridged senseless miles
And glow about their thoughts in waves of love.

'Twas time already! Now? As soon as this?
Did his voice hold? How did he look to them?
Poor craven little crowd of human mites!
Now they were crawling over the scarred cheese,
Silently going towards that roaring sea,
Each thinking his own thought, craving perhaps
A body that would fail, or with set teeth
Pitting a human will against the world.
Now every step seemed an eternity:
Each stretch of earth unreachable until it lay
Behind and a stretch longer lay beyond.
Would it never be ended? Crumbling earth,
Dry with the cracks of earthquake, dumbly showed
Death had just trodden there - and there he lay,
Foully deformed in what was once a man.
'Lo! as these are, so shalt thou be', he thought,
Shuddered: then thrilled almost to ecstasy,
As one from hell delivered up to heaven.

How slow they moved in front! Yes, slower still.
Then we must stop: we were not eighty yards.
But to stop here - to wait for it! Oh no!
Backward or forward, anything but not stop -
Not stand and wait! There's no alternative.
And now he rasps out, 'Halt!' They stand and curse,
Eyes furtive, fingers moving senselessly.
There comes a roar nearer and louder till
His head is bursting with noise and the earth shakes.
'A bloody near one, that!' and 'What the hell
Are we stuck here for?' come with sudden growls.
He moves without a word, and on they trudge.
So near! Yet nothing! Then how long? How long?...

And slowly in his overheated mind
Peace like a river through the desert flows,
And sweetness wells and overflows in streams
That reach the farthest friend in memory.
Peace now, and dear delight in serving these,
These poor sheep, driven innocent to death:
Peace undisturbed, though the poor senses jump,
And horror catches at the heart as when
Death unsuspected flaunts his grisly hand
Under the very eye of quietness:
Peace, peace with all, even the enemy,
Compassion for them deep as for his own:
Quietness now amid the thunderous noise,
And sweet elation in the grave of gloom.

We are going to the trenches. That little knot of men two hundred
yards ahead, just disappearing over the barren crest of the rise, is Hill's
platoon. Two hundred yards behind us is Smalley's. This afternoon the
sun glares down on earth that has lost its nature, for, pitted everywhere
with shell-holes, it crumbles and cracks as though it has indeed been
subject to earthquake. Up here we can be seen by the enemy; but there
is no hurrying, for we have to keep distance between platoons. Hill has
halted: we must halt, too. The men behind me swear with nervous
irritation and mutter about being stuck out here to be fired at. I turn to
look at them. Standing loaded up with boxes of bombs and sandbags
of rations, how utterly unlike the red-coats of romance they appear.

We are off again, now traversing the slope that leads to the valley of
Longueval. "Death Valley", it is nicknamed, and it has earned its title,
for everywhere there are signs of death: an inverted bottle with a bit of
paper in it: a forage-cap hung on a stick: a rough wooden cross
bearing the pencilled inscription, "To an Unknown British Soldier."
These signs recur: pathetic, temporary memorials; will they outlast the
war? In the bottom of the valley lie broken trucks and the shattered
rails of a tramway. As we come to the end of the tram-line we have to
pass the body of a dead horse, foul and distended, poisoning the air.
Suddenly, like a rat, a human figure comes out of the earth. Who
would have thought there were dug-outs here? As quickly it
disappears, and we pass on. We march in silence, broken occasionally
by a jest that fails to catch on, or by an irritable rebuke from one
jogged by his companion. There is no singing now; 'tis as if we moved
under an invisible cloud.

We halt for a moment in a chalk-pit where the M.O. has his dug-out, and then follow the narrowing sunken road that leads up St. George's Hill. By the time we have reached the top we are moving in single file round the horseshoe bend of the trench we are to occupy, pushing by the troops that wait for us to relieve them.

This is an old German trench that has been reversed and now forms part of our second line facing High Wood, just distinguishable as such, about five hundred yards away on the hill opposite. We have hardly entered the trench before we come on a stretcher lying on the ground. It bears the body of a boy: the face quite black. He has just been killed. It appears there was an old German latrine close to the parapet of the trench; two boys had gone to it when a shell came over and killed them both. As we push along I find that this particular sector falls to my platoon. The shell has made a big breach. To-night we shall have to repair it and clean up the mess which is beyond description.

The men are posted and the relieved troops scuttle out. In this narrow gap between two deep walls of clay we shall spend the next four days. The air is tainted with the sickly-sweet odour of decaying bodies. At certain corners this odour, intensified by the heat, becomes a stench so foul the bay cannot be occupied. Just now I tripped over a lump in the floor of the trench. It was necessary to get a shovel and quickly cover the spot. Literally we are the living among the dead.

Shelling is incessant. There is not a moment when something is not passing overhead; but the fire is not upon this trench, it is meant for the batteries now crammed up close behind on the rearward slope of the hill. Our batteries are replying, shell for shell. Somewhere very close to my sector a French seventy-five barks deafeningly.

I look for a place to lay my ground-sheet and rations, and find a hole burrowed in the side of the parapet and a new German saxe-blue coat lying on the floor. This hole will give cover from shrapnel and serve to deaden the noise if there's any chance of sleep; but it would prove an ugly death-trap if a shell dropped near. I lay my things in the hole and turn to see Rowley [the Company Commander] and the company-sergeant-major coming along to inspect. We go round together till we come to a spot in a traverse behind my sector where the smell of decay is so strong they are convinced there is a body lying out. Sure enough, just behind the parados, the dead body of a gunner lies on a stretcher, evidently left in haste. Both shin-bones are broken, but otherwise the poor fellow looks unhurt. We have the corpse carried out along the narrow trench: a difficult, awkward business.

I see Jackson considering the gap in our parapet and speak to him about it. He has the whole thing sized up, and without any fuss makes himself responsible for a particularly filthy job, telling me just what he proposes to do as soon as it is dark. He seems more at his ease in the trenches. I shall like this man.

Wondering how Hill fares I go down the trench to see him, and we decide we shall have to spread out our platoons, that are much under strength, if we are to keep in touch. I am just returning along the unoccupied gap between us when rapid rifle-fire suddenly starts in the valley below. What does it mean? I get up on a firestep and peer over. There's nothing to see, but the firing continues, causing a cloud of smoke that begins to fill the air. Are they coming over? If they do - well, I've this bit of the line to myself. I pull out my revolver, load it and wait, wondering ironically what anyone would give for my chances. If they come as soon as this, it will have been quick work. The firing continues so that the smoke obscures all view. Then to my relief the sergeant-major comes along. He too is wondering what is going to happen, and we wait together silently. Gradually the firing dies down. It ceases. We go back to my platoon and beyond to see Smalley on the right. He has put his men into the P.H. helmets, mistaking the smoke for a gas attack. "All's well that ends well." But we do not fail to chaff Smalley about his precaution...

Night has fallen. The stars shine brilliantly and (these trenches facing north) I gaze at The Plough dipping towards High Wood. What joy it is to know that you in England and I out here at least can look upon the same beauty in the sky! We've the stars to share. Look at them! They have become seers - images of divine stability - guardians of a peace and order beyond the power of weak and petty madness. Upon what havoc and ruin have they looked down in days of Greece and Rome and centuries beyond! Still they shine and keep their calm serenity. They, at least, will outlast the war and still be beautiful. We cannot shoot the stars.

If only those two guns on the horizon beyond High Wood could stop! They flash a pair of devilish eyes and we, trembling, wait the result; for they are firing on us. Already they have knocked the trench in twice, luckily at unoccupied places. It's all because of that damned machine-gun that keeps hammering away on our left. Why on earth do they want to keep firing into the dark like that?

Hill and I think it our duty to find out. After some difficulty we discover the machine-gun, and ask the gunners if they can't stop for a while. Sorry, but they've instructions to carry on overhead fire all night on a road beyond the hill which it is reported the Germans use every night.

We come back to my burrow and crawl in, drawing the ground-sheet across the opening so that we can strike a match and by the light of a candle eat and smoke.

This is the first time in the trenches for us both, and we marvel at the continuous shelling, wondering if it is ever going to stop. Hill falls asleep, and with friendship's pity I look upon his sleeping face. Then a whizz-bang bursts just above us and he wakes, scared like a child. We climb out and parade, for the rest of the night, up and down the trench...

Morning breaks shrouded in mist: pale pink veils in the sky above announce the coming of the sun... The shelling goes on, now heaviest over Delville Wood. We go and look down over it, from the horseshoe bend in the trench on Smalley's right flank, as the mist begins to clear. We can only guess very roughly the lie of our own and the German trenches: not a living thing is to be seen. The wood itself is just a collection of stakes stuck upright in the ground, looking like the broken teeth of some vicious beast. Shells drop everywhere, making little Etnas as they burst, but we cannot tell which are the hits...

As dark comes on we are filing out to dig a new communication-trench down in the valley between the front line and our own. Passing a dump, the men draw picks and shovels alternately. It is strange and exciting to be in the open again. The men are extended in line while the tape is being laid. They begin to chatter - too loudly it seems, for half a dozen whizz-bangs come fizzing right among us, glaring red as they burst. The men flop, and I, knowing no better, do the same. Down along the line comes Rowley cursing the men furiously.

"What the hell do you think you are doing lying there?"

I get up feeling badly chagrined, and the work is begun. For a couple of hours it is continued, practically undisturbed. Then we file hurriedly back to the trench, learning as we enter it that we are to return to the work in the morning...

Another perfect day; but against the blue sky beyond High Wood an observation-balloon hangs ominously. If we were shelled in the dark, how shall we fare in such daylight as this with that balloon hanging over there?

Anyway - merciful and delicious relief! - the shelling here has ceased at last.

At moments there is real silence. To our tired ears this absence of sound is positive and acute pleasure: we drink it like wine, loathe to break it even with conversation.

Wondering what will happen, we file down the hillside. To our surprise the silence continues. Out in the bright sunlight the trench is deepened and widened and not a shot is fired at us, though looking across the valley we can see shrapnel falling, ironically enough, on the trenches we have left.

Soon after noon we return, very hot, to eat our bully beef and bread, sitting on the firestep. Castlereagh, bright lad, has made me a drink of tea, which I am thankful to accept even from his mess-tin. But while drinking it, I feel a smack on the neck and look round to see who is throwing earth about. No one looks guilty, and putting my hand up I find my neck bleeding; and there at my feet lies an inch of shrapnel I had not seen before. Luckily it must have been the flat side that hit and split the skin. Hill ties me up and we laugh over our first "casualty". Then Rowley comes along and, brushing my ridicule aside, insists that I must report to the M.O. for anti-tetanus inoculation. I can go on at once with Hardy's sergeant, and afterwards, on behalf of the company "take over" at Pommiers Redoubt where the battalion is due again to-night. We shall pass the dressing-station on the way out.

That greasy-looking M.O! Rowley says that he covers his skin with the fat of bully beef to save washing and keep off the lice, and though that is probably gross libel, unfortunately it looks true. I suffer his attentions, wondering what devil of malice he must house to make him scornful of our easy spell, and together the sergeant and I go into the fearsome valley.

Suddenly those black-bursting shells known as "coal-boxes" begin to fall. They come with terrifying explosions, and we scuttle in search of a deep communication-trench there should be hereabouts. At the far end of the valley a limber is moving along the road. A shell comes over, and when the cloud of smoke clears, the wagon is gone and the horses are bolting down the road. A moment later and we are mopping our hot faces in the comparative security of the deep trench...

– 8th AUGUST 1916 –

SERGEANT FREDERICK LESLIE A. COULSON

1st/12th Battalion London Regiment (The Rangers)

Leslie Coulson, who served in the same Battalion as Edward Liveing (qv), was in trenches east of Hébuterne and Fonquevillers and billeted behind the line in the villages of Sailly and Bayencourt. He wrote 'The Rainbow' on 8th August when parties were drawn from the Battalion to work in the front line trenches.

THE RAINBOW

I watch the white dawn gleam,
    To the thunder of hidden guns.
I hear the hot shells scream
Through skies as sweet as a dream
    Where the silver dawnbreak runs.
And stabbing of light
Scorches the virginal white.
But I feel in my being the old, high, sanctified thrill,
And I thank the gods that the dawn is beautiful still.

From death that hurtles by
    I crouch in the trench day-long
But up to a cloudless sky
From the ground where our dead men lie
    A brown lark soars in song.
Through the tortured air,
Rent by the shrapnel's flare,
Over the troubleless dead he carols his fill,
And I thank the gods that the birds are beautiful still.

Where the parapet is low
    And level with the eye
Poppies and cornflowers glow
And the corn sways to and fro
    In a pattern against the sky.
The gold stalks hide
Bodies of men who died
Charging at dawn through the dew to be killed or to kill.

I thank the gods that the flowers are beautiful still.

When night falls dark we creep
   In silence to our dead.
We dig a few feet deep
And leave them there to sleep -
   But blood at night is red,
Yea, even at night,
And a dead man's face is white.
And I dry my hands, that are also trained to kill,
And I look at the stars - for the stars are beautiful still.

– 12th - 13th AUGUST 1916 –

LIEUTENANT ALAN ALEXANDER MILNE
11th Battalion Royal Warwickshire Regiment

Until July 1916, A.A. Milne was a Signalling Instructor in England and he joined the Battalion shortly before it was sent into action. Between the 6th and 9th August the Battalion was in trenches at the west edge of Mametz Wood and was heavily shelled. On the 11th the artillery bombardment was very intense and there were sixty-three casualties many of whom were buried by high explosive shells. During the afternoon Second Lieutenant Harrison, the signals officer, Milne and three men went out to lay a telephone cable to the front trench. They came under heavy fire and Harrison was wounded. Milne then became signalling officer. At 4 a.m. on the 12th he went out again and this time managed to lay the cable. The Battalion was ordered to attack east of the Bazentin-le-Petit - Martinpuich road. It was driven back and once again many men were lost. The following day the Battalion Diary recorded: "At daybreak many of our men were still finding their way back to our trenches. The Germans showed themselves and shouted friendly remarks to our men and appeared anxious for a peaceful spell."

H.Q. was in a deep German dug-out, facing, of course, the wrong way. In an adjoining dug-out was the H.Q. of the East Lancashires with whom the attack was being made. In the space between these two underground rooms were my signallers. At eleven o'clock that night the Colonel, the Major, the Adjutant and I sat round a table by candle-light smoking and talking, waiting for our barrage to begin. But the Germans, who knew all about it, began first. And the line went.

The sergeant-major of the East Lancashires went up the steps with some idea, I suppose, of getting information, and was blown out of existence before he reached the top. My signallers announced this, and added that the line to Brigade was also down. We sat there completely isolated. The depth of the dug-out deadened the noise of the guns, so that a shell-burst was no longer the noise of a giant plumber throwing down his tools, but only a persistent thud, which set the candles dancing and then, as if by an afterthought, blotted them out. From time to time I lit them again, wondering what I should be doing, wondering what signalling officers did on these occasions. Nervously I said to the Colonel, feeling that the isolation was all my fault, "Should I try to get a line out?" and to my intense relief he said, "Don't be a bloody fool."

It was about two o'clock in the morning that a runner got through.

The attack, as was to be expected, was a complete failure. In his Company, So-and-so and So-and-so were killed - I remembered them, two boys under the apple trees in the little village where I had joined them in billets; we had dined in the garden to the gramophone, and there were peaches which one of them had fetched from Amiens, and the war was just a happy picnic to them, the guns rolling so far, far away in the distance that one would never catch up with them - no, sir, he couldn't say about the captain - no, sir, he was all right, but he couldn't rightly say about any of the others, it had been coming over something cruel.

"All right," said the Colonel.

"Am I to go back, sir?"

"No." He caught the Major's eye. The Major got up and strapped on his revolver. It was all too clearly the moment for me to strap on mine...

"Use your common sense," said the Colonel. "If it's impossible, come back. I simply cannot lose three signalling officers in a month."

I promised, but felt quite unable to distinguish between common-sense and cowardice. The whole thing was so damned silly.

I told my sergeant that we were now going to run out a line, and asked him to pick two men for me. I knew nothing of the section then, save that there was a Lance-Corporal Grainger who shared my passion for Jane Austen, unhelpful knowledge in the circumstances. My sergeant said at once: "I'll come for one, sir," which I thought was sporting of him, although it was obviously wrong for both of us to go. He picked on another man, a company signaller who had joined headquarters for the occasion, and we attached ourselves to the Major. We dashed. The Major went first - he was going to "reorganize the troops"; I went second, God knew why; the sergeant and the signaller came behind me, running out a line neatly and skillfully. No laddering now, no text-book stuff, it was just dropped anywhere. From time to time the Major flung himself down for a breather, and down we flopped and panted, wondering if he would get up again. To our relief each time he was alive, and so were we. We passed one of the signal-stations, no longer a station but a pancake of earth on top of a spread-eagled body; I had left him there that evening, saying "Well, you'll be comfortable here." More rushes, more breathers, more bodies, we were in the front line. The Major hurried off to collect what men he could, while I joined up the telephone. Hopeless, of course, but we could have done no more. I pressed the buzzer, and incredibly heard Daffy's slow, lazy voice: not my Daffy [his wife Daphne] in England, but Corporal Daffy, ex-gardener from Buxton, with the gardener's heavy drooping moustache and heavy stoop, unalterably a civilian...

I asked to speak to the Colonel. I told him what I knew. I ordered - what were telephones for? - a little counter-bombardment. Then with a sigh of utter content and thankfulness and the joy of living, I turned away from the telephone. And there behind me was Lance-Corporal Grainger.

"What on earth are you doing here?" I said.

He grinned sheepishly.

"You weren't detailed, were you?"

"No, sir."

"Well, then —-"

"I thought I'd just like to come along, sir."

"But why?"

He looked still more embarrassed.

"Well sir, I thought I'd just like to be sure you were all right."

Which is the greatest tribute to Jane Austen that I have ever heard.

– 13th - 17th AUGUST 1916 –

LIEUTENANT GRAHAM H. GREENWELL, M.C.
4th Battalion Oxfordshire and Buckinghamshire Light Infantry

During July and the first few weeks of August Graham Greenwell was in and out of the trenches and in billets at Mailly Maillet, Hebuterne, Sailly, Bouzincourt and Agenville. On 12th August he was bivouacked in Bouzincourt 'a sort of ante-chamber to the Chamber of Horrors beyond' and on 13th August, a twenty-year old Company Commander, he was in trenches at Ovillers. His letters were written to his mother.

I have just taken over some trenches, such as they are, full of equipment, filth and bodies and am being heavily shelled. I have had four casualties already, one killed and three wounded: my poor men are rather windy I am afraid, and I can't really blame them as most of them have only been three months in the army and this is their first introduction to the trenches.

The village we passed through just now is literally abolished, absolutely flat, not a sign even of a wall and the stink is awful.

The Huns are in a miserable state, absolutely craven and disheartened: some prisoners have just passed down the trench, rotten specimens. But they have a devil of a lot of guns here which give us hell.

One of my boys has just come down rather badly wounded and whimpering, but he will be all right directly he gets back to the dressing station.

August 14th... I have seldom felt such a miserable wreck. I have had my boots on since 8 a.m. of the day before yesterday and have had no hot food for thirty-six hours, only a small piece of bread and cheese and a hunk of melted chocolate.

We were heavily shelled all yesterday without a stop and I had a few more casualties. The bombardment increased in violence about 9 p.m. and the Germans attacked our front line, the garrison of which had been hopelessly reduced by the afternoon's shelling and by our own shells falling short. Our men were driven out and back, and receiving an urgent message for reinforcements and bombs, I sent up two of my subalterns with their Platoons and two bombs a man. They appear to have lost their way and couldn't find anyone except the Anzacs, who were also having the devil of a time.

I then got a message from King [a platoon commander] that they believed the trench in front of them was occupied by the Germans, and the next thing I saw was the boy himself, with his whole face bathed and streaked in gore and roughly bandaged. He said that Lakin, my Second-in-Command, was killed and that a good many of the men were casualties. I passed him on to the dressing station and then went round to Battalion headquarters to get some information. I was told to remain in my trench and hold it with the remaining Platoons of my Company, reinforced by a party of Berkshires who had turned up carrying bombs.

Later I saw Pickford - who had been in charge of the front line all day. He said he had lost nearly all his Company and all his officers - among them Leslie Hunter, a Wykhamist and a Fellow of New College who had only just joined us.

I got my officer out: he was wounded in the head and leg and was suffering very severely indeed from shock.

The Berks counter-attacked the trench at 4 a.m. to try to regain it and I was present at their conference at my Company headquarters just before. I don't know what has happened to them, but a friend of mine, commanding one of the Companies, has been killed and another badly wounded. I believe they are having a pretty bad time of it up there.

The Bosche is still shelling us, but not quite so heavily.

I took over as my Headquarters a deep German mine shaft, but it isn't a very good place and I have chosen instead a narrow little sap running out of the main trench - as safe as anywhere can be, I think. The whole place simply reeks, and I am filthy from head to foot. I am hoping we may be relieved tonight or early to-morrow morning, as this will be our third night without sleep and some of the men are rather ill I'm afraid. Carew Hunt [a platoon commander] and I are the only officers in the Company at present, but I have one lad whom I left behind on a machine gun course and who will rejoin afterwards.

I can't describe the awful destruction and the litter and waste: shattered trenches and dug-outs with equipment, bodies, food, bombs and rifles everywhere...

August 15th. Reserve Trenches behind Ovillers...

After writing my yesterday's letter to you we settled down to the most awful hell of shelling I have ever been in... From 11.30 a.m. to 2.30 p.m. the Germans shelled like the devil with big stuff; it was a most trying ordeal; I was in a shaft full of filth and flies with my servant, bugler, sergeant-major and a wounded man (with a huge gash in his back and wounded in the leg), a stretcher-bearer and anyone who happened to blow in. The wounded man was very good and cheerful though his arm was nearly off and his lung pierced. We spent the time getting hold of iodine and dressings and trying to patch up his wounds. Finally, the other Battalion came up and I began to pass my men out of the trench back through what is left of the village of Ovillers.

The trench was all blown in and littered with filth and bodies. I think the awful stench is much worse than the shelling. My men told me that this thirty-six hours in the trench was far worse than their attack on July 23rd. But I had only twenty-two casualties in my Company and two officers wounded.

Lakin is very seriously wounded and King rather seriously.

Hunter was seen to be hit and is either a prisoner or dead, probably the latter. He will be a great loss, as he was a most brilliant man and a splendid officer. Another Company Commander, Willie Wayman, is missing and probably killed, and two other officers wounded slightly. The regiment had nearly one hundred and forty casualties I'm afraid - of course a few men are still unaccounted for.

We found our cookers, with tea waiting behind Ovillers. There I formed my Company up and called the roll. A groom came up to me as I emerged from the trenches, saluted and said: "Would you like a horse?" Of course I was delighted: they hadn't brought my own up but I got the Padré's - a little polo pony full of buck, but I was so delighted to get on again and not to have had to walk a step further that I would have ridden anything.

It was curious to ride all through our old line of trenches and the old German front line. The Huns have already got a superiority of artillery here and give our people the most ghastly time of it; they know the exact range of all our trenches as they are their old ones. However, each night we push on a bit somewhere; unfortunately it is very expensive.

We are now back in some trenches cut in the chalk hills instead of bivouacking in the bare field which was alloted to us...

August 17th. Skyline Trench, Ovillers... I am sitting in the bottom of an old German dug-out about ten or twelve feet under the earth with three other officers and about ten men, orderlies and runners; the table is littered with food, equipment, candle grease and odds and ends. The floor is covered with German clothing and filth. The remains of the trench outside is blown to pieces, and full of corpses from the different regiments which have been here lately, German and English. The ground is ploughed up by enormous shell-holes; there isn't a single landmark to be seen for miles except a few gaunt sticks where trees once were. The stench is well-nigh intolerable, but thank God I have just found the remains of a tube of frozacalone Bridge sent out, which I have rubbed under my nose. Everyone is absolutely worn out with fatigue and hunger.

Yesterday while trying to find the regiment we were relieving, I was very slightly wounded by a piece of shrapnel to the left of my left eye. It knocked me over and stunned me a bit, but was only a flesh wound and is healed now except for a bruise.

I wandered on round these awful remains of trenches with my bugler, simply sickened by the sights and smells, until I found some poor devils cowering in the filth, where they had been for forty-eight hours. I moved them back. Soon after this I felt rather dizzy and went back to Battalion headquarters where the Colonel was very kind and made me lie down on a German bed for a rest. Later in the afternoon I went down to the doctor, who has a fine dressing station in a huge German dug-out. There I rested and spent the night and came back here this morning.

Thank Heaven we are due to be relieved in an hour or two, when we shall go back to some trenches behind, though they will, of course, be only comparatively better. To-morrow morning I hope the whole regiment will be relieved and go back...

I shall never look on warfare either as fine or sporting again. It reduces men to shivering beasts: there isn't a man who can stand shell-fire of the modern kind without getting the blues...

– 18th AUGUST 1916 –

LIEUTENANT ADRIAN CONSETT STEPHEN, M.C.
Trench Mortar Battery, Royal Field Artillery.

By 13th August Adrian Stephen's position was in Mash Valley, which ran parallel and to the left of Sausage Valley. The Battery's guns were just behind the parapet of the old German 1st line. The men slept in an old, very infested, German dug-out. Stephen was to witness the forthcoming daylight attack on Thièpval supported by a creeping barrage.

The first attack was on August 18th at 5 p.m., and this was the first time I had seen the Infantry "go over the top". From the O.P., which was in an old German trench, and which was simplicity itself, as it merely consisted in sticking one's head over the parapet, I could look from a distance of about 500 yards on the scene of operations. On the left, squatting on its hill, was Thièpval, a mass of ruins but apparently impregnable - a thorn in the British left flank. To the right was a maze of mangled trenches - one's first impression was that of a ploughed field; for half a mile not a shrub or blade of grass, just chalk heaps and timbers strewn around after being uplifted from the depths of dug-outs. It was indeed a different front, needing hours of study and consultation among the various observers, and when one had mastered the system of trenches - system is a euphemism - the Infantry would attack, and the whole landscape be re-shuffled. Artillery work was a sensitive business. Well, at 5 p.m. on the 18th, the brigade opened the ball by attacking about 1000 yards of trench. A second or two before the hour the Infantry clambered out of the trenches, and a few guns began to clear their throats with stray shells. For a dangerous second the Infantry seemed to stand up without protection, then with the roar and hiss of a flood our barrage swept along in front of them. The infantry walked quickly forward, shoulders bent, rifles at the trail. Right to the edge of the barrage they seemed to walk; then they vanished into shell holes and trenches. One or two still stood up and seemed to be arguing as to the direction. It was uncanny to see them standing there in the open; but the barrage which now flayed and churned the German trenches into a line of smoke and dust, had dropped in front of them like a solid shield. Not one had fallen in crossing the open.

Now the smoke drifted behind them and we saw nothing for an hour except a misty figure here and there. News came from the Battery that prisoners were pouring in. Later when the smoke had cleared no movements were to be seen, the ploughed landscape was as lifeless and sullen as before, yet a battle had been fought. Someone had won. But who? We knew nothing. Here is the curse of all modern trench battles - How to get information?... By six o'clock things had quietened, and we had a cup of tea... Bullets were whistling round the O.P. I am glad to say. Glad, that is, that we were even slightly involved in the big game being played down there below us, and not mere spectators at some gladiatorial show... Not till after the battle is over do you realise that the so called "show" has been paid for in blood and tears. Hateful to think that people may even watch these fights in a picture palace. Returning to the Battery, I passed files of men carrying bombs to the firing line. I also met an orderly carrying soda water for some general and his staff. Not till next morning did we hear full news of the complete success of the fight - the objective gained, casualties few, prisoners numerous. The daylight attack seemed to have justified itself...

– 18th - 19th AUGUST 1916 –

PRIVATE FRANK RICHARDS, D.C.M., M.M.
2nd Battalion Royal Welch Fusiliers

During August two separate attacks had been made to drive the Germans out of the part of High Wood they still held, but both attacks had failed with heavy losses. However, communication trenches had been dug and troops could enter the wood by day. On 18th August the 2nd Battalion Royal Welch Fusiliers took over trenches in High Wood relieving the 2nd Battalion Argyll and Sutherland Highlanders. Frank Richards and A Company, in support, were in a trench which ran from just inside to the centre of the wood.

We dumped our telephone on the fire-step in a bay by ourselves. Anyone leaving the centre of the wood would have to pass us to make their way to the communication trenches. Some parts of the parapet had been built up with dead men, and here and there arms and legs were protruding. In one bay only the heads of two men could be seen; their teeth were showing so that they seemed to be grinning horribly down on us...

About 8 a.m. the enemy started shelling us very heavily. It was big stuff they were sending over and by 10 a.m. we had sixty casualties in the Company. Great trees were uprooted and split like matchwood, some falling over the trench. We were throwing our dead on the back of the parapet, from where in some cases they were blown up again and thrown further afield. All communication had gone West and the young signaller was huddled up in a heap on the fire-step and shaking like a madman. I told him to buck up and that it would be better if he moved about. I asked him to go halfway along the lines to the Battalion Headquarters and repair any breaks, pointing out to him that we were just as liable to be blown to bits where we were as in any part of the trench, but he wouldn't move. I then told him to stick on the telephone and that I would go along the lines and also run any messages received. For thirty-six hours he hardly moved off that fire-step to do anything. He took no food but was constantly drinking out of his water bottle until it was empty. The lines had been repaired between us and Battalion Headquarters by one of their signallers, so I made my way along the other lines to C Company. When I was about halfway there I was told that a large shell had burst right on top of the dug-out C Company signallers were in, killing and burying them at the same time.

In the afternoon the shelling ceased and about an hour later I heard the sharp explosions of bombs somewhere on the left of us. A few minutes later about half a dozen newly-joined men came running down the trench towards us. They had no rifles and looked properly scared. I barred their way and asked what was the matter, but they couldn't get a word out. A young Platoon-Sergeant who had been with us a decent time now, came running down the trench in rear of the men. He shouted, "Don't let any of them pass you, Dick. They're running away." He told me that some German bombers, dodging from tree to tree, had crept close up and hurled their bombs in the trench and these men had dropped their rifles and ran away. He now drove them back to their part of the trench, but never reported them. They would have been all court-martialled and probably shot if he had. If a proper look-out had been kept those German bombers should have been shot down before ever they came in bombing range. Then the shelling started again and kept on more or less until we were relieved...

– 18th - 19th AUGUST 1916 –

CAPTAIN FRANCIS HITCHCOCK, M.C.

'C' Company 2nd Battalion Leinster Regiment

During August Captain Hitchcock was in camp on the ridge north of Bray. On the 18th the Battalion moved from Carnoy to the Briqueterie near Montauban. Later that day the men prepared for the attack on the village of Guillemont, in support of the 13th Battalion Middlesex Regiment.

Each man was given sand-bags and bombs in addition to his cumbersome "battle order". It was a sweltering day, and the men were too heavily equipped. All had been issued with a white metal plate, which attached to a string was to be worn round the neck, the disc hanging on the back between the shoulders. The Staff told us that these plates were for co-operation with aircraft, and that they would be conspicuous from the air. For the most part, officers and men treated these discs as a huge joke... Every aeroplane was fitted with a "Klaxon" horn which they sounded when they wanted to co-operate with the Infantry. We were then supposed to do the ostrich trick, i.e., bury our heads in the ground and show these discs. As might be imagined, the lives of the discs were short; they were found to be of no practical use, and were discarded. Another issue was in the shape of morphine tablets by the regimental M.O. to all officers.

This attack was not only a divisional operation; there was to be a general advance along the whole corps front. On our left the 14th Division, and on our right the 3rd Division, were advancing, and at Péronne, the French were attacking in conjunction.

The main topographical feature of this country was the Guillemont-Maltz Horn Farm ridge. The ruins of Guillemont stood on the highest point of this ridge, predominating the surrounding country. Guillemont was, therefore, the key of the position, and once it was captured we would have command of the whole area. Three of our attacks on Guillemont had been written off as failures. The Germans fully realised its important strategic position, and had turned it into almost an impregnable fortress to bar the way of the Allies in their advance up the slopes of the Somme plateau in Picardy. I got an excellent view of the attack from the top of some old ruined walls near the Briqueterie. This place was about 1000 yards as the crow flies from the jumping-off trenches before Guillemont. It stood up on another ridge smaller and separated from the Guillemont ridge by a wide valley known as "The Valley of Death".

Before Zero hour, the leading companies of the Battalion (B and D) were moving across this valley and winding up the Guillemont ridge. We were now going to witness the much talked of creeping barrage.

The men were silent, and did not volunteer any ideas about the new system of shell-fire, but I overheard my platoon-sergeant (Sergeant Henry) telling the "toughs" when in training, "to use their imagination and follow the shells" (the Battalion drummers).

This explanation seemed to satisfy all. Here to-day was the reality, and no imagination was needed. Up till now there had only been intermittent shelling; mostly counter-battery work. Suddenly a crashing roar resounded over the whole area; the preliminary bombardment of the Hun lines had started punctually to the second. All the British batteries were giving tongue simultaneously. Thousands of tons of shells were crashing down on the enemy's trenches on the sky line. Shells came from places unthought of and unseen, so excellently were they camouflaged; field-guns in pits with only a covering of rabbit wire interlaced with grass and leaves to conceal them. Behind them again were rows of howitzers all staked to the ground so tremendous was their recoil every time they fired. The noise of the explosions, the whine of the shells, and the concussion produced, was unlike anything I had ever imagined. Here and there shrapnel bursts flashed in the inky darkness. Above this curtain of fire one could see numerous German SOS rockets of all colours shooting up into the sky. We passed some of our gunners on our way up; they were all stripped to the waist, their sweat-begrimed bodies showed one the almost superhuman effort of endurance they were making under the blazing heat of the August sun at midday. How long would this furious bombardment last? The flash of our shell bursts seemed further away, the gunners were lengthening their fuses. The barrage had lifted - "Zero".

Simultaneously out got a line of forms from the British trenches, the first wave, and disappeared into the smoke. This cloud of smoke grew denser with the debris of brick and mortar from the ruins of Guillemont. The enemy was now retaliating with a vengeance on the slopes of the ridges to wipe out our supports, and the rattle of musketry or machine-guns could now be heard above the roar of the guns. Their artillery was not to be frustrated, and reaped a harvest. Laville and Handcock were killed, and our gallant C.O. Lieut.-Colonel R.A.H. Orpen-Palmer, D.S.O, O'Morchoe, Burns, D.C.M., Todd, and Magner were wounded, as well as 100 rank and file. L/Corpls, Jenkins and Egan were the first to be hit in C Company. Over 100 casualties just going up that ridge without seeing the enemy. Fodder for guns indeed!

Something had happened on the right. The Highlanders of the 3rd Division were coming back, and so were the attacking regiments of our Brigade. They were not "walking wounded" coming out of the smoke - wounded do not come back in lines. "A failure!" It had been a fine sight seeing the leading battalions advancing into action, but it was a most depressing one seeing them retiring.

Streams of wounded, walking and on stretchers, were now beginning to drift by; men with smashed arms, limping, and with the worst of all to see - facial wounds. They all muttered of machine-guns in a sunken road, which enfiladed them and had broken up the attack...

The order for attack on Guillemont: 73rd Brigade. Two Battalions in the front line. 7th Northampton Regiment on left, and 13th Middlesex Regiment on right. The 2nd Leinster Regiment in support, and the 9th Sussex Regiment in reserve. First objective the German front line before Guillemont to be taken by leading units. Second objective the village of Guillemont to be taken by the regiment in support (us), who would leap-frog the front-line battalions. Our role was to exploit the success of the leading regiments, but as the attack had failed, we had now to cope with the task of replacing a disorganised battalion, and holding the original British front line against counter-attacks.

We were informed that everything had gone splendidly for the attacking troops, until they had got to within 30 yards of their objective. Our barrage had then to lift off the Hun lines and, when it did, up rushed the Boche from his deep dug-outs with machine-guns and directed a withering fire on the attackers. Machine-guns which had been lying out concealed in a sunken road which ran between the advancing battalions, also enfiladed the flanks of the two units.

Surprise being the greatest element in warfare, and the attacking troops being caught in an unexpected hail of well-directed machine-gun fire, were held up and then retired back across No-Man's-Land. On our left, the 17th Brigade had captured some small posts near Waterlot Farm, and a party of the 7th Northamptons under the leadership of Major A.D. Murphy, M.C. (who was acting O.C. 7th Northamptons), captured a small post at the Quarries near the Railway Station. The 3rd Division had also failed to gain any of their objectives.

The Leinsters got orders to take over the front-line trenches from the remnants of one of the attacking battalions. The officers in reserve joined their Companies - so Newport, Crowe, McCann, and I started off across country for Guillemont. We moved through a terribly devastated area - every inch churned up by shell-fire, everywhere were shell-holes, most of them over-lapping. We struck up against communication trenches, most of them were obliterated. Here and there lay huddled-up figures in khaki. It was getting dusk when we reported, at Battalion Headquarters, to Poole, upon whom command of the Battalion had devolved, as senior officer. I will never forget the scene in that small dug-out or shelter off the main C.T. [communication trench].

Poole was sitting on the ground, giving his orders in a clear and concise manner. Palin, the Adjutant, writing on a message form by candle-light, with two of the Battalion signallers lying on the ground beside him, and Lieut-Colonel J. Greene, C.O. of the 13th Middlesex, sitting on an ammunition box, thanking Poole for having come so speedily to take over from his Battalion. I got orders to bring up bombs from the sunken road to the barricade in our front line. On my way I met John Burns limping down the C.T. He had been hit for the second time during the afternoon. I got up to the barricade on the sunken road at 5.30 p.m. It was being held by the Battalion bombers, with a gun and crew of the Machine-Gun Corps. Everything seemed extraordinarily still after the furious pandemonium of the afternoon. A solitary shell burst over us occasionally, and some went whining over our heads in the direction of our transport dumps. I peered over the barricade at the Hun lines and Guillemont, barely 150 yards away. Our stretcher bearers, Morrissey (now L/Corpl.), Reid, Dooley, and Merriman, all heroes of Premesques '14 and Hooge '15, were out searching No-Man's-Land for wounded. Occasionally one could hear the cries of some who had been missed in the torn-up and shell-pitted ground. What had been the ruins of a village some six hours previously, was now only heaps of red bricks and debris. A few trees which had been left standing were now all torn up by the roots. Arrow Head Copse on our left flank had ceased to exist. The ploughed-up yellow earth stank of lyddite and powder. From the constant firing of Very lights by the enemy, we could judge his nervous state. There were no wire entanglements left, they too had disappeared in the bombardment. It was the picture of desolation. L/Corpl. Delaney took out a patrol to make a reconnaissance of the enemy position. I overheard Poole saying that he wanted to carry out a night attack, and telephoned Brigade for sanction. The morale of the Battalion, in spite of its casualties, was very high, and a determined bayonet charge that night would have wrested Guillemont from the enemy. Poole walked about on our parapets under shell and occasional bursts of M.G. fire, restoring the line.

Brigade refused to hear of an attack, and gave us orders for relief. At 9.30 p.m. the Battalion was relieved by the 1st Battalion North Staffordshire Regiment, 72nd Brigade. Having handed over, C Company got orders to move to the Brigade left flank, and support the 7th Northamptons. Here we lay for some time in another sunken road. The enemy had attempted to counter-attack, but were beaten off, and the Company was not required. We got orders to take up our position for the night in the sunken road. On our way back we passed Padré Doyle, making cover for our wounded near an advanced dressing-station. Later, this fine man had his leg blown off by a shell and died. The Battalion M.O. was also wounded. [The dressing station was totally distroyed by shell fire that night]. We took up our position in a sunken road, which ran parallel to our front line, near Arrow Head Copse.

In the dim light we could make out a lot of figures lying in huddled-up heaps in the middle of the road. A Company of the 1st North Staffords had "caught it" when coming up to relieve us earlier in the night.

We posted sentries at intervals, a task that was rendered difficult by the dead of the 1st North Staffords, whom we stumbled over in the darkness, and got the men under what cover was available. There were numerous undercuttings in the sunken road, known as "funk holes". Whitby, Jameson, and I crawled into these and, leaving our legs exposed to the rain which was now falling, went to sleep.

19th August. Woke up at dawn, wet and cold. Discovered that lying on either side of Jameson and myself were two dead men of the 1st North Staffords. The whole sunken road was taken up with the dead of the same regiment - at least 30. Our men had no rations, so we turned out the kits of the dead for iron rations; got some cigarettes too. I had a strange species of fodder in my haversack - tinned lobster and crab. With the help of some bread, Whitby, Jameson, and I had a weird breakfast.

At 6 a.m. orders came to move lower down into the valley, where the Battalion was. We fell in and moved off. Everything very wet and clammy! Enemy shelling spasmodic. R.S.M. Smith came round and collected a party of our men for the burial of the 1st North Stafford dead, and a few of our own.

We got to a reserve trench some 800 yards away, where we found the Battalion. The men were walking about under cover of a thick mist, making their breakfasts...

– 18th - 23rd AUGUST 1916 –

SECOND-LIEUTENANT ROBERT ERNEST VERNEDE
3rd Battalion The Rifle Brigade

On 8th August Robert Vernède's battalion moved from sandpits south of Albert to positions behind the front line in craters north of Carnoy. He wrote to his wife on the 18th that he was to go on a Lewis gun course but directly he finished the letter he received a wire ordering him to rejoin the Battalion which was preparing for an attack on the Guillemont front. On 23rd August he wrote again telling her of his five days in the trenches.

The attack came off at 2.30 p.m., and at 3.30 five of us were sent for to Brigade H.Q. No time to pack anything, a blazing hot day, and I had to borrow the Quartermaster's revolver as I'd lent mine. An hour-and-a-half's walk to Brigade H.Q., where we heard that things were going very well, but more officers were needed...

We had a three hour walk to the front line. Shells most of the way, and the wounded streaming down an open road between the downs. We passed A.D., hit through the leg, but filled with delight because he was going back to Blighty alive and kicking... then heaps of bandaged men, including two of my platoon. Then men of all regiments, and wounded in every variety of way. To read in the papers you might suppose the wounded were whisked from the battlefield in a motor ambulance. I get rather tired of all that false and breezy representation of a battle.

I've never been so hot in my life as when we came to Batt. H.Q. just behind our jumping-off trench... From there we went on to join our Coys in the various bits of Boche trench they had taken. No guide, a hail of shells and a sort of blind stumble through shell-holes to where we fancied the new line was. I found C Company at last. H.Q. in a 30 ft. deep Boche dug-out, choked with dead Germans and bluebottles, and there we had our meals till we started back at 4 a.m. this morning (five days). In between that time I certainly spent some of the most unpleasant hours of my life. It seems that the Batt. had done extraordinarily well and gained the first of two objectives. The second was to be won that night, and next day we were to be relieved. Unfortunaely a Batt. on our right had been held up and we had to wait for them in a trench choked with our dead and Boche wounded and dying for two days and then do another attack. The men had been in high spirits over the first part, but naturally the reaction was great when they found that instead of being relieved they were to dig in, and I had never seen them so glum. Here again the breezy reporter is revolting. The Push itself is done in hot blood; but the rest is horrible, digging in when you are tired to death, short rations, no water to speak of, hardly any sleep, and men being killed by shell-fire most of the time.

I was given the C line in front of H.Q. to hold with two-and-a-half platoons, and luckily the Boches never really found it, and I had fewer casualties than anybody. I slept in the bottom of the trench, sometimes in rain (in shorts), without any cover and really never felt very cold. Also, though I don't suppose I got more than an hour at a time, I never felt done for want of sleep. C. and Buxton were the only officers left.

The second attack was made yesterday, and only our D Coy was sent off at the start. C Coy was to support it if it needed reinforcement. My dear, you never saw anything more dramatically murderous than the modern attack - a sheet of fire from both sides in which it seems impossible for any one to live. I saw it from my observer's post about 100 yds away. My observer was shot through the head in the first minute. The O.C. of D Company had been badly wounded, and Butler led them on most gallantly. The last I saw of him was after a huge shell had burst just over him (laying out several men) waving on the rest. None of the D officers came back, and very few of the men.

Again the right Batt. failed, and this time the Rifle Brigade was inevitably involved in it, as far as D Coy went. We gained a certain amount of France back by digging a trench in front of my bit of line about 100 yds. from the Boches in the dark, lit by terrific flares from the German lines. After that we hunted for our wounded till 4 a.m. I found S.S. about 50 yds. from the Boche trench, shot through the heart. R. got back wounded in several places. Butler was last heard of in a shell-hole about 10 yds from the Boches. He was an awfully gallant fellow. The whole thing was almost too bloody for words, and this, mind you, was victory of a sort for us. We fancy the Boches lost far more heavily, as our guns got on them when they were reinforcing.

I'm too sleepy to tell you any more. The Batt. did magnificently: captured many prisoners and advanced several hundred yards; but the cost is very great...

PRIVATE FREDERIC MANNING (19022)
7th Battalion King's Shropshire Light Infantry

Private Frederic Manning, aged 34, joined the Battalion in the middle of August at Méaulte. On 18th August the Battalion took part in an attack near Maltzhorn Farm; the following day, with the loss of thirty-eight men, the Battalion captured Lonely Trench close to the village of Guillemont. The trench was subsequently renamed Shropshire Trench.

THE FACE

Out of the smoke of men's wrath,
The red mist of anger,
Suddenly,
As a wraith of sleep,
A boy's face, white and tense,
Convulsed with terror and hate,
The lips trembling...

Then a red smear, falling...
I thrust aside the cloud, as it were tangible,
Blinded with a mist of blood.
The face cometh again
As a wraith of sleep:
A boy's face delicate and blonde,
The very mask of God,
Broken.

– 23rd - 28th AUGUST 1916 –

LIEUTENANT GRAHAM H. GREENWELL, M.C.
4th Battalion Oxfordshire and Buckinghamshire Light Infantry

After four days resting at Aveluy, Graham Greenwell and his Company were back in Ovillers Trenches on 23rd August.

Here I am again seated about thirty feet down in a late German residence surrounded with maps and papers and trying to convey to Battalion head-quarters what piece of captured German trench I am holding.

But really it is most difficult to discover where one is: the ground is honeycombed with old trenches and maps are published every day, each giving different versions. Of course the situation changes every hour owing to small attacks and bombing stunts - in fact everything is loathsomely unsettled compared to the dear quiet old days of proper trench warfare.

You can scarcely hear a sound at the bottom of these mined shafts except a dull booming. The stink is rather bad, but these trenches are a positive paradise compared to the ones next door which we had before, no corpses and comparatively deep and clean.

I really hope we shall go back after this tour for a rest: this is our third go in and quite enough.

I am bucked to death with my lads though I have got a poor chap who has suddenly gone groggy with shell-shock. He can't keep his hands still and waggles them the whole time. I have brought him down here and he is buried somewhere in the depths of the dug-out. I have just had to interrupt this letter on receiving three messages from the Adjutant and a visit from a strange officer who wanted to find some obscure trench in my area in order to do some digging at 1 o'clock to-morrow morning. I was up at 3.45 this morning in order to go round with the Colonel and look at the trenches, and of course I shall be up all night to-night and probably to-morrow night as well; you can imagine one gets slightly fatigued. Living on bread and jam and bully, lemonade and water, doesn't make one's spirits exactly bound; however, it's all in the day's work.

August 24th... We are still in these vile trenches and I am feeling rather more tired than before.

Thank Heaven we had a quiet night and day, but of course I was up all the time receiving and sending messages until I dropped asleep over the table. All I can get to eat are dog biscuits (rations), which are very hard, but still do fill up the gaps.

I have been relieved from the responsibility of the front line and am just a little bit further back in another flea-invested German dug-out. It isn't much of a change or rest and we shall have to work all night I think. There is a faint chance of relief to-morrow, but I am afraid only a faint one - and we shall probably have to stick twenty-four hours more of it.

Just on our left there is a strong point to which the Bosche is clinging passionately and our C.O. has determined that we have got to have it. Bombing goes on round it all the time and we are constantly withdrawing our men in order to shell the spot; but the Hun sticks there, and as our left Company can't make much of it we shall perhaps be given a try if there is no relief to-morrow...

August 25th. Still in the trenches for the third night and feeling filthy and tired.

Plagues of flies, but still going strong.

Hope to get relieved tomorrow.

I have run out of writing-paper and everything else.

This is a disgusting hole: if only the people at home could imagine a tenth of the vileness of this part of the world that figures so gloriously in all our cold official communiques!...

August 26th. Reserve Trenches behind Ovillers. At last I can write to you in comparative safety again, though scarcely in peace or comfort.

After another night up in the trenches we were relieved at 8.30 this morning and got out of it without accident and I felt delighted with myself, especially when I found my horse waiting for me in the old spot, although we are only just in some rickety dug-outs and trenches about a mile behind. I can't tell you how tired and filthy we all are and hungry too - much too hungry to want to go to sleep at once.

Your dear anxious letter about my "wound" arrived in the trenches with a parcel containing - oh! sacred joy! a Fuller's cake and some Haversack chocolate which dropped like manna from Heaven in our midst. The cake reposed - a veritable Snow Queen - among the variegated litter of the German dug-out which was my headquarters - a huge place in which I was able to crowd forty men and which was most useful, as my stretcher-bearers were able to work there in safety.

We had a comparatively quiet night and I only had about five casualties in all, together with a few shell-shock cases.

I had a lot of letters last night. Two of my late brother-officers have died of wounds, Newman Hall, who was wounded in the battle of July 23rd has died at Rouen, and now I have just heard that Lakin, who was my Second-in-Command, has also died, as I was afraid he would. I can't help feeling more and more like the survivor of some great disaster, when I look back a few weeks and remember that we had nine officers in this Company alone, and of them only myself and two others are left.

I must say that my two officers are the best I could have had: Carew Hunt is a marvel. Can you imagine a tall, very delicate man, suffering constantly from laryngitis and neuralgia, living more or less cheerfully up in this hell and taking patrols out into the outer darkness in search of vague Anzac regiments on our right; entirely devoted to the amenities of University life and respectable comfort, he has managed to throw himself entirely into this new and really horrible job: to me it is quite extraordinary.

My other officer, Pearson, is quite a lad and is really worth his weight in gold. He is exceedingly cool and brave, which is saying a lot now-a-days when the oldest and strongest of the soldiers get affected by the constant shelling: and he is very cheery and eager - just like a schoolboy. You would have loved to see him walking into your cake last night when he came in for a rest after four hours in the open trench. It went down splendidly with a dollop of rum and water. I should certainly like to recommend both these officers to the C.O.'s notice and I have already sent in a report on a young lance-corporal of mine who did some splendid work reconnoitring last night.

There has been a big attack again this afternoon, and as we are near the guns, the noise has been loud and incessant - but nothing will stop me from sleeping to-night.

I really don't think we shall be put back into these trenches again - we are so very reduced and exhausted, and are expecting in a day or two to go right back. I must really knock off now and have a little dinner before a blessed sleep - my first for four nights. I had quite a respectable beard this afternoon.

August 28th. Bouzincourt, Somme. You remember how joyful I was when I last wrote to you yesterday. Well, that same evening just as I was waiting for the savoury to be brought in for dinner, I got an urgent order to parade my Company at once in fighting order and to proceed to the trenches. Can you imagine anything more hateful? We were tired out, we had at last got clean and we hoped to have seen the last of the trenches for many days.

Two other regiments in our Brigade had, we knew, done an attack at 7 o'clock that evening; it was clear that our job would be to go and support them if not actually to take over the captured trench from their wearied soldiers, a most dangerous and unpleasant task.

We arrived panting hot after groping our way for miles and miles behind a guide along the old German trenches in the old nauseating surroundings and with plenty of shelling. I reported to the O.C. of the Gloucesters, an old friend of mine, a younger brother of their Colonel and actually Second-in-Command but who was now acting C.O. He told me to make my way to advanced headquarters and carry up bombs, lights, tools, aeroplane signals and rockets to the captured trench: to start a digging party on getting communication through to the captured trench and to hold myself in readiness for a German counter-attack, which was, of course, expected.

The trench was full of men, wounded, and stretcher cases blocking the way, Bucks and Oxfords carrying bombs and tools, German prisoners being brought down, and runners trying to get through with messages.

I was up all night, but at 6 this morning I came back with the whole Brigade, the Division being at last relieved by an entirely new lot; so now we are at last free of this awful battle and to-morrow we hope to march away to quieter climes.

But you can imagine how I loathed that last long night in the trenches. I may add that the attack was a brilliant success and not very costly, though I am sorry to say I lost a friend of mine in the Gloucesters, Winterbotham (qv), who was killed...

– 31st AUGUST 1916 –

CAPTAIN FRANCIS HITCHCOCK, M.C.
2nd Battalion Leinster Regiment

On 30th August the Battalion marched in torrential rain from its camp near Dernancourt to Carlton Trench, a Support Trench in the Longueval area. After a long tramp along Caterpillar Valley it arrived at Green Dump, near Longueval, where each man was given two sandbags and two hand-grenades, and continued until they reached the crest of a ridge where they took over the support line in preparation for their part in a forthcoming action in Delville Wood.

I had about ten heavy boxes of bombs with me. As we scrambled over the top, the Padré blessed us. We had to go down into a small valley before getting to the ridge, where Longueval was situated. The enemy probably expected that we were massing troops in this dead ground. At any rate, he gave it a thorough searching with shrapnel, and a systematic strafing with "Black Marias" and "Jack Johnsons". There was a C.T. [communication trench] but we did not use it. Besides it was full of wounded making their way back.

A fatigue party of Maoris passed us; thick-set, brown-skinned men from New Zealand, all carrying cork-screw wire entanglement stakes. The shelling did not seem to worry them in the least. The going was terribly heavy, and my men were laden with cumbersome boxes of bombs. In the smoke and noise, I used my whistle to hurry and direct the men; away in our rear I could still see Colonel Murphy standing up like a statue on the horizon.

Men were now streaming back without arms or equipment, a number unwounded, and in these circumstances our advance was made "nerve-racking". It is a severe test to both officers and men to advance through demoralized troops who are retiring in disorder. On we went without hesitation. The men were splendid; no troops can touch them as regards behaviour in action. I got orders to halt at the trench on the ridge, and so far we had arrived unscathed.

The rest of B Company now came up under Crowe and halted in this trench called Pont Street. Across on our right we watched khaki-clad figures running back from the southern edge of Delville Wood and through Longueval.

I was now detailed to bring my platoon up, and support the 9th Royal Sussex. My way lay up a slope on the top of which we scrambled into a shallow communication trench, as we were quite visible to the enemy, who was now sniping at us.

From the ridge one could discern khaki-clad figures in a disconnected line, due west of Delville Wood. We made our way direct to these, taking full advantage of all available cover. Here I found the C.O. of the 9th Sussex. The exact position was at the junction of Plum Street with Chesney Walk. The O.C. 9th Sussex ordered me to advance up Plum Street with my platoon and bomb the enemy, who had a position at the "T" junction formed by Orchard Trench, which we knew they were holding in strength.

In broad daylight I was ordered to advance up an exposed C.T. with my platoon in file! Had I been ordered to take up my platoon in extended order over the top I would have had a much more sporting chance of carrying out the instruction "to capture the enemy post in Orchard Trench".

I got my platoon into the correct bombing formation, of bombers, bayonet men, and carriers, placing myself as No. 3 in the line, and with bent heads we turned into Plum Street, which was at right angles to Chesney Walk. We advanced very cautiously, as 150 yards ahead of us, on commanding ground, was the Boche post. Along the left-hand side of Plum Street were the shattered stumps of trees, and when we had advanced some 20 yards only, where we came to an iron 5-barred gate thrown into the shallow trench, bombs rained down all round us. My bombers retaliated, and after a short exchange, the Boches whom we could see quite distinctly wearing their coal-scuttle shaped helmets, retired. We again advanced, but crawling on our hands and knees, as the trench was completely obliterated. Enemy snipers now started to worry us, as our screen of smoke from the bombs cleared off. Some men were hit behind me.

We were now (i.e., the head of the platoon) taking advantage of some cover from a flattened-out traverse. To cover our advance, I detailed two men to observe the Huns from some shell-holes on either side of the C.T. and snipe. They were put in position, and had only fired a few rounds when they were both shot straight through the head. Within a few seconds two more men were killed, and I narrowly missed one myself, the bullet hitting the earth beside my head, and driving some stone splinters into my neck. We were now out of bombing range and we watched the Boches climbing back over the barrier which they had erected at the head of the C.T. These we fired at, and probably hit a few. Simultaneously as the last Hun disappeared a Maxim opened on us, and I had six men killed instantly.

Advancing was now out of the question, as the trench was completely obliterated, so I withdrew my men. All the Lewis Gun Section being casualties, we brought back the gun.

In this attempt I had twelve men of my platoon killed by snipers and machine-gun fire. Crowe joined me, and we returned to Pont Street to bring up the other two platoons, leaving Powell with his platoon and the remnants of mine at Sussex Headquarters. We picked up an officer of the 13th Middlesex on our way back. During the attack in the morning, he had got cut off from his unit, but had gallantly remained with a mere handful of men in an isolated trench on the fringe of Delville Wood.

We brought the remainder of the Company up without casualties, though all the back areas were being heavily shelled by "big stuff". There were a number of stretcher cases lying about under cover, waiting until darkness set in to be carried off to the dressing station.

B Company was now allotted a line of sorts, connected shell-holes on the extreme edge of Delville Wood... In this trench [Bugle Trench] we were approximately situated. We experienced difficulty in getting to this line. We all ran the gauntlet from the enemy snipers, who were extremely vicious. One by one we ran from shell crater to shell crater, bullets whizzing past and slapping the earth beside us. Our dead lay all over the place. I remember in the fold of the ground two dead men sitting up straight, their mouths wide open, and full of horrible black flies.

It was about 6 p.m. when we manned our so-called trench and prepared for eventualities. C Company, less Powell's platoon attached to D Company, was now reduced to some thirty-five strong. The enemy now began putting over gas shells, and gas helmets were donned. Most of the shells passed over us, and fell into the wood, but the gas hung about our area, which was in a hollow. All the time heavy shelling was smashing up Delville Wood. Our guns were very silent, and did not fire in the enemy trenches during the evening.

September
1916

– 1st SEPTEMBER 1916 –

CAPTAIN FRANCIS HITCHCOCK, M.C.
'C' Company 2nd Battalion Leinster Regiment

During the night of 31st August/1st September the Battalion endeavoured to extend the position to the right and restore the front line by bombing attacks but these were unsuccessful. The Germans had consolidated their positions.

Later C Company successfully attacked under Lieut-Colonel Murphy, and they succeeded in regaining all the left position of the original front line. In this attack, a stretcher-bearer - Merriman - showed great daring in rescuing a wounded man who had fallen behind a German barricade...

At about 4 p.m. there was a sudden lull in the fighting which seemed rather uncanny. Artillery, machine-guns, and snipers seemed to pause, as it were, for breath.

The stillness was rudely broken by the crisp bark of a bomb. All strained our eyes towards the ridge on the left which C Company was holding.

A khaki figure, minus steel helmet, the only human figure visible on this vast stretch of desolation, could be seen throwing bombs with extraordinary rapidity into what was presumably an enemy advanced post. He fell, but quickly regained his feet and continued hurling hand-grenades.

Then he became enveloped in a cloud of smoke which screened him from view. Clearing, it revealed him once more throwing bombs. A machine-gun opened fire and steadily traversed along the front. The bomber fell to an invisible foe, having courted death for some sixty seconds of what seemed a charmed life, and disappeared into a shell-hole... Investigations failed to discover the name of this hero; he was one of C Company, undoubtedly, who was trying to regain our lines after the night attack. And so this unknown Irish warrior of a daring exploit was swallowed up in the weeping countryside of tortured Picardy.

It was a sweltering hot day, and gas from the shells hung all round the place. We had now turned our line of connected shell-holes into a useful fire trench... Dobbie and Powell were wounded.

The enemy certainly "had their tails well up" at the commencement of this engagement. They had gained a huge piece of ground; they had the complete superiority of fire, both by snipers and machine-guns, and they must have known that they had caused us heavy casualties. Whether it was a coincidence, or whether it was because the Boches' intelligence was especially good, will never be known, but at any rate the 13th Middlesex, which came in for the gruelling, was the unit which had had such a terrible ordeal in front of Guillemont, just a fortnight earlier. Its depleted ranks had been filled with a large draft of young and inexperienced troops.

All afternoon enemy aeroplanes hovered over us, and the edges of Delville Wood, like a lot of angry hornets. They were obviously observing for their gunners, and making a reconnaisance of our lines with a view to another attack.

At 5 p.m. after a short preliminary bombardment, the 3rd Rifle Brigade and the 8th Battalion The Buffs attacked on our left in waves and drove back the Huns. The attack was in full view of our sector, and we watched the riflemen advancing at the "high port", and the Huns running like rabbits. All the ground which had been lost had now passed back into our hands.

This attack was a fine sight. Our infantry steadily advancing in perfect waves, their R.S.M. standing on a flank dressing them as they went by. Enemy shells were bursting, and taking their usual toll, but there was no hesitation, except for the casualties and the stretcher bearers, who dodged about in the rear picking up the wounded.

During the attack the enemy was particularly active with his artillery. The outer edges of Delville Wood and our trench came in for a rough time. However, we did not mind the shelling in the least, as we were all so excited watching the attack. The 3rd Rifle Brigade and 8th Buffs lost rather heavily consolidating the regained line...

– 1st SEPTEMBER 1916 –

SECOND-LIEUTENANT ROBERT ERNEST VERNEDE
3rd Battalion The Rifle Brigade

On the evening of 1st September the Battalion, in reserve behind the lines, was ordered to counter-attack and retake two trenches, which had been lost the night before, near Delville Wood. The attack was launched without proper preparation and although the Battalion took Orchard Trench, Tea Trench was very strongly held by the Germans and the Battalion was unable to progress further. There were over two hundred casualties, including Robert Vernède, who was temporarily in command of his Company. The following day he wrote to his wife.

A pleasing Blighty one at last, and almost before you get this I shall, with luck, be in Angleterre with you a-coming to see me. It's shrapnel through the thigh, and hasn't been pronounced on yet by the medical authorities, who have to extract a bit of iron that didn't go quite through. But as I plunked through the trenches knee-deep in mire for six hours afterwards, more or less, it can't be very bad; and I ought to get back before you can think of coming here. I got it in another show suddenly forced upon us, in which I was in charge of the Coy. with C. only subaltern. A shell plumped neatly between six of us, killed Sgt. Oliver and hit the rest in divers ways. It was rather a funny sensation. I thought I'd been bruised. Handed over to C., who a little later got badly hit in the arm. So C Coy., when I last heard of it, is without officers - three platoon sergeants knocked out - two killed - both awfully nice fellows, and A. rather badly hit.

AT DELVILLE

At Delville I lost three Sergeants -
And never within my ken
Had one of them taken thought for his life
Or cover for aught but his men.

Not for two years of fighting
Through that devilish strain and noise;
Yet one of them called out as he died -
"I've been so ambitious, boys"...

And I thought to myself, "Ambitious!"
Did he mean that he longed for power?
But I knew that he'd never thought of himself
Save in his dying hour.

And one left a note for his mother,
Saying he gladly died
For England, and wished no better thing...
How she must weep with pride.

And one with never a word fell,
Talking's the one thing he'd shirk,
But I never knew him other than keen
For things like danger and work.

Those Sergeants I lost at Delville
On a night that was cruel and black,
They gave their lives for England's sake.
They will never come back.

What of the hundreds in whose hearts
Thoughts no less splendid burn?...
I wonder what England will do for them
If ever they return?

SEPTEMBER 1916

– 3rd SEPTEMBER 1916 –

LIEUTENANT EDMUND BLUNDEN, M.C.
11th Battalion Royal Sussex Regiment

The Battalion arrived on the Somme from the Arras area at the end of August and was billetted in tents in a wood outside Mailly-Maillet, three miles from the German lines. During the next few days Edmund Blunden organised dumps of 'rations, rifle ammunition, grenades, reels of barbed wire, planks, screw pickets, wire netting, sandbags' in readiness for the attack on Beaucourt Ridge. All this time Thièpval Wood was being heavily bombarded. The Battalion Commanding Officer, Colonel George Harrison, later wrote: "Blunden, always known to me as 'The Rabbit', with his gentle ways and his unassuming manner, was not born to be a soldier but he became one in spite of himself. His acute brain was tuned for instant action and he performed arduous duties with conspicuous success and courage..." On the evening of 2nd September, the Battalion moved from Mailly-Maillet and assembled in the Hamel trenches. The Headquarters were in the 'rambling but remarkable dug-out' in a chalk cliff, known as Kentish Caves. These were near Jacob's Ladder, a long communication trench which ran north-east from Mesnil to Hamel village and then turned south-eastwards, connecting up with Hamel Bridge across the River Ancre.

The British barrage opened. The air gushed in hot surges along that river valley, and uproar never imagined by me swung from ridge to ridge. The east was scarlet with dawn and the flickering gunflashes; I thanked God I was not in the assault, and joined the subdued carriers nervously lighting cigarettes in one of the cellars, sitting there on the steps, studying my watch. The ruins of Hamel were crashing chaotically with German shells, and jags of iron and broken wood and brick whizzed past the cellar mouth. When I gave the word to move, it was obeyed with no pretence of enthusiasm. I was forced to shout and swear, and the carrying party, some with shoulders hunched, as if in a snowstorm, dully picked up their bomb buckets and went ahead. The wreckage around seemed leaping with flame. Never had we smelt high explosive so thick and foul, and there was no distinguishing one shell-burst from another, save by the black or tawny smoke that suddenly appeared in the general miasma. We walked along the river road, passed the sand-bag dressing-station that had been built only a night or two earlier where the front line crossed the road, and had already been battered in; we entered No Man's Land, but we could make very little sense of ourselves or the battle. There were wounded Highlanders

151

trailing down the road. They had been in the marshes of the Ancre, trying to take a machine-gun post called Summer House. Ahead, the German front line could not be clearly seen, the water-mist and the smoke veiling it; and this was lucky for the carrying party. Halfway between the trenches, I wished them good luck, and pointing out the place where they should, according to plan, hand over the bombs, I left them in charge of their own officer, returning myself, as my orders were, to my colonel. I passed good men of ours, in our front line, staring like men in a trance across No Man's Land, their powers of action apparently suspended.

"What's happening over there?" asked Harrison, with a face all doubt and stress, when I crawled into the candled, overcrowded frowsiness of Kentish Caves. I could not say. "What's happening the other side of the river?" All was in ominous discommunication. A runner called Gosden presently came in, with bleeding breast, bearing a message written an hour or more earlier. It did not promise well, and, as the hours passed, all that could be made out was that our attacking companies were "hanging on," some of them in the German third trench, where they could not at all be reached by the others, dug in between the first and the second. Lintott wrote message after message, trying to share information north, east and west. Harrison, with sweat standing on his forehead, thought out what to do in this deadlock, and repeatedly telephoned to the guns and the general. Wounded men and messengers began to crowd the scanty passages of the Caves, and curt roars of explosion just outside announced that these dugouts, shared by ourselves and the Black Watch, were now to be dealt with. Death soon arrived there, among the group at the clumsy entrance. Harrison meanwhile called for his runner, fastened the chin strap of his steel helmet, and pushed his way out into the top trenches to see what he could; returned presently, with that kind of severe laugh which tells the tale of a man who has incredibly escaped from the barrage. The day was hot outside, glaring mercilessly upon the burned, choked chalk trenches. I came in again to the squeaking field telephones and obscure candlelight. Presently Harrison, a message in his hand, said: "Rabbit, they're short of ammunition. Get round and collect all the fellows you can and take them over - and stay over there and do what you can." I felt my heart thud at this; went out, naming my men among headquarters "odds and ends" wherever I could find them squatted under the chalk banks, noting with pleasure that my nearest dump had not been blown up and would answer our requirements; I served out bombs and ammunition, then thrust my head in again to report that I was starting, when he delayed, and presently cancelled, the enterprise. The shells on our breathless neighbourhood seemed to fall more thickly and the dreadful spirit of waste and impotence sank into us, when a sudden report from an artillery observer warned us that there were Germans in our front trench. In that case Kentish Caves was a death-trap, a hole in which bombs would be bursting within a moment; yet here at last was something definite, and we all seemed to come to life, and prepared with our revolvers to try our luck.

The artillery observer must have made some mistake. Time passed without bombs among us or other surprise, and the collapse of the attack was wearily obvious. The bronze noon was more quiet but not less deadly than the morning. I went round the scarcely passable hillside trenches, but they were amazingly lonely: suddenly a sergeant-major and half a dozen men bounded superhumanly, gasping and excited, over the parapets. They had been lying in No Man's Land, and at last had decided to "chance their arm" and dodge the machine-guns which had been perseveringly trying to get them. They drank pints of water, of which I had luckily a little store in a dugout there, now wrecked and gaping. I left them sitting wordless in that store. The singular part of the battle was that no one, not even these, could say what had happened, or what was happening. One vaguely understood that the waves had found their manoeuvre in No Man's Land too complicated; that the Germans' supposed derelict forward trench near the railway was joined by tunnels to their main defence, and enabled them to come up behind our men's backs; that they had used the bayonet where challenged, with the boldest readiness; "used the whole damn' lot, minnies, snipers, rifle-grenades, artillery"; that machine-guns from the Thièpval ridge south of the river were flaying all the crossings of No Man's Lane. "Don't seem as if the 49th Div. got any further." But the general effect was the disappearance of the attack into mystery.

Orders for withdrawal were sent out to our little groups in the German lines towards the end of the afternoon. How the runners got there, they alone could explain, if any survived. The remaining few of the battalion in our own positions were collected in the trench along Hamel village street, and a sad gathering it was. Some who had been in the waves contrived to rejoin us now. How much more fortunate we seemed than those who were still in the German labyrinth awaiting the cover of darkness for their small chance of life! And yet, as we filed out, up Jacob's Ladder, we were warned by low-bursting shrapnel not to anticipate. Mesnil was its vile self, but we passed at length. Not much was said, then or afterwards, about those who would never again pass that hated target...

PREPARATIONS FOR VICTORY

My soul, dread not the pestilence that hags
The valley; flinch not you, my body young,
At these great shouting smokes and snarling jags
Of fiery iron; as yet may not be flung
The dice that claims you. Manly move among
These ruins, and what you must do, do well;
Look, here are gardens, there mossed boughs are hung
With apples whose bright cheeks none might excel,
And there's a house as yet unshattered by a shell.

"I'll do my best," the soul makes sad reply,
"And I will mark the yet unmurdered tree,
The tokens of dear homes that court the eye,
And yet I see them not as I would see.
Hovering between, a ghostly enemy
Sickens the light, and poisoned, withered, wan,
The least defiled turns desperate to me."
The body, poor unpitied Caliban,
Parches and sweats and grunts to win the name of Man.

Days or eternities like swelling waves
Surge on, and still we drudge in this dark maze;
The bombs and coils and cans by strings of slaves
Are borne to serve the coming day of days;
Pale sleep in slimy cellars scarce allays
With its brief blank the burden. Look, we lose;
The sky is gone, the lightless drenching haze
Of rainstorm chills the bone; earth, air are foes,
The black fiend leaps brick-red as life's last picture goes.

ESCAPE

A Colonel -
There are four officers, this message says,
Lying all dead at Mesnil.
One shell pitched clean amongst 'em at the foot

Of Jacob's Ladder. They're all Sussex men.
I fear poor Flood and Warne were of that party.
And the Brigade wants them identified...

A Mind -

Now God befriend me,
The next word not send me
To view those ravished trunks
And hips and blackened hunks.

A Colonel -

No, not you, Bunny, you've just now come down.
I've something else for you.
Orderly!

(Sir!)

Find Mr. Wrestman.

THE ANCRE AT HAMEL: AFTERWARDS

Where tongues were loud and hearts were light
   I heard the Ancre flow;
Waking oft at the mid of night
   I heard the Ancre flow.
I heard it crying, that sad rill,
   Below the painful ridge,
By the burnt unraftered mill
   And the relic of a bridge.

And could this sighing river seem
   To call me far away,
And its pale word dismiss as dream
   The voices of to-day?
The voices in the bright room chilled
   And that mourned on alone,
The silence of the full moon filled
   With that brook's troubling tone.

The struggling Ancre had no part
   In these new hours of mine,
And yet its stream ran through my heart;
   I heard it grieve and pine,

As if its rainy tortured blood
  Had swirled into my own,
When by its battered bank I stood
  And shared its wounded moan.

PREMATURE REJOICING

What's that over there?
                     Thièpval Wood.
Take a steady look at it; it'll do you good.
Here, these glasses will help you. See any flowers?
There sleeps Titania (correct - the Wood is ours);
There sleeps Titania in a deep dugout,
Waking, she wonders what all the din's about,
And smiles through her tears, and looks ahead ten years,
And sees her Wood again, and her usual Grenadiers,
    All in green,
    Music in the moon;
  The burnt rubbish you've just seen
  Won't beat the Fairy Queen;
      All the same, it's a shade too soon
      For you to scribble rhymes
      In your army book
     About those times;
    Take another look;
That's where the difficulty is, over there.

THIEPVAL WOOD

The tired air groans as the heavies swing over, the river-hollows
    boom;
The shell-fountains leap from the swamps, and with wildfire and
    fume
  The shoulder of the chalkdown convulses.
Then jabbering echoes stampede in the slatting wood,
Ember-black the gibbet trees like bones or thorns protrude
  From the poisonous smoke - past all impulses.
To them these silvery dews can never again be dear,
Nor the blue javelin-flame of thunderous noons strike fear.

– 3rd - 4th SEPTEMBER 1916 –

LIEUTENANT THOMAS MICHAEL KETTLE
9th Battalion Royal Dublin Fusiliers

At the end of August 1916 the Irish Brigade was sent from the Hulloch sector to the Somme. On 3rd September from bivouacs at Billon Farm, Tom Kettle wrote his political testament with instructions that it should be published if he was killed. The following day the Battalion was at Carnoy and Kettle wrote the poem 'To my Daughter Betty, the Gift of God'.

Had I lived I had meant to call my next book on the relations of Ireland and England: The Two Fools: A Tragedy of Errors. It has needed all the folly of England and all the folly of Ireland to produce the situation in which our unhappy country is now involved. I have mixed much with Englishmen and with Protestant Ulstermen, and I know that there is no real or abiding reason for the gulfs, salter than the sea, that now dismember the natural alliance of both of them with us Irish Nationalists. It needs only a Fiat Lux, of a kind very easily compassed, to replace the unnatural by the natural.

In the name, and by the seal of the blood given in the last two years, I ask for Colonial Home Rule for Ireland - a thing essential in itself and essential as a prologue to the reconstruction of the Empire. Ulster will agree.

And I ask for the immediate withdrawal of martial law in Ireland, and an amnesty for all Sinn Fein prisoners. If this war has taught us anything it is that great things can be done only in a great way.

TO MY DAUGHTER BETTY, THE GIFT OF GOD

In wiser days, my darling rosebud, blown
To beauty proud as was your mother's prime,
In that desired, delayed, incredible time,
You'll ask why I abandoned you, my own,
And the dear heart that was your baby throne,
To dice with death. And oh! they'll give you rhyme
And reason: some will call the thing sublime,
And some decry it in a knowing tone.
So here, while the mad guns curse overhead,
And tired men sigh with mud for couch and floor,

Know that we fools, now with the foolish dead,
Died not for flag, nor King, nor Emperor,
But for a dream, born in a herdsman's shed,
And for the secret Scripture of the poor.

– 5th SEPTEMBER 1916 –

FATHER WILLIAM DOYLE, S.J., M.C.
Attached 8th Battalion Royal Irish Fusiliers

On 1st September the 8th Battalion Royal Irish Fusiliers, recently arrived from the Loos sector, was in bivouacs in Happy Valley, near Bray-sur-Somme; on 5th September the Battalion was in Chimpanzee Trench, south of Bernafay Wood, near the brickworks on the Montauban Road. From here the men, accompanied by their Chaplain, advanced towards Leuze Wood.

The first part of our journey lay through a narrow trench, the floor of which consisted of deep thick mud, and the bodies of dead men trodden under foot. It was horrible beyond description but there was no help for it, and on the half-rotten corpses of our own brave men we marched in silence, everyone busy with his own thoughts...

Half an hour of this brought us out on the open into the middle of the battlefield of some days previous. The wounded, at least I hope so, had all been removed, but the dead lay there stiff and stark, with open staring eyes, just as they had fallen. Good God, such a sight! I had tried to prepare myself for this, but all I had read or pictured gave me little idea of the reality. Some lay as if they were sleeping quietly, others had died in agony, or had had the life crushed out of them by mortal fear, while the whole ground, every foot of it, was littered with heads or limbs, or pieces of torn human bodies. In the bottom of one hole lay a British and a German soldier, locked in a deadly embrace, neither had any weapon, but they had fought on to the bitter end. Another couple seemed to have realised that the horrible struggle was none of their making, and that they were both children of the same God; they had died hand-in-hand praying for and forgiving one another. A third face caught my eye, a tall, strikingly handsome young German, not more, I should say, than eighteen. He lay there calm and peaceful, with a smile of happiness on his face, as if he had had a glimpse of Heaven before he died. Ah, if only his poor mother could have seen her boy it would have soothed the pain of her broken heart.

We pushed on rapidly through that charnel house, for the stench was fearful, till we stumbled across a sunken road. Here the retreating Germans had evidently made a last desperate stand, but had been caught by our artillery fire. The dead lay in piles, the blue grey uniforms broken by many a khaki-clad body. I saw the ruins of what was evidently the dressing station, judging by the number of bandaged men about; but a shell had found them out even here and swept them all into the net of death.

A halt for a few minutes gave me the opportunity I was waiting for. I hurried along from group to group, and as I did the men fell on their knees to receive absolution. A few words to give them courage, for no man knew if he would return alive. A 'God bless and protect you, boys', and I passed on to the next company. As I did, a soldier stepped out of the ranks, caught me by the hand, and said: 'I am not a Catholic, sir, but I want to thank you for that beautiful prayer.' The regiments moved on to the wood, while the doctor and I took up our positions in the dressing station to wait for the wounded. This was a dug-out on the hill facing Leuze Wood, and had been in German occupation the previous afternoon.

To give you an idea of my position. From where I stood the ground sloped down steeply into a narrow valley, while on the opposite hill lay the wood, half of which the Fusiliers were holding, the Germans occupying the rest; the distance across being so short I could easily follow the movements of our men without a glass.

Fighting was going on all round, so that I was kept busy, but all the time my thoughts and my heart were with my poor boys in the wood opposite. They had reached it safely, but the Germans somehow had worked round the sides and temporarily cut them off. No food or water could be sent up, while ten slightly wounded men who tried to come back were shot down, one after another. To make matters worse, our own artillery began to shell them, inflicting heavy losses, and though repeated messages were sent back, continued doing so for a long time. It appears the guns had fired so much that they were becoming worn out, making the shells fall 300 yards short.

Under these circumstances it would be madness to try and reach the wood, but my heart bled for the wounded and dying lying there alone. When dusk came I made up my mind to try and creep through the valley, more especially as the fire had slackened very much, but once again the Providence of God watched over me. As I was setting out I met a sergeant who argued the point with me. 'You can do little good, Father,' he said, 'down there in the wood, and will only run a great risk. Wait till night comes and then we shall be able to bring all the wounded up here. Don't forget that, though we have plenty of officers and to spare, we have only one priest to look after us.' The poor fellow was so much in earnest I decided to wait a little at least. It was well I did so, for shortly afterwards the Germans opened a terrific bombardment and launched a counter-attack on the wood. Some of the

Cornwalls, who were holding a corner of the wood, broke and ran, jumping right on top of the Fusiliers. Brave Paddy from the Green Isle stood his ground and drove the Germans back with cold steel.

Meanwhile we on the opposite hill were having a most unpleasant time. A wounded man had reported that the enemy had captured the wood. Communication was broken and Headquarters had no information of what was going on. At that moment an orderly dashed in with the startling news that the Germans were in the valley, and actually climbing our hill. Jerusalem! We non-combatants might easily escape to the rear, but who would protect the wounded? They could not be abandoned. If it were day-light the Red Cross would give us protection, but in the darkness of the night the enemy would not think twice about flinging a dozen bombs down the steps of the dug-out. I looked round at the bloodstained walls and shivered. A nice coward, am I not? Thank God, the situation was not quite so bad as reported; our men got the upper hand, and drove back the attack, but that half-hour of suspense will live long in my memory...

– 7th SEPTEMBER 1916 –

LIEUTENANT RAYMOND ASQUITH
3rd Battalion Grenadier Guards

Towards the end of August Raymond Asquith commented in a letter to his wife Katherine that his father had not written to him once during his ten months 'exile' in France. Two weeks later the Battalion was at Morlancourt.

Our 5 minutes notice to move has been cancelled again, as one guessed it would be, and we are continuing our strenuous training. Yesterday we had a Brigade Field Day under John Ponsonby illustrating all the newest and most elaborate methods of capturing German trenches with the minimum of casualties. It involved getting up at 5 a.m. but in other respects was funny enough. The "creeping barrage" i.e. the curtain of shell fire which moves on about 50 yards in front of the advancing infantry, was represented by drummers. The spectacle of the whole four battalions moving in lines across the cornfields at a funeral pace headed by a line of rolling drums, produced the effect of some absurd religious ceremony conducted by a tribe of Maoris rather than a brigade of Guards in the attack. After it had gone on for an hour or two I was called up by the Brigadier and thought at first that I must have committed some ghastly military blunder (I was commanding the Company in Sloper's absence) but was relieved to find that it was only a telegram from the corps saying "Lieut. Asquith will meet his father at cross roads K.6d at 10.45 a.m." So I vaulted into the saddle and bumped off to Fricourt where I arrived exactly at the appointed time. I waited for an hour on a very muddy road congested with troops and lorries and surrounded by barking guns. Then 2 handsome motors from G.H.Q. arrived, the P.M. in one of them with 2 staff officers, and in the other Bongie, Hankey, and one or two of those moth-eaten nondescripts who hang about the corridors of Downing Street in the twilight region between the civil and domestic service.

We went up to see some of the captured German dug-outs and just as we were arriving at our first objective the Boches began putting over a few 4.2 shells from their field howitzer. The P.M. was not discomposed by this, but the G.H.Q chauffeur to whom I had handed over my horse to hold, flung the reins into the air and himself flat on his belly in the mud. It was funny enough.

The shells fell about 200 yards behind us I should think. Luckily the dug-out we were approaching was one of the best and deepest I have ever seen - as safe as the bottom of the sea, wood-lined, 3 storeys and electric light, and perfect ventilation. We were shown round by several generals who kept us there for half an hour or so to let the shelling die down, and then the P.M. drove off to luncheon with the G.O.C. 4th Army and I rode back to my billets...

– 8th - 10th SEPTEMBER 1916 –

MAJOR ROWLAND FEILDING, D.S.O.
6th Battalion Connaught Rangers

On 6th September Rowland Feilding was given temporary command of the 6th Battalion Connaught Rangers who were part of the 47th Brigade, 16th (South Irish) Division. He joined the remnant of the Battalion on a slope alongside the ruins of Carnoy where it was resting after having suffered heavy casualties, including the Colonel and Second in Command, at Guillemont a few days previously. Within twenty-four hours of taking command he moved up to trenches in front of Ginchy 'with 200 fighting men, plus signallers and Battalion Headquarters' in readiness for an attack on the village.

September 8th. In Trenches, facing Ginchy. At 5.50 last evening I paraded my 250 Irishmen, who, before moving off, were addressed by the Senior Chaplain of the Division. Then, kneeling down in the ranks, all received General Absolution: - after which we started to move forward, timing our arrival at Bernafay Wood for 8.20, when it would be dark.

At Bernafay Wood we were met by a guide, who led us through Trones Wood - that evil place... Thence, to what once was Guillemont.

All former bombardments are eclipsed by the scene here. Last year, in the villages that had been most heavily bombarded, a few shattered houses still stood, as a rule: last month, occasionally, a wall survived. But to-day, at Guillemont, it is almost literally true to say that not a brick or stone remains intact. Indeed, not a brick or stone is to be seen, except it has been churned up by a bursting shell. Not a tree stands. Not a square foot of surface has escaped mutilation. There is nothing but the mud and the gaping shell-holes; - a chaotic wilderness of shell-holes, rim over-lapping rim; - and, in the bottom of many, the bodies of the dead. Having reached this melancholy spot, we left the cover of a battered trench which we had followed since leaving Trones Wood, and took to the open.

The guide was leading. I came next, and was followed by the rest of the party in single file. The moon shone brightly, and, as the enemy kept sending up flares from his trenches at intervals of a minute or less, our surroundings were constantly illuminated, and the meandering line of steel helmets flickered, rather too conspicuously, as it bobbed up and down in crossing the shell-holes.

I do not know if the Germans saw it or not. They soon started shelling, but as the ground we were passing over is commonly being shelled, there was nothing peculiar in that. We plodded on. The guide soon began to show signs of uncertainty. I asked him if he had lost his bearings - a not uncommon thing on these occasions. He admitted that he had. I crawled past the body of a dead German soldier into the doorway of a shattered dug-out, and with an electric torch studied the map.

As we started off again the shelling increased, and once I was hit by a small splinter on the chest, which stung. The men began to bunch in the shell-holes. They are brave enough, but they are untrained; and 91 of my 200 fighting men were from a new draft, which had only just joined the battalion.

I shall not forget the hours which followed. I had only the slightest acquaintance with the officers, and as for the rank and file I did not know them at all; - nor they me.

The shells were now dropping very close. One fell into a group of my men, killing seven and wounding about the same number. My guide was hit and dropped a yard or two in front of me. I told him to lie there, and I would have a stretcher sent for him: but he pulled himself together, saying, "It's all right, sir", and struggled on.

About 10.30 p.m. we reached our destination - only to find the rear Company detached and missing, as well as the medical officer and my servant. However, they turned up just before daybreak, having spent the night wandering among the shell-holes.

At the position of assembly, which was at the junction between the Guillemont-Combles road (known officially as Mount Street) and the sunken road leading to Ginchy, we found things in a state of considerable confusion. The battalion we had come to relieve had apparently thought it unnecessary to await our arrival, and as, consequently, there was no one to allot the few shallow trenches that were available, a sort of general scramble was going on, each officer being naturally anxious to get his own men under cover, before the daylight of the morning should reveal them to the enemy.

Luckily, the enemy was now quiet, and before it was light enough to see, the troops were disposed more or less in their "jumping off" positions, where they were to wait some forty hours or more for "Zero" - the moment of attack...

September 9th. In Trenches, facing Ginchy... This morning (Saturday), between eight and nine o'clock, our artillery began to bombard the German lines.

This preliminary bombardment, in so far as I have observed it, has, up to the present, been disappointing, a very large proportion (about half) of the shells having failed to explode. Many, too, have fallen short, some upon my parapet, and one has fallen into the trench, wounding four of my men...

The trenches in which we are waiting are very restricted and so irregular in form that it has been possible only by distributing the Companies in scattered portions, and by dovetailing them with another battalion, to fit them in at all. Things have not been made easier by the fact that my adjutant went sick yesterday with trench fever and had to be sent down. In his place I have appointed young Jourdain - a boy of 18 and a half - who seems to be possessed of wisdom far beyond his years.

My headquarters are in a trench which runs alongside the sunken road, and which was German till a few days ago. There is a hole in the side (marked in pencil with the name of a German soldier) - about 4 feet square by 8 feet deep, which serves as a sleeping-place for two or three at a time. The first German trench is some 300 yards in front, and has been reported by the patrols of the battalion that preceded us to be unoccupied, or only lightly held. We shall know more about this to-morrow.

On our left front, some 750 yards away, is the village of Ginchy: on the right is Leuze Wood (universally known among our people as Lousy Wood).

September 10th. Happy Valley. It is over. After a wait of forty-two hours, the leading Companies of the Brigade went over the parapet yesterday afternoon at forty-seven minutes past four o'clock.

The scheduled moment of "Zero", as a matter of fact, was two minutes earlier, but at the last moment orders came to postpone the assault two minutes, to give time for a final intensive bombardment of the German lines.

Perhaps there were good reasons for this, though it might be thought by the critical, that a bombardment would be as effective during the two minutes preceding, as those following Zero; and, having regard to the difficulty of insuring the delivery of messages to the front line at such times as these, that it would have been wiser to avoid interference with the Infantry Time-table.

The prearranged plan was that the 6th Royal Irish Regiment on the right and the 8th Royal Munster Fusiliers on the left should lead the attack for the 47th Brigade, in four waves, at distances of 50 paces, and that they should be followed, at 15 paces, by two more waves, composed of the 6th Connaught Rangers, with one Company of the

7th Leinster Regiment and two of the 11th Hampshire (Pioneers). The 168th Brigade was to be on our right.

The right battalion of the 48th Brigade - which like ourselves belongs to the Irish Division - to our immediate left, moved forward at 4.45, having, presumably, failed to hear of the postponement.

I cannot say whether this influenced our artillery, and caused them to abandon or to modify the intended last two minutes of "intensive" bombardment, though it certainly had the effect of bringing on the enemy's counter-barrage before its time. I can say that on my immediate front our artillery fire continued to be ineffective, and it is a fact that the Germans seemed very little disturbed by it, their snipers coolly continuing their operations even after the attack had been launched.

The leading wave of 47th Brigade, as I have said, left the trench at 4.47. It was immediately mowed down, as it crossed the parapet, by a terrific machine-gun and rifle fire, directed from the trench in front and from numerous fortified shell-holes. The succeeding waves, or such as tried it, suffered similarly.

Then Captains Steuart and Bain, who commanded C and D Companies of the Connaught Rangers, observing a check, got out of the trench, and started to rush their men forward: but they had only gone a few yards when both fell wounded.

On the right, there being no suitable jumping-off trench, it had been arranged that the Leinster and Hampshire parties, which were under my command for the day, should cross the open to their starting-point, but before they were able to reach it all the officers but one of the latter battalion had been hit, in addition to many of the rank and file. The officer commanding the Hampshire Companies had already been wounded by a sniper earlier in the day.

The trench in front of us, hidden and believed innocuous, which had in consequence been more or less ignored in the preliminary artillery programme, had - perhaps for this very reason - developed as the enemy's main resistance.

This, in fact, being believed to be the easy section of the attack, had been allotted to the tired and battered 47th Brigade. Such are the surprises of war! Supplemented by machine-gun nests in shell-holes, the trench was found by the few who reached close enough to see into it to be a veritable hornets' nest. Moreover, it had escaped our bombardment altogether, or nearly so. While the battle was in progress one of our aeroplanes, after flying over-head, dropped a map reporting the enemy in force there, but the news came too late to be of value. To the left of the Brigade, where heavy opposition had been expected and provided for, comparatively little was encountered. The artillery had done its work well, and the infantry was able to push forward and enter Ginchy.

In the meantime, the jumping-off trench soon became packed with the returned attacking troops and their wounded. The former were disordered and obviously shaken. Indeed, it was more than ever apparent that - apart altogether from the effects of the ordeal through which they had passed and were still passing (since the enemy artillery was still pounding furiously, while the machine-guns were raking up the parapets of our shallow trench) - they were in no condition for battle of this strenuous order, as I had thought before.

Those that were not raw recruits from the new drafts were worn out and exhausted by their recent fighting, and much more fitted for a rest camp than an attack.

One of the first sights I saw was poor Steuart being carried back on a stretcher. A few minutes before I had been talking and laughing with him, and, as I stopped to speak to him, now, his face wore the same cheery expression. I had known him only two days, but had formed the very highest opinion of his character, and since our first meeting, had counted much on his help during the trying times that were before us. He was full of life and spirits and daring - the acme of the perfect soldier. But such men are rare: they often die young; and this, I fear, is to be his fate. The bullet that hit him penetrated his hip, and, glancing upwards, is reported to have touched a vital part. He lay some hours in the trench, till his turn came, and the firing had quieted down sufficiently to send him away, never once by word or gesture betraying the pain he must have been enduring.

Later during the afternoon another of my officers - Seppings Wright - was killed in the trench by shrapnel. I came upon his body during one of my rounds, and helped to lift him - he was a big and heavy man - into a shell-hole, beside the place where he had fallen. He had been in charge of the machine-guns.

Heavy shelling continued throughout the rest of the day and during the night - a lurid night of countless rockets and star-shells from the enemy, who was nervous; a night of wild bursts of machine-gun and rifle fire - delaying our relief by the 4th Grenadier Guards from 9 p.m. (when it was due) til 4.40 the following - that is to say - this morning.

Then, after three practically sleepless nights, under shell-fire most of the time - often heavy, we marched back to Carnoy Craters, as the old front line of June 30, at the point where it is crossed by the Carnoy-Montauban road, is called.

Here we are bivouacked, and I have just had a good sleep on the ground, under the canopy of a transport wagon...

During the three days my casualties have amounted to 92 (9 officers and 83 other ranks), out of the 16 officers and 250 other ranks with which I started, bringing the total casualties of the battalion for the past nine days to 23 officers and 407 N.C.O.s and men. Of the latter, 63 are missing; 54 were killed, and others have since died.

Thanks to my splendid doctor - Knight, a Newfoundlander - we got them all out.

LIEUTENANT THE HON. EDWARD WYNDHAM TENNANT

4th Battalion Grenadier Guards

Aged just seventeen, 'Bim' Tennant was commissioned in the 4th Battalion Grenadier Guards in August 1914. He celebrated his nineteenth Birthday in the trenches at Ypres. The 4th Battalion was transferred from the Ypres sector to the Somme area during August 1916. After spending some time in the trenches at Beaumont Hamel the Battalion was re-deployed to Ville-sur-Ancre near Albert at the end of the month. On 7th September the Battalion moved in buses to Carnoy with orders to repair a road running from there to Wedge Wood. It bivouacked in shelters near Talus Boisé two and a half miles west of Leuze Wood where it came under incessant artillery fire. Tennant wrote frequent letters home to his parents.

8th September. We left our billets yesterday morning at 8 a.m. in motor lorries, and came up here about seven miles. We are bivouacked here on a slope, with old trenches all round, and our old original trench is 500 yards in front of us. I walked right across all the old trenches last night, and again this morning. Last night Mitchell and I were on a five-hour fatigue, repairing a road about three miles away to our front. We worked till dark, being rather hampered by a constant stream of men, waggons, and horses which cut up the road as fast as we mended it. However, we did good work. The whole place up there is littered with rifles, ammunition, clothing, wire, shells, and every sort of stuff. At one point the road had been previously repaired, and instead of rows of staples put across and covered with mud, they had used rifles. Just think of the waste. We were shelled a bit as we prepared to move off about 8.30 p.m., and though only about three shells came, all were uncomfortably close. I am thankful to say that only one man was slightly wounded and we got back here with no further trouble.

Directly we got in last night (about 10.15), we, that is Mitchell and I, had dinner and went to bed in a 'bivvy' made of coloured canvas and sticks, in which the other three were also in bed. The C.O. then sent round to say that he wanted me to go up and inspect the work done, at 6.20 this morning. I rose at 5.40 and went up to last night's place with him, only we went much further. It was awfully interesting, and I would not have missed it, though it is horribly grisly in places.

The wastage of material all the way is something terrific. I saw a lot of machine-gun magazines lying about, still wrapped up in brown paper, as they came from the makers. We got back to breakfast, and I have seized about four hours' sleep through the day since.

There are big guns all round us as I write, but none near enough to be unpleasant, as they were at Vermelles last year. We have nothing to do here, and it is quite fine, though wind-swept. I now hear that we shall probably take over the most newly won line to-morrow night, which will probably not be a very quiet locality. However, I trust implicitly in God, and am in very high spirits...

September 11th... Up to now I am safe and well; but we have had a fairly uncomfortable time, though we have been lucky on the whole. Poor Thompson (in my Company) was killed yesterday. I shall miss him so, he was such a charming fellow. We have been heavily shelled everywhere of the line.

We had very good luck getting up here, having hardly any casualties in the whole Battalion. I was flying up and down the batt. with messages to different people from the Commanding Officer all the time, it was quite a busy time for me; but since then, apart from helping to write messages, and being generally useful and cheerful, it's been less strenuous. I keep my 'Oxford Book of English verse' with me...

September 12th... We were safely relieved last night and are now going back for a day or two. We have had all the kicks and none of the ha'pence in this show, as other batts. had the fun of repulsing attacks and killing hundreds, while we had to just sit and be shelled. No doubt we shall have a better chance soon. The C.O. is very envious of what he calls the 'other chaps' hellish good shoot'.

We are delighted to be out, and should be in comfortable quarters by midnight to-night. I have not changed my clothes yet, so shall be glad.

I forgot to tell you that I was developing an abcess in a back molar on the morning of the day we went into action. So I forthwith mounted a prehistoric bicycle, rode eight miles in sweltering heat, had gas and tooth out in a brace of shakes, and rode back, getting one or two lifts in lorries...

– 9th -10th SEPTEMBER 1916 –

FATHER WILLIAM DOYLE, S.J., M.C.
Attached 8th Battalion Royal Irish Fusiliers

The 8th Royal Irish Fusiliers, having lost so many officers at Leuze Wood, were held in reserve for the battle for Ginchy. For the part he played in the assault on Leuze Wood on 5th September, and the subsequent fight for the village of Ginchy, Father Doyle was awarded the Military Cross. On Saturday 9th September he celebrated a Mass for the Dead.

By cutting a piece out of the side of the trench I was just able to stand in front of my tiny altar, a biscuit box supported on two German bayonets. God's angels, no doubt, were hovering overhead, but so were the shells, hundreds of them, and I was a little afraid that when the earth shook with the crash of the guns, the chalice might be overturned. Round about me on every side was the biggest congregation I ever had: behind the altar, on either side, and in front, row after row, sometimes crowding one upon the other, but all quiet and silent, as if they were straining their ears to catch every syllable of that tremendous act of Sacrifice - but every man was dead. Some had lain there for a week and were foul and horrible to look at, with faces black and green. Others had only just fallen, and seemed rather sleeping than dead, but there they lay, for none had time to bury them, brave fellows, every one, friend and foe alike, while I held in my unworthy hands the God of Battles, their Creator and their Judge, and prayed Him to give rest to their souls. Surely that Mass for the Dead, in the midst of, and surrounded by the dead, was an experience not easily to be forgotten...

Shortly before 5 p.m. I went up to the hill in front of the town, and was just in time to see our men leap from their trenches and dart up the slope, only to be met by a storm of bullets from concealed machine guns. It was my first real view of a battle at close quarters, an experience not easily forgotten. Almost simultaneously all our guns, big and little, opened a terrific barrage behind the village, to prevent the enemy bringing up reinforcements, and in half a minute the scene was hidden by the smoke of thousands of bursting shells, British and German. The wild rush of our Irish lads swept the Germans away like chaff. The first line went clean through the village and out the other side, and were it not for the officers, acting under orders, would certainly be in Berlin by this time! Meanwhile the supports had cleared the cellars and dug-outs of their defenders; the town was ours and all was well. At the same time a feeling of uneasiness was about. Rumour said some other part of the line had failed to advance, the Germans were breaking through, etc. One thing was certain, the guns had not ceased. Something was not going well.

About nine o'clock the Fusiliers were getting ready to be relieved by another regiment. But one further experience was to be theirs. There came an urgent order to hurry up to the Front. To my dying day I shall never forget that half-hour, as we pushed across the open, our only light the flash of bursting shells, tripping over barbed wire, stumbling and walking on the dead, expecting every moment to be blown into Eternity. We were halted in a trench at the rear of the village, and there till four in the morning we lay on the ground listening to the roar of the guns and the scream of the shells flying overhead, not knowing if the next moment might not be our last. Fortunately, we were not called upon to attack, and our casualties were very slight. But probably because the terrible strain of the past week was beginning to tell, or the Lord wished to give me a little merit by suffering more, the agony and fear and suspense of those six hours seemed to surpass the whole of the seven days.

We were relieved on Sunday morning, 10th, at four o'clock and crawled back (I can use no other word) to the camp in the rear. My feet, perhaps are the most painful of all, as we were not allowed to remove our boots even at night...

– 9th - 10th SEPTEMBER 1916 –

SECOND-LIEUTENANT ARTHUR CONWAY YOUNG
7th Battalion Royal Irish Fusiliers

The 7th Battalion arrived on the Somme from the Loos sector at the beginning of September. On 5th September the Battalion was ordered to attack Combles Trench near Leuze Wood but when the men waded waist-high through standing corn they discovered belts of wire sown in the crop. While attempting to get through these the Battalion was caught by machine-gun fire; another attempt in the evening was also unsuccessful, and by the end of the second day the Battalion had suffered over two hundred and forty casualties. On the 9th the worn out men of the depleted 7th Battalion took part in gaining ground north of Leuze Wood and the village of Ginchy, and once again received heavy casualties. The village, which stood on a high plain, had already endured several fierce attacks and was 'a mass of wreckage and tangled trees'. In a letter to his aunt, Arthur Young described his part in the battle in which he was wounded.

Our right flank was down near the bottom of the valley; our left extended up to the higher ground towards the ruins of Waterlot Farm. The trench was very shallow in places, where it had been knocked in by shell-fire. I had chosen it as the only one suitable in the neighbourhood, but it was a horrible place. British dead were lying round everywhere. Our men had to give up digging in some places, because they came down to bodies which were lying in the bottom, having been buried there when the parapet blew in. The smell turned us sick. At last, in desperation I went out to look for another trench, for I felt sure the Germans must have the range of the trench we were in, and that they would give us hell when dawn broke. To my joy I found that a very deep trench some distance back had just been vacated by another regiment, so we went in there.

The night was bitterly cold. I have felt hunger and thirst and fatigue out here to a degree I have never experienced them before, but those are torments I can endure far better than I thought I could. But the cold - my word! it is dreadful...

However, dawn broke at last. It was very misty. All night we had been trying to get in touch with the unit on our left, but without success. So the Captain sent me out with an orderly to see whether I could manage it. We two stumbled along, but the mist was so dense we could see nothing. We came to one trench after another, but not a living thing could we see - nothing but dead, British and German, some of them mangled beyond recognition. Bombs and rifles and equipment were lying all over the place, with here and there a greatcoat, khaki or grey according to the nationality of their one-time owners, but of living beings we could see no sign whatsoever. There was a *horrible* stench in places which nearly turned our stomachs. To make matters more wretched, we could not make sure of our direction, and were afraid of running into a German patrol, or even into a German trench, for such accidents are by no means uncommon in this region. However, we managed to find our way back, and report that up to such and such a point on the map (approximately) there was no-one on our left. The Captain was not content with this, so I went out again, this time with another officer. Having a compass on this second occasion I felt far more self-confidence, and to our mutual satisfaction we discovered that the unit on our left was the right flank of an English Division. Captain Edwards was very bucked when we brought back this information. As the mist continued for some time afterwards we were able to light fires and make breakfast...

It was about 4 o'clock in the afternoon when we first learned that we should have to take part in the attack on Ginchy... Well, even at the risk of making you feel ashamed of me, I will tell you the whole truth and confess that my heart sank within me when I heard the news. I had been over the top once already that week, and knew what it was to see men dropping dead all round me, to see men blown to bits, to see men writhing in pain, to see men running round and round gibbering, raving mad. Can you wonder therefore that I felt a sort of sickening dread of the horrors which I knew we should all have to go through? Frankly, I was dismayed. But, I know you will think the more of me when I tell you, on my conscience, that I went into action that afternoon, not with any hope of glory, but with the absolute certainty of death. How the others felt I don't exactly know, but I don't think I am far wrong when I say that their emotions were not far different from mine...

We were ordered to move up into the front line to reinforce the Royal Irish Rifles... The bombardment was now intense. Our shells bursting in the village of Ginchy made it belch forth smoke like a volcano. The Hun shells were bursting on the slope in front of us. The noise was deafening. I turned to my servant O'Brien, who has always been a cheery, optimistic soul, and said, "Well, O'Brien, how do you think we'll fare?" and his answer was for once not encouraging. "We'll never come out alive sir!" was his answer. Happily we both came out alive, but I never thought we should at the time.

It was at this moment, just as we were debouching on to the scragged front line of trench, that we beheld a scene which stirred and thrilled us to the bottommost depths of our souls. The great charge of the Irish Division had begun, and we had come up in the nick of time... Between the outer fringe of Ginchy and the front line of our own trenches is No Man's Land - a wilderness of pits, so close together that you could ride astraddle the partitions between any two of them. As you look half-right, obliquely along No Man's Land, you behold a great host of yellow-coated men rise out of the earth and surge forward and upward in a torrent - not in extended order, as you might expect, but in one mass, - I almost said a compact mass. The only way I can describe the scene is to ask you to picture five or six columns of men marching uphill in fours, with about a hundred yards between each column. Now conceive those columns being gradually disorganised, some men going off to the right, and others to the left to avoid shell-holes. There seems to be no end to them. Just when you think the flood is subsiding, another wave comes surging up the beach towards Ginchy. We joined in on the left. There was no time for us any more than the others to get into extended order. We formed another stream, converging on the others at the summit. By this time we were all wildly excited. Our shouts and yells alone must have struck terror into the Huns, who were firing their machine-guns down the slope. But there was no wavering in the Irish host. We couldn't run. We advanced at a steady walking pace, stumbling here and there, but going ever onward and upward. That numbing dread had now left me completely. Like the others, I was intoxicated with the glory of it all. I can remember shouting and bawling to the men of my platoon, who were only too eager to go on. The Hun barrage had now been opened in earnest, and shells were falling here, there, and everywhere in No Man's Land. They were mostly dropping on our right, but they were coming nearer and nearer, as if a screen were being drawn across our front. I knew that it was a case of "now or never" and stumbled on feverishly. We managed to get through the barrage in the nick of time, for it closed behind us, and after that we had no shells to fear in front of us. The din must have been deafening (I learned afterwards that it could be heard miles away) yet I have only a confused remembrance of it. Shells which at any other time would have scared me out of my wits, I never so much as heard and not even when they were bursting quite close to me. One landed in the midst of a bunch of men about seventy yards away on my right: I have a most vivid recollection of seeing a tremendous burst of clay and earth go shooting up into the air - and even parts of human bodies - and that when the smoke cleared away there was nothing left. I shall never forget that horrifying spectacle as long as I live, but I shall remember it as a sight only, for I can associate no sound with it...

We were now well up to the Boche. We had to clamber over all manner of obstacles - fallen trees, beams, great mounds of brick and rubble, - in fact over the ruins of Ginchy. It seems like a nightmare to me now. I remember seeing comrades falling round me. My sense of hearing returned to me for I became conscious of a new sound; namely the continuous crackling of rifle-fire. I remember men lying in shell-holes holding out their arms and beseeching water. I remember men crawling about and coughing up blood, as they searched round for some place in which they could shelter until help could reach them. By this time all units were mixed up: but they were all Irishmen. They were cheering and cheering and cheering like mad. It was Hell let loose. There was a machine-gun playing on us near-by, and we all made for it. At this moment we caught our first sight of the Huns. They were in a trench of sorts, which ran in and out among the ruins. Some of them had their hands up. Others were kneeling and holding their arms out to us. Still others were running up and down the trench distractedly as if they didn't know which way to go, but as we got closer they went down on their knees too. To the everlasting good name of the Irish soldiery, not one of these Huns, some of whom had been engaged in slaughtering our men up to the very last moment, was killed. I did not see a single instance of a prisoner being shot or bayoneted. When you remember that our men were now worked up to a frenzy of excitement, this crowning act of mercy to their foes is surely to their eternal credit. They could feel pity even in their rage.

By this time we had penetrated the German front line, and were on the flat ground where the village once stood surrounded by a wood of fairly high trees... As I was clambering out of the front trench, I felt a sudden stab in my right thigh: I thought I had got a "Blighty" but found it was only a graze from a bullet, and so went on... McGarry and I were the only two officers left in the company, so it was up to us to take charge. We could see the Huns hopping over the distant ridge like rabbits, and we had some difficulty in preventing our men from chasing them, for we had orders not to go too far. We got them - Irish Fusiliers, Inniskillings and Dublins - to dig in by linking up the shell-craters, and though the men were tired (some wanted to smoke and others to make tea) they worked with a will, and before long we had got a pretty decent trench outlined.

While we were at work, a number of Huns who had stopped behind and were hiding in shell-holes commenced a bombing attack on our right. But they did not keep it up for long, for they hoisted a white flag (a handkerchief tied to a rifle) as a sign of surrender. I should think we must have made about twenty prisoners. They were very frightened. Some of them bunked into a sunken road or cutting which ran straight out from the wood in an easterly direction, and huddled together with hands upraised. They began to empty their pockets and hand out souvenirs - watches, compasses, cigars, penknives - to their captors, and even wanted to shake hands with us! There was no other officer about at the moment so I had to find an escort to take the prisoners down. Among the prisoners was a tall, distinguished looking man, and I asked him in my broken German whether he was an officer "*Ja! Mein Herr!*" was the answer I got. "*Sprechen Sie English?*" "*Ja!*" "Good," I said, thankful that I didn't have to rack my brains for any more German words. "Please tell your men that no harm will come to them if they follow you quietly." He turned round and addressed his men, who seemed to be very gratified that we were not going to kill them. I must say the officer behaved with real soldierly dignity, and not to be outdone in politeness by a Hun I treated him with the same respect that he showed me. I gave him an escort for himself and told off three or four men for the remainder. I could not but rather admire his bearing, for he did not show anything like the terror that his men did.

There were a great many German dead and wounded in the sunken road. One of them was an officer. He was lying at the entrance to the dug-out. He was waving his arms about. I went over and spoke to him. He could talk a little English. All he could say was, "Comrade, I die, I die." I asked him where he was hit and he said in the stomach. It was impossible to move him, for our stretcher bearers had not yet come up, so I got my servant to look for an overcoat to throw over him, as he was suffering terribly from the cold. Whether or not he survived the night I don't know...

After the counter-attack had subsided I was ordered to take my men and join up with the rest of the battalion on our right. There we spent the night in a trench. We must have been facing south. It was a miserable night we passed, for we were all very cold and thirsty. We had to keep digging. When morning broke it was very misty. We expected to be relieved at 2 in the morning, but the relief did not come till noon. Never shall I forget these hours of suspense. We were all hungry. The only food we could get was Hun black bread, which we picked up all over the place; also Hun tinned sausages and bully beef. We had to lift up some of the dead to get at these things. Some of them had water-bottles full of cold coffee, which we drank. We all craved a smoke. Fortunately, the Hun haversacks were pretty well stocked with cigarettes and cigars. I got a handful of cigars off a dead Boche, and smoked them all morning. Also a tin of cigarettes. His chocolates also came in handy. Poor devil, he must have been a cheery soul when living, for he had a photograph of himself in his pocket, in a group with his wife and two children, and the picture made him look a jolly old sport, and here he was, dead, with both legs missing! The trench (between ours and the wood) was stacked with dead. It was full of debris - bombs, shovels, and whatnot - and torn books, magazines and newspapers. I came across a copy of Schiller's "*Wallenstein*".

Hearing moans as I went along the trench, I looked into a shelter or hole dug in the side and found a young German. He could not move as his legs were broken. He begged me to get him some water, so I hunted round and found a flask of cold coffee which I held to his lips. He kept saying "*Danke, Kamerad, danke, danke.*" However much you may hate the Huns when you are fighting them you can only feel pity for them when you see them lying helpless and wounded on the ground. I saw this man afterwards on his way to the dressing station. About ten yards further on was another German, minus a leg. He too craved water, but I could get him none, though I looked everywhere. Our men were very good to the German wounded. An Irishman's heart melts very soon. In fact, kindness and compassion for the wounded, our own and the enemy's, is about the only decent thing I have seen in war. It is not at all uncommon to see a British and German soldier side by side in the same shell-hole nursing each other as best they can and placidly smoking cigarettes. A poor wounded Hun who hobbled into our trench in the morning, his face badly mutilated by a bullet, - he whimpered and moaned piteously as a child - was bound up by one of our officers, who took off his coat and set to work in earnest. Another Boche, whose legs were hit, was carried in by our men and put into a shell hole for safety, where he lay awaiting the stretcher-bearers when we left. It is with a sense of pride that I can write this of our soldiers...

– 16th - 20th SEPTEMBER 1916 –

LIEUTENANT THE HON. EDWARD WYNDHAM TENNANT
4th Battalion Grenadier Guards

On 13th September the Battalion moved from bivouacs near Carnoy. 'Bim' Tennant's Company (No. 4) and Battalion Headquarters were established in an old German trench 500 yards to the east of Guillemont. On the 14th Tennant wrote to his mother explaining that there was little information as to what would happen in the next few days. He concluded the letter 'I pray I may be all right, but in any case 'Where is Death's sting?'. The following day the Battalion took part in further attacks in the heavy fighting east of Ginchy; later, Tennant described the events. On 20th September, before the assault on the village of Lesboeufs, 'Bim' Tennant wrote his last letter home.

18th September... We were in support and went up about 7.45 and sat down again further up just the right side of the German barrage. Then I was sent across to another Guards Regiment to go with them, find out where they proposed going, and lead the Battalion up beside it. Off I went, and joined them, and went forward with them. When we had skirted Ginchy and were going through a little dip in the ground, we were shot at by Boches on the high ground with rifles, there must have been about twenty shooting at us. I was walking in front with their C.O. and Adjutant, and felt sufficiently uncomfortable, but didn't show it. Bullets scuffed up dust all around with a wicked little 'zump', but they were nearly all short and none of us, at least who were in front, were hit. Thus we went on, and they took up their position between two of these huge steel tanks on the near side of the ridge. Then they lent me an orderly, and I started back to bring the Battalion along; it was an unpleasant journey of about half a mile over nothing but shell-holes full of dead and dying, with any amount of shells flying about. Several whizz-bangs landed very close to me, but I got back to the Battalion and explained the position to them, and then we all went down there and took up a position on the right. The C.O., the Adjutant, the Doctor, and I spent that afternoon, evening and night in a large rocky shell-hole. We were severely shelled on and off the whole time, and about four men were done in in the very next shell-hole a couple of yards away. That night was one of the coldest and most uncomfortable it has ever been my fortune to spend - 'with the stars to see'. Meanwhile most of the Battalion had gone up to support the

Brigades who had done the attack at five that morning and lost heavily. At seven or eight on the 16th we moved our Battalion Headquarters to the line of trenches in front which had been dug the night before. This was safer than our shell-hole, and as we had the worst shelling I have ever experienced during that afternoon and evening, it was probably a very wise move.

An attack took place at 1.15 p.m. that day, and I will tell you more about it when I see you, d.v. My worst job was that of taking messages down the line of trenches to different captains. The trenches were full of men, so I had to go over the open. Several people who were in the trench say they expected every shell to blow me to bits. That night we were again shelled till about 8 p.m. and were relieved about midnight. We got in about 2.30. I was dog-tired and Churchill [Captain Spencer-Churchill], who now commands No. 4 Company, was even more tired. Soup, meat, champagne, and cake, and I went to bed till about 2 p.m. That is the time one really does want champagne, when one comes in at 3 a.m. after no sleep for fifty hours. It gives one the strength to undress... I suppose you have heard who are dead? Guy Baring, Raymond Asquith, Sloper Mackenzie and many others. It is a terrible list... Death and decomposition strew the ground...

20th September... Tonight we go up to the last trenches we were in, and tomorrow we go over the top. Our Brigade has suffered less than either of the other two Brigades in Friday's biff (15th), so we shall be in the forefront of the battle. I am full of hope and trust, and pray that I may be worthy of my fighting ancestors. The one I know best is Sir Henry Wyndham, whose bust is in the hall at 44 Belgrave Square, and there is a picture of him on the stairs at 34 Queen Anne's Gate. We shall probably attack over about 1200 yards, but we shall have such artillery support as will properly smash the Boche line we are going for, and even (which is unlikely) if the artillery doesn't come up to our hopes, the spirit of the Brigade of Guards will carry all resistance before it. The pride of being in such a great regiment! The thought that all the old men 'late Grenadier Guards', who sit in the London Clubs, are thinking and hoping about what we are doing here! I have never been prouder of anything, except your love for me, than I am of being a Grenadier. Today is a great day for me. That line of Harry's rings through my mind, '*High heart, high speech, high deeds, 'mid honouring eyes*'. I went to a service on the side of a hill this morning, and took the Holy Communion afterwards, which always seems to help one along, doesn't it? I slept like a top last night, and dreamed that someone I know very well (but I can't remember who it was), came to me and told me how much I had grown. Three or four of my brother officers read my poems yesterday, and they all liked them very much which pleased me enormously. I feel rather like saying 'If it be possible let this cup pass from me', but the triumphant finish 'nevertheless not what I will but what Thou Willest, steels my heart and sends me into this battle with a heart of triple bronze.

I always carry four photies of you when we go into action, one is in my pocket-book, two in that little leather book, and one round my neck, and I have kept my little medal of the Blessed Virgin. Your love for me and my love for you, have made my whole life one of the happiest there has ever been; Brutus' farewell to Cassius sounds in my heart: 'If not farewell; and if we meet again, we shall smile.' Now all my blessings go with you, and with all we love. God Bless you, and give you peace. Eternal Love from Bim.

– 17th - 24th SEPTEMBER 1916 –

CAPTAIN ARTHUR GRAEME WEST
6th Battalion Oxfordshire and Buckinghamshire Light Infantry

Arthur West served as a Private in the 16th Public Schools Battalion, Middlesex Regiment, in the trenches in the Béthune area for four months between November 1915 and March 1916. He was commissioned in the 6th Battalion Oxfordshire and Buckinghamshire Light Infantry in August 1916, but during his leave his strong pacifism made him so against the idea of rejoining the Army that he decided to desert. However, he did not carry this through and 'in a state of cynical wrath', and certain that he was wrong to go on, he joined his new Battalion which was in billets in Corbie and Méaulte in the middle of September. On the 17th, a Sunday, West was in Triangle trench.

The trenches I am in are near Guillemont, were originally German, and have been recently captured by the British. I have not been really in the trenches for a long time, and find the renewal of the experience particularly trying.

We got up here about 2.20 a.m. Sunday morning - a terribly long relief, for we started out for this line from Guillemont Ridge at 8.30 p.m. Saturday night. The men were dog-tired when they got here, and though ordered to dig, complied very unwillingly, and were allowed to sit about or lean on their spades, or even to stand up and fall asleep against the side of the trench. It was a smelly trench. A dead German - a big man - lay on his stomach as if he were crawling over the parados down into the trench; he had lain there some days, and that corner of trench reeked even when someone took him by the legs and pulled him away out of sight, though not out of smell, into a shell-hole. We sat down and fell into a comatose state, so tired we were. On our right lay a large man covered with a waterproof, his face hidden by a sandbag, whom we took to be a dead Prussian Guardsman, but the light of dawn showed him to be an Englishman by his uniform. From where I sit I can see his doubled-up knees.

The men lay about torpidly until 4.30 a.m... We tried to keep awake merely for form's sake while the light very slowly grew...

One always feels better with daylight - of this kind of life alone is the psalmist's saying true - in ordinary modern life, where unhappiness consists so much in *mental* agitation, it is startlingly false.

We joke over the tea and biscuits, go into the next bay and talk to the men about the German things they have found and are determined to get home somehow - a rifle, a belt-buckle with "Gott mit uns" on it, a bayonet, and so on.

We try and make out where we are on the map, and find we are at least 1,000 yards away.

Then we resolve that as we had practically no sleep last night nor the night before, and I had little even the night before that, we will try and get some. We lie...

Wednesday, 20th September. So far I had written when it became evident that our quiet Sunday was to be of the usual kind and we were to be bombarded. H.E. shells, about 6-inch ones, came over with a tremendous black smoke, making an explosion and sending up a column of earth about thirty feet high. The first intimation I had was when I went round the corner to the next bay to see where one had fallen, and found a man with a little ferrety nose and inadequate yellow moustache, in a very long great-coat, sitting muttering away on the firing-step like a nervous rabbit and making vague gestures with his hands and head. He would return no answer to questions, and I was told two men had just been buried in a dug-out near by. I went round and found two more pale men, rather earthy. I talked to them and did my best to comfort them. A few more shells came over, unpleasantly near, but it was not yet certain whether they were definitely after us.

Soon this was clear. They worked down a winding trench, and blew in the walls; we lost six men by burying and ten others wounded or suffering from shell-shock. It was horrible. A whistle would be heard, nearer and nearer, ceasing for a mere fraction of a second when the shell was falling and about to explode. Where was it coming?

Men cowered and trembled. It exploded, and a cloud of black reek went up - in the communication trench again. You went down it; two men were buried, perhaps more you were told, certainly two. The trench was a mere undulation of newly-turned earth, under it somewhere lay two men or more. You dug furiously. No sign. Perhaps you were standing on a couple of men now, pressing the life out of them, on their faces or chests. A boot, a steel helmet - and you dig and scratch and uncover a grey, dirty face, pitifully drab and ugly, the eyes closed, the whole thing limp and mean-looking: this is the devil of it, that a man is not only killed, but made to look so vile and filthy in death, so futile and meaningless that you hate the sight of him.

Perhaps the man is alive and kicks feebly or frantically as you unbury him: anyhow, here is the first, and God knows how many are not beneath him. At last you get them out, three dead, grey, muddy masses, and one more jibbering live one.

Then another shell falls and more are buried.

We tried to make them stand up.

It is noticeable that only one man was wounded; six were buried alive.

I shall always remember sitting at the head of this little narrow trench, smoking a cigarette and trying to soothe the men simply by being quiet. Five or six little funk-holes dug into the side of the trench served to take the body of a man in a very huddled and uncomfortable position, with no room to move, simply to cower into the little hole. There they sit like animals for market, like hens in cages, one facing one way, one another. One simply looks at his hands clasped on his knees, dully and lifelessly, shivering a little as a shell draws near; another taps the side of his hole with his finger-nails, rhythmically; another hides himself in his great-coat and passes into a kind of torpor. Of course, when a shell falls on to the parapet and bores down into the earth and explodes, they are covered over like so many potatoes. It is with the greatest difficulty that we can shift the men into another bit of trench and make them stand up. I found myself cool and useful enough, though after we had been shelled for about two and a half hours on end my nerves were shaky and I could have cried for fright as each shell drew near, and longed for nothing so much as to rush down a deep cellar. I did not betray any kind of weak feeling.

It was merely consideration of the simple fact that a shell, if it did hit me, would either wound me or kill me, both of which were good inasmuch as they would put a pause to this existence - that kept me up to my standard of unconcern. And the more I experience it, the more fear seems a thing quite apart from possible consequences, which may occur in a person even when he assents fully to the proposition I have noted above.

I feel afraid at the moment. I write in a trench that was once German, and shells keep dropping near the dug-out. There is a shivery fear that one may fall into it or blow it in.

Yet *what* do I fear? I mind being killed because I am fond of the other life, but I know I should not miss it in annihilation. It is not that I fear.

I don't definitely feel able to say I *fear* the infliction of pain or wound. I cannot bind the fear down to anything definite. I think it resolves itself simply into the realisation of the fact that being hit by a shell will produce a new set of circumstances so strange that one does not know how one will find oneself in them. It is the knowledge that something may happen with which one will not be able to cope, or that one's old resolutions of courage, etc., will fail one in this new set of experiences. Something unknown there is. How will one act when it happens? One may be called upon to bear or perform something to which one will find oneself inadequate.

The shelling went on - on this Sunday, I mean - for about five hours, and we had a few biscuits and a tot of whisky about 1 o'clock. By then the whole of the little communication trench had been battered by successive shells, and we had left off going down it after each one, as the Germans had turned machine-gun fire on to the levelled portion of trench. We stood in the only undamaged bay, eating and drinking, and watching the huge columns of earth and smoke as the work of destruction went on. They had worked rather off this particular trench, and the men still stood all about it, but I believed for certain that they would return towards the end and smash in the only bay to which they would naturally have hoped to have driven us. I had had enough whisky to enable me to view this prospect with nothing but interested excitement, and really did not flinch as the shells fell, seemingly groping their way towards their mark.

Just as they drew near, a runner from the X...'s came down to say the Germans had broken through on their left and were attacking, would we look after the third line and the flank? This news woke us all up from this rather unreal alertness of impending destruction and we rushed off with rifles, bayonets, and all manner of weapons to man the trench. No foe appeared, but it cheered us, and they did not shell very much more that night. The strain of the whole thing was very much worse than anything we had ever had at the Béthune section.

24th September. A Tent [Billets at Ville-sur-Ancre]... I am unhappier than I ever was last year, and this not only because I have been separated from my friends or because I am simply more tired of the war.

It is because my whole outlook towards the thing has altered. I endured what I did endure last year patiently, believing I was doing a right and reasonable thing. I had not thought out the position of the pacifist and the conscientious objector, I was always sympathetic to these people, but never considered whether my place ought not to have been rather among them than where I actually was. Then I came back to England feeling rather like the noble crusader or explorer who has given up much for his friend but who is not going to be sentimental or overbearing about it, though he regards himself as somehow different from and above those who have not endured as he has done.

I have described how I modified this feeling after much company with Joad. It would certainly be much pleasanter if I could regard myself still in this rather sublime light as the man who goes into the pit for his friends: but I cannot do so, for I am beginning to think that I never ought to have gone into it at all. "This war is trivial, for all its vastness," says B [Bertrand] Russell, and so I feel. I am being pained, bored, and maddened - and to what end? It is the uselessness of it that annoys me. I had once regarded it as inevitable; now I don't believe it was, and had I been in full possession of my reasoning powers when the war began, I would never have joined the Army. To have taken a stand against the whole thing, against the very conception of force, even when employed against force, would have really been my happier and truer course.

The war so filled up my perspective at first that I could not see anything close because of it: most people are still like that. To find a growing body of men who can really be "au-dessus de la mêlée," who can comprehend and condemn it, who can live in the world beside the war and yet not in it, is extremely encouraging to anyone who can acclaim himself of their brotherhood. Spiritually I am of it, but I am prevented from being among them. I am a creature caught in a net.

Most men fight, if not happily, at any rate patiently, sure of the necessity and usefulness of their work. So did I - once! Now it all looks to me so absurd and brutal that I can only force myself to continue in a kind of dream-state; I hypnotise myself to undergo it. What *good*, what *happiness* can be produced by some of the scenes I have had to witness in the last few days?

Even granting it was necessary to resist Germany by arms at the beginning - and this I have yet most carefully to examine - why go on?

Can no peace be concluded?

Is it not known to both armies that each is utterly weary and heartsick?

Of course it is. Then why, in God's name, go on?

It must be unreasonable to continue. The victorious, or seemingly victorious side, ought to offer peace: no peace can be worse than this bloody stupidity. The maddening thing is the sight of men of fairly goodwill accepting it all as necessary; this angers me, that men *must* go on. Why? Who wants to?

Moreover, I feel quite clearly that I ought to have stood aside. It is these men who stand aside, these philosophers, and the so-called conscientious objectors, who are the living force of the future; they are full of the light that must come sooner or later; they are sneered at now, but their position is firm.

If all mankind were like them there would not have been war. Duty to country and King and civilisation! Nonsense! For none of these is a man to be forced to leave his humanity on one side and make a passionate destroying beast of himself. I am a man before I am anything else, and all that is human in me revolts. I would fain stand beside these men I admire, whose cause is the highest part of human nature, calm reason, and kindliness.

The argument drawn from the sufferings of the men in the trenches, from the almost universal sacrifices to duty, are not valid against this. Endurance is hard, but not meritorious simply because it is endurance. We are confronted with two sets of martyrs here: those of the trenches, and those of the tribunal and the civil prison, and not by any means are the former necessarily in the right.

And it is not even as if the Army men were content simply to do their dirty work: they sneer at the pacifist, they encourage the sentiments of the *Spectator* and such poisonous papers, or, at any rate, they are profoundly indifferent to the cause of Internationalism; they are ready to fight and beat the Boche (as they will call him), and there is the end.

Yes! There was but one way for me, and I have seen it only when it was too late to pursue it. Even be the thing as necessary as you like, be the constitution of this world really so foul and hellish that force must be met by force, yet I should have stood aside, no brutality should have led me into it. Had I stood apart I should have stood on firm logical ground; where I was truth would have been, as it is among my friends now.

To defy the whole system, to refuse to be an instrument of it - this *I* should have done.

– 25th - 27th SEPTEMBER 1916 –

SECOND-LIEUTENANT ALEXANDER AITKEN
1st Otago Battalion (New Zealand Expeditionary Force)

After suffering terrible casualties at Gallipoli, the New Zealand Division was reinforced and sent to the Western Front; on 15th September they took part in their first action at Flers. Nine days later the 1st Otago Battalion assembled in Grove Alley, which ran in a south-westerly direction between Gueudecourt and Flers, to the left of the Flers-Eaucourt road. The New Zealanders were to attack the German trenches in Goose Alley and then go on to capture Gird Trench.

Now it was the evening of the 24th September; we were to attack some time next day. All details of the plan were known except zero time, which was usually not divulged until a few hours before action... My Platoon, Platoon 1, was to be the first wave on the left half of the Battalion sector; and if ever I prepared for an examination it was now, to learn by heart, relative to zero time, every particular of the time-table and of the ground. Maps had been run off on a duplicating machine from the official ones of scale 1 in 10,000; every officer and many of the senior N.C.O.s had one of these. Small study groups had been formed, and the scheme of attack had been discussed down to its finest details; each platoon commander was responsible that every man should understand both it and his own share in it...

The first German line had been broken, but on the southern part only of the front attacked, on 1st and 2nd July; the second line in the night attack on Contalmaison on the 14th; the third, the Martinpuich-Flers line, had fallen to us only lately, on 15th September. Parallel to this and about a mile farther back was the strongly fortified fourth line, from Le Sars to Eaucourt l'Abbaye and thence to Gueudecourt and Le Transloy; its code name was Gird Trench; it had still to be captured. The lately captured third line, Flers Trench, was joined to the fourth line by communication trenches each about a mile long, Grove Alley and Goose Alley. Grove Alley was ours as far as the point where it crossed the Flers-Ligny-Thilloy road; the projected new line was to run from the south-western part of the next switch trench on the west, Goose Alley, to a point on the Flers-Ligny road called Factory Corner. This whole line was the Brigade objective; our Battalion was to capture the left third or so of Goose Alley. Assembly trenches were to be in Grove Alley, to the left of the Flers-Eaucourt road. The advance would be at first downhill to a hollow, below the 120-metre contour containing a road forking into two parallel avenues; then uphill on a similar slope 300 or 400 yards to Goose Alley, on a ridge above the 130-metre contour, looking north-west to Eaucourt l'Abbaye and south-east backward to Flers. The total distance from assembly to objective was 700 yards...

The rate of progress behind the barrage, fifty yards per minute, was everything. There were also to be fixed barrages playing on side-trenches, machine-gun nests, and so on; these we might take for granted. All ranks had been drilled in the plan and their own part in it; lance-corporals even, or senior privates, in extreme emergency, could have taken charge. Such thoroughness bred confidence everywhere...

At midnight we packed up, passed on the right of High Wood to the line beyond Flers and filed into the assembly trenches at Grove Alley... Zero time was now announced with precision as 12.35 p.m... Once more, and finally, watches were accurately synchronized with 'Brigade time', and now every precaution, so far as we could see, had been taken. We must have had a slight meal - though meals before an attack are eaten in a kind of absentness and not remembered; we arranged ourselves in order for going over. All the platoons densely filled the assembly trench from end to end, in readiness to move out in successive waves. The men of my Platoon were extended right and left of me at intervals of eight or ten yards, with N.C.O.s uniformly spread among them, in such a way that in emergency they could take over according to seniority. Ten minutes before zero all platoons were arranged in this way, dove-tailed and interwoven. All was ready, but for these last few minutes we kept the men spacing themselves still more evenly, in the congested trench, merely to keep their minds, and ours, occupied up to the last. My watch is showing 12.34. One more minute.

Zero! Crash of explosions in the best barrage yet seen, bursts of cotton-wool smoke at different heights but all in one vertical plane. The air twanging like a bow-string; seconds-hand moving round. Now, 12.37! Platoon, lifted like one man, clears parapet. Very evenly; but it must be fifty yards a minute, exactly half ordinary marching pace. Mentally count seconds, nought, *a*, *b*, *c*, one, *a*, *b*, *c*, and make a full pace at each second. The trees down there - as if I had known them always. A glance back; that is Captain Herbert, wearing a private's tunic and carrying a rifle, as we all are, to avoid being picked out by snipers; for our own men the stars on our shoulders are enough. Grove Alley, now all platoons are out, begins to go up in air behind us. Halt here till barrage moves on - man three to my left, 13th

Reinforcements, has dropped on one knee but is looking my way and will come on all right. Trees quite near now, no casualties yet, everything running wonderfully... Count seconds again. Something disturbs from half left; birds, six or eight, panic-running across front, now rising, flying away half-right. My watch, my piece of paper, the barrage are everything, but - not quail, not grouse, *perdix* of course, partridges! Something else also running from left - a hare, not three yards in front. Man two to my left makes mock point at it with his bayonet, grins at me in this blazing barrage! This is a green slope with only a few fresh shell-holes. Company on right, under Rutherford in first wave, seems a little too far forward. Corporal Gilmour there, keeping contact, a little too far - pass the word along to Corporal - too late! One of our own shells has exploded short, very little. Five or six men in the 8th Company fall forward; Arthur Gilmour, friend and fellow student, also. My Platoon otherwise still intact.

The trees; just as imagined always. Through here; barrage forward; 35 plus 18 equals 12.53 and everything is still right. Same man grins and jerks his bayonet upward towards a tree. Nought, *a*, *b*, *c*, hardly time to glance up, but - an owl! How in the name of all that shrapnel? Cross parallel roads, double drive, light all red flares along this ditch. Horn-blasts from left, contact aeroplane above, red streamer flying low down along line of trees. Everything incredibly right so far.

Three hundred yards more, up farther slope same way. Lessening gradient, the ridge, line of thrown-up earth, Goose Alley! My watch dead on 1.00, barrage forward. 'Platoon! Rush trench with lowered bayonets and jump in!'

We met with no resistance. The Germans, seeing the unbroken lines coming at speed with fixed bayonets, fled, most of them away to the right, like the partridges and the hare, north-east along Goose Alley to Gird Trench, a few the other way, over towards Eaucourt l'Abbaye. I could not believe that we had been twenty-three minutes in no-man's-land; it felt like twenty-three seconds. Ordinary time came back the instant my feet touched trench bottom. A few machine-guns were seized at once; a handful of prisoners, Bavarians, surrendered and were sent to the rear; several others, including a company officer, had been badly wounded, while dead lay in the floor of the trench at every few yards. Most of these seemed very young, eighteen or nineteen years old; myself only two years older, I felt a compunction. The officer, dignified, distinguished, was bleeding from a grave wound in the upper part of the leg. We bandaged him as soon as we could and sent him back on a stretcher... Deathly white and in grievous pain, he made no complaint and thanked me in French. One can have no quarrel with such a man. As for my own Platoon, Arthur Gilmour died of wounds later...

Shell-fire and counter-attack were now to be expected. All men were carrying pick and shovel, inserted in the braces of the web equipment behind the shoulders. They had already set to work deepening the trench against machine-gun fire and shrapnel. Suitable sites were chosen, facing Eaucourt l'Abbaye, for a shield of machine-gun posts. We divided up our sector, each platoon commander making himself responsible till night for his own quarter; mine was farthest to the right, where we joined the 10th Company under Captain Hargest. On the extreme left, where once again we rested on air, Sutherland jumped up to pick a site; he was sniped fatally on the instant. Sergeants Carnegie and Malcolm leapt up to pull him in; both were severely wounded. Our left flank must be badly exposed... By nightfall Goose Alley was deeper and safer, but digging continued unremittingly. High explosive was now crashing down in enfilade from the north-east, not so much on us as on the 10th Otagos, who were suffering losses. So far there was no sign of a counter-attack...

Darkness fell. The remaining three platoon commanders divided the night into two-hour watches and took turns on duty, those off duty not sleeping but sitting in a waking-sleeping state; the mind might try to sleep, but obscure fears would seize it the moment the head drooped, making one sit up with a start. So it passed, a 'quiet night'... quiet except for the kettle-drum rat-a-tat of machine-guns and the occasional howl and crash of a heavy shell. On our rounds we tramped in the dark over the dead bodies of those young Germans in the floor of the trench; once, for a few minutes, I was pillowed in broken sleep between two of them, and now and then, stumbling thus upon some dead man's head, I shook off our conditioned callousness, shook off the feeling, now taking root, that this world of arbitrary violence and random death was the real world, and that justice, mercy, peace, and love were phantasms that had never been...

26th September. Dawn broke at last; our fears of a night attack down Goose Alley, were for the time being dispelled. In daylight Goose Alley appeared a worse shambles than ever. On my rounds I reached the extreme left of our sector, Flers Trench, where we were now presumed to be in contact with the Black Watch. I saw none of them alive, but many of them dead. I saw, too, what cannot be described, a sergeant of the Black Watch, a powerful red-haired man with magnificent shoulders, and five Germans lying radially extended from him. They had closed in upon him and he had let off a Mills bomb... I set the men to collect systematically the large quantities of equipment, rations, and ammunition that had been abandoned. The greatcoats we abstracted for our own use in keeping warm by night...Numbers of machine-guns, complete with cartridge-belts, had been abandoned, as well as quantities of the familiar stick-grenades and hundreds of small black-lacquered bombs of a new type of the shape and size of a goose-egg. Belts lay about, inscribed *'Gott mit uns'*, also a saw bayonet, intended of course, in spite of atrocity stories in the newspapers, to be really used as a saw; lastly, numerous rifles of Spandau make. I appropriated one of these; my own, left for a minute in the corner of a bay, was twisted and stripped of all woodwork by a shell while I was, fortunately, in the next bay. We found a few diaries - we were not allowed to keep any ourselves, and these seemed rather pathetic - and handed them in to Stuart Macdonald, the Battalion Intelligence Officer. Food in plenty was found: large numbers of white bags, containing small loaves of palatable black or brown bread, small square biscuits like our own emergency 'iron rations', and tins of *Rindfleisch*, the German equivalent of our bully beef. Dozens of small bottles of soda-water lay about, and were soon sampled...

All day for every shell arriving in Goose Alley many of ours went over in the opposite direction. The upper air was full of roaring and whining noises, long high notes, sinister descending chromatic scales. The green carpet of fields that I had seen as a mirage of peace above the smoke and dust ten days before was being torn up; the ground in and far behind the German lines was spouting in great brown geysers. The enemy were keeping so low in cover under all this that it was possible to lean over the trench-wall and make observations, even to send parties across the open to Flers Dump. Men who had been killed were now lifted over the trench, on the south-east side, and buried by their friends, the spot being marked by any spare rifle and bayonet driven into the ground...

The counter-attack did not materialize; the night of 26th-27th September passed off for us in relative quiet. Now from headquarters came more precise details of a new objective, to be captured if possible some time during the afternoon of the 27th, time-table and barrage scheme to be communicated to all ranks about the middle of the morning...

27th September. The objective this time was Gird Trench itself, on a frontage of about 400 yards, the very strong fourth line of the Germans, with its thick hedge of barbed wire in front and its support line, which we were also to capture, 150 yards in rear... In order to attack Gird Trench we should have to file along Goose Alley to our extreme point, scramble out there on the right, and deploy into line at the double across the enemy's front, finally inclining half left to face Gird Trench and move forward in the usual waves. Those were in fact our eventual instructions; but let anyone imagine such a movement carried out under machine-gun fire! Yet again, Goose Alley was almost at right angles to Gird Trench, and half of it, several hundred yards, was still occupied by Germans, who while we were attacking would have to be dislodged by our bombers. Finally, Gird Trench was concealed from periscope scrutiny by a slight ridge, almost imperceptible but significant, along the Eaucourt-Factory Corner road...

The time-table, communicated later in the morning relative to an unspecified new time, was even more discouraging. The careful arrangements of the 25th had allowed twenty-three minutes for the crossing of 700 yards; these of the 27th allowed a bare eight minutes for the crossing of 1,000 yards far more exposed to fire of all kinds. We should have to move at 150 paces a minute. As for barrages, there was nothing remotely resembling the elaborate creeping and stationary barrages of the Monday; little more than the bare statement that the barrage would lift and move forward at zero time, when we should make our dash...

The attack being as usual by waves of platoons, I saw that I should go forward in the middle of the ninth wave. We must have had a midday meal, but I forget it. At noon zero time was given out as 2.15 p.m., watches were synchronized with Brigade time and the interval was spent in instructing N.C.O.s and men. There was little to say; no one could feel any conviction in the opening manoeuvre and the brief and apparently inadequate barrage. There was the lurking suspicion that the Staff (but which Staff - Army, Army Corps, or Division?) were counting on our making a flying dash and capturing Gird Trench by luck.

At 2.15 the barrage, which seemed a perfunctory affair, moved forward and the first two companies, in eight platoon waves, scrambled out and over to the right. My Platoon followed quickly up Goose Alley and climbed out on the right at the point where the sunken road from Flers to Eaucourt l'Abbaye crossed it. When the last man was clear we inclined left and hurried forward after the other waves. This deployment was carried out without loss, so far as I could judge from a quick survey, which gave me my last glimpse in this world of Captain Herbert at the gap, directing the next wave. Like all the other officers I was wearing a private's tunic and equipment and carrying a rifle and bayonet, the Spandau rifle I have mentioned. We had not gone a furlong when it became clear that there was something wrong ahead; the leading waves were not to be seen, except for isolated men straggling here and there. The reason became clear as we neared the road running due east and west from Factory Corner to Eaucourt.

We were about half-way across when German high explosive mixed with shrapnel, of the greenish-black kind, began to fall thickly. Not ten yards ahead a group of the 8th Company vanished in the smoke of a shell-burst, some falling where they stood, the others walking on dreamlike. I passed through the smoke. In a dim way I wondered why I had not been hit by the flying pieces, but the mind would not trouble itself with problems at that moment, the over-mastering impulse being to move on. On! On! In an attack such as this, under deadly fire, one is as powerless as a man gripping strongly charged electrodes, powerless to do anything but go mechanically on; the final shield from death removed, the will is fixed like the last thought taken into an anaesthetic, which is the first thought taken out of it. Only safety, or the shock of a wound, will destroy such auto-hypnosis. At the same time all normal emotion is numbed utterly. Close upon this road now, I heard a voice abusing the Germans; crossing the road, I realized it had been my own.

As I took the bank I looked left and saw Private Nelson, one of my men, fall forward on his knees and elbows, his head between his hands. I mentally registered 23598, Nelson, W.P., and the terrific electro-magnetic force pulled me on. He was dead.

Now from two directions, half-right, half-left, came the hissing of many bullets, the herring-bone weave of machine-gun cross-fire. I saw some cut long straight scores in the ground, sending up dust; some, as I found later, cut my tunic, frayed the equipment, and made rents in the cloth cover of my shrapnel helmet; many seemed to whizz past my ear, some to bury themselves under my feet as I walked... Suddenly at my left side my platoon sergeant, Livingston, dropped on one knee and looked up at me in a curious doubtful gaze. 'Come on, sergeant!' I said, stepping forward myself. He was killed, I think, the next instant; I never saw him again.

All this occurred within a few yards of crossing the road. I glanced right and left and saw the Platoon, thirty of them, crumple and fall, only two going on, widely apart, and no N.C.O. A few yards farther on I was nearly knocked down by a tremendous blow in the upper right arm and spun sideways; simultaneously the right hand unclenched and the Spandau rifle and bayonet fell to the ground. Even then no thought of death came, only some phrase like 'sledge-hammer blow', from a serial read years before in a boys' magazine. Pain came the next moment; the spurious self-hypnotism vanished and gave way to an overwhelming desire to run, anywhere. Of three men - as I heard later - crouching wounded in a shell-hole that afternoon, one tried to keep the other two in safety, but they broke away and made a wild dash in no particular direction, both being killed by machine-gun fire within a few yards. I had the same wild wish, but it was crossed and quelled by the resurgent rhythm of the first impulse, so that I found myself walking on mechanically, yet wondering what I should do, disarmed now, if I reached Gird Trench. A second wound dismissed the question. As the right foot was coming to the ground a bullet passed through in front of the ankle and fractured the several tarsal bones. I crumpled and fell sideways to the right into a providential shell-hole, curling up like a hedgehog.

Sleeve sopping, boot oozing blood through the holes, I settled in as compactly as I could, lying back with head towards the enemy, tilting the shrapnel helmet in the direction of the bullets and waiting for the hours to pass. It was 2.23 p.m. summer time; the attack had begun only eight minutes before; firing could not be expected to cease before nightfall at least. The wounds, numb at first, soon throbbed recurrently. I drank very little water, reserving it for emergency. At one stage I wondered for a few seconds whether the arm-wound would affect the bowing of the violin, supposing I should ever get out of this; it seemed a foolish and unimportant thought. The hours seemed to pass very slowly; I wondered again whether any of us had reached Gird Trench...

Bullets still hissed above my shell-hole, a raised hand would have been perforated at once; it was out of the question to think of crawling back. I saw the head and shoulders, and once or twice the hands also, of a field telephonist running forward from shell-hole to shell-hole and unrolling his wire; he was still unwounded as he drew level with my crater and passed behind me towards the front, but I fear he could not long have remained so.

Soon afterwards I was myself forced to move, by noticing amid the uproar a regularity, a periodicity, in a particular type of explosion. I watched carefully, and saw that shells from a 5.9 or 4.1 howitzer were coming closer every two minutes, apparently in a straight line. When first seen, their burst seemed close to the part of Goose Alley, perhaps 500 yards back, where we had emerged and strung out. I visualized the German gunners lowering their howitzers by a fraction of angle each time; I reckoned that in about ten minutes one of these shells would fall near my crater, possibly on it. Being blown to pieces or killed by blast seemed worse than the machine-guns. Using what cover I could, I crawled from my shell-hole over to our original right, now my left, out of the line of fire. This brought me in a few minutes to the Factory Corner road again, at a point some 200 yards to the original right of Goose Alley, which I could trace by its thrown-up earth at that distance down the road. It was a narrow country road with very little camber - even so slight a detail meant life or death at such a moment - and with a low bank eighteen inches high on the side towards Gird Trench; not much protection in itself, not enough even for explicit mention on the map, but enough for me. Under the lip of the bank was a fresh shallow crater. I fitted myself into it. The road here and the ground to either side were strewn with bodies, some motionless, some not. Cries and groans, prayers, imprecations, reached me... A few yards back from the road a man lay forward supported on his elbows, not letting his body touch ground; one could but surmise why he did this...

Relieved for the time being, I attended to things near at hand and saw - how had I failed to notice him earlier? - a man lying flat on his face almost within reach on the road, his eyes shut but his face twitching. I studied him; wounded in the arm, able to move elbows and knees. While I looked his eyes opened and looked back at me, but their gaze was unfocused; he was in a state of shock and fear. But suppose - I thought - suppose he could manage to crawl on his stomach under the lee of this slight bank as far as Goose Alley, then drop in, turn left, and make a dash for it! It was what I should have done in his place. I spoke peremptorily and ordered him to do this. 'No, no,' he almost gibbered, 'they nearly got me, they'll get me.' I threatened him; he was of another company but I knew his face. I said, 'You know me. When you get back, say that when last seen Mr. Aitken was on this road, but all right. Now, off you go!' He crawled five yards and flattened down quivering. He plucked up courage and crawled a few more; then after a while the same. I watched his disappearing heels. Down towards Goose Alley I lost him for some time in a hollow, then suddenly I saw him throw himself in, turn left, and run; his shrapnel helmet appeared for a moment flying past a gap farther down. The Germans had not yet begun to shell Goose Alley as heavily as they did later; and I learned when I myself got in that he was safe and had delivered his message.

About 4 p.m. the sky clouded over and drizzle fell. I angled for a German waterproof sheet a yard away, and this, though riddled with bullet-holes, gave me some shelter... The rain was fortunately not heavy, the ground became wet and greasy but the craters did not fill with water. I had thought of crawling like that other man down the road to Goose Alley, but now a dense barrage of green-black shrapnel mixed with heavy shells fell on the junction of trench and road; the trench was in bad repair and the shrapnel swept it on enfilade. There was nothing for it but to wait until dark, when, if machine-gun fire should die down, I might hope to crawl back overland to somewhere near the starting-point of our attack, where the trench would be occupied by the 10th Company and would be in better repair. The distance would be about 500 yards.

About 8 p.m. the rain had stopped, the sky had cleared; in the dusk I could just distinguish our observation balloons. The stars shone in a moonless night, the Great Bear swinging low with the Pole Star above. I turned my back on them, fixed south by other constellations and began the long crawl...

From shell-hole to shell-hole I side-crawled on left elbow and knee; perhaps taking three or four hours - though I had ceased to consult the luminous wrist-watch, now daubed with mud. Many times I was tempted to curl up and wait for the stretcher-bearers, but I crawled the few yards farther, rested, and crawled again... At length I saw outlined, in black against the rain-washed night sky, the figures of two men on a mound, digging. I recognized them, Alf Ellis of my old section and Lou Mylchreest, a Manxman, also of the 10th Company, which had evidently come up from supplies to hold the line. Both men were killed next day. I called 'Alf!' Instantly the figures vanished. Three or four minutes passed, and then I felt a prod in the rear with a bayonet, a foot pressed into the hollow of my back and 'Who's this? Speak!' 'Your old corporal, Alf', I said; 'steady with that bayonet.' They bent down, recognized me, and returned to the trench for a stretcher; but all stretchers must have been in use... The next thing I remembered is the earthy parapet, I had evidently crawled the last fifteen yards. I fell in...

– 26th SEPTEMBER 1916 –

LIEUTENANT ADRIAN CONSETT STEPHEN, M.C.
Trench Mortar Battery, Royal Field Artillery

On 23rd September Adrian Stephen, whose Battery gun positions were still in Mash Valley, reconnoitred the ground nearer the front line, clambering 'from one shell hole to another'. He came upon a piece of high ground somewhere behind Mouquet Farm and from this vantage point registered targets preparatory to the forthcoming assault on Thièpval fortress by the 18th Division.

Noon on the 26th found me at the O.P. with the Captain. Zero was at 12.35, and as yet the trenches were silent and motionless. Then suddenly, at the appointed minute, the slopes of Thièpval seemed to move with small brown figures, like a field alive with rabbits, and the guns swept down on Thièpval and the country to the right of it. At first the men advanced in disordered masses, but gradually, taking their own time they opened out like a stage crowd falling into their allotted places. I could see the first wave walking towards Thièpval, and then a second wave sprang up and spread out behind them, then the last wave took shape and followed up in artillery formation; small bunches of men, with an interval between each bunch, or more often six men advancing in single file with a stretcher bearer in the rear. It was a wonderful sight. Never have I seen such a calm, methodical and perfectly ordered advance. It seemed incredible that this parade could be marching on Thièpval, the most sinister of German strongholds, yet hardly a man fell. The barrage was as perfect as it was terrible. The white smoke of shrapnel ran like a rampart along the trenches that were the first objective, as clear as though it were made of tape carefully placed and measured. Indeed, the barrier of white smoke, broken now and again by a black puff from an enemy gun, might have been an ermine fur with its little black tufts.

From my vantage point I could even look over the barrage on to the trenches beyond, but it was hard even for a moment to drag one's eyes away from the little brown figures that were slowly but steadily drawing upon Thièpval. Sometimes a wave of men would dip and disappear into a trench only to emerge on the other side in perfect line again. Now they are into Thièpval! No, the line suddenly telescopes into a bunch and the bunch scurries to right or left, trying to evade a machine-gun in front, and then with a plunge the first wave, broken now into little groups, vanished amidst the ruined houses. What desperate resistance they encountered in the dark and mysterious passages beneath those ruins, only the men who fought will know, but the other waves swept on up to the slope, till they too were lost amidst the village. Farther to the right, where the barrage had lifted, more brown figures streamed across the open. A black dog ran out of a dug-out to meet them; a man stooped down and fondled it. When they drew near to a line of chalk heaps I saw black masses emerge and march towards our lines. Prisoners were giving themselves up without a fight. Prisoners were pouring in from all sides, sometimes in black batches, guided by a brown figure and a shining bayonet, sometimes a single Boche would race, hands above head, panic-stricken till he reached our lines. Thièpval was now a closed book, though runners would sometimes emerge and dash stumbling to our trenches. The Boche retaliation was feeble and badly placed. His barrage fell behind all our men, and very few shells had burst among them, and even then never did they cause a man to turn his head or swerve out of place - unless he fell. At this stage a tank crawled on to the scene and crept laboriously, like a great slug, towards Thièpval. It disappeared among the ruins, puffing smoke. Subsequently it caught fire. Thièpval now became as stony, as devoid of life, as it was before the attack. Away to the right, however, a fresh assault was being launched. A new barrage opened, and our men swept forward to another objective, wheeling slightly as the trench in front ran diagonally across their path. Suddenly, as though spirited away, they vanished, sank into the ground. Watching carefully we could distinguish a movement among the long grass and wire, and sometimes a man would leap up, dash forward, or run backward. It seemed they were playing at hide and seek. Probably they were. It is certain they were held up by something, and the bitter fighting which continued the next day for Hessian Trench - the trench in question - made one wonder how they ever got as far as they did. Yet all this time men were streaming backwards and forwards to the Zollern Trench just in the rear. How astounding, this careless movement across the open! Even during my exploration I had found myself strolling about in places where I could sometimes see Boches running along their trenches. It made one smile to remember the old Corp Summaries of "peace time" warfare. "Our snipers shot two of the enemy today." Slaughter now has become so wholesale that one is careless of the mere individual.

When the light failed, our men were still playing hide and seek. We had taken the Zollern Redoubt, part of the Stuff Redoubt on the right, and part of Schwaben Redoubt on the left. Above all, Thièpval had fallen. Thièpval, the proud fortress garrisoned by one regiment since September 1914, had at last, after three big attacks, yielded. It was a good conquest, for the slopes of Thièpval are surely as tragic and bloody as any in this war, except, of course, Gallipoli, but the battle of Thièpval was significant, not so much for the actual ground gained, as for the sudden appearance in the conflict of an element hitherto unseen. Not only the battle of Thièpval, but the whole battle of the Somme, must be judged from three points of view:-

1. Strategic progress.
2. Material progress.
3. Moral progress.

Now, strategically, the battle of the Somme is a great British reverse. We had failed to do what we intended to do. The battle was lost on July 1st. The Boche line still held. Moreover, it had taken us months to accomplish what, according to time-table, should have been done in as many hours. Let us not hesitate to confess that strategically the battle was a failure. Of course we are now threatening the communications of Bapaume, Vely and Achiet after four months. We had meant to do that in as many hours.

Materially we have turned the battle into a success. We have killed Germans, taken guns, villages and men. Our material progress is as obvious as the map.

Morally we have never obtained complete mastery. The Boche morale remained as hard as his line and as unbreakable. But here we come to Thièpval. For the first time I saw Germans surrendering in droves before putting up a fight. For the first time his hitherto faultless military machinery failed to swing reserves where they were wanted. On the 26th September I felt our moral ascendancy. It was as obvious, also, as the map at my elbow or the ground under observation. It was not pronounced, but it was there.

We must push on - on - on without rest and without mercy, even to ourselves. Our moral ascendancy, however slight, makes one feel like that. It fires one with fresh enthusiasm.

October
1916

– 8th OCTOBER 1916 –

SERGEANT FREDERICK LESLIE A. COULSON
'D' Company attached 1st/12th Battalion London Regiment
(The Rangers)

The Battalion took part in the attack on the Transloy Ridges, planned for 5th October which was postponed because of poor weather, until 7th. The task of the 56th Division, of which the Battalion was part, was to capture trenches to the north east of Lesboeufs and establish a line on the forward slope of the ridge overlooking Le Transloy. After a long supporting bombardment the assault itself began at 1.45 pm.

The Rangers attacked on a 3 platoon front in 4 waves. After 50 yards only about 15 men of the leading wave from Rainy trench were left and the advance was checked. The second wave suffered a similar fate - neither of the succeeding waves were able to get up in sufficient strength to carry the attack forward. The remnants of the leading waves stayed in shell holes until dusk when they reoccupied Rainy trench. It was during one of the charges that Coulson was shot in the chest. He lived until he reached the Casualty Clearing Station, thanked the stretcher bearers, and sent a last message home to his family. He died a few hours later.

During the weeks before his death Leslie Coulson wrote two poems 'But a Short Time to Live' and 'From the Somme'. After his death the poem 'Who Made the Law?' was found among his possessions and returned to his family.

BUT A SHORT TIME TO LIVE

Our little hour, - how swift it flies
   When poppies flare and lilies smile;
How soon the fleeting minute dies,
   Leaving us but a little while
To dream our dream, to sing our song,
   To pick the fruit, to pluck the flower,
The Gods - They do not give us long, -
   One little hour.

Our little hour, - how short it is

When Love with dew-eyed loveliness
　Raises her lips for ours to kiss
　And dies within our first caress.
Youth flickers out like wind-blown flame,
　Sweets of to-day to-morrow sour,
For Time and Death relentless claim
　Our little hour.

Our little hour, - how short a time
　To wage our wars, to fan our hates,
To take our fill of armoured crime,
　To troop our banners, storm the gates.
Blood on the sword, our eyes blood-red,
　Blind in our puny reign of power,
Do we forget how soon is sped
　Our little hour?

Our little hour, - how soon it dies:
　How short a time to tell our beads,
To chant our feeble Litanies,
　To think sweet thoughts, to do good deeds.
The altar lights grow pale and dim,
　The bells hang silent in the tower -
So passes with the dying hymn
　Our little hour.

FROM THE SOMME

In other days I sang of simple things,
　Of summer dawn, and summer noon and night,
The dewy grass, the dew-wet fairy rings,
　The lark's long golden flight.

Deep in the forest I made melody
　While squirrels cracked their hazel nuts on high,
Or I would cross the wet sand to the sea
　And sing to sea and sky.

When came the silvered silence of the night
    I stole to casements over scented lawns,
And softly sang of love and love's delight
    To mute white marble fauns.

Oft in the tavern parlour I would sing
    Of morning sun upon the mountain vine,
And, calling for a chorus, sweep the string
    In praise of good red wine.

I played with all the toys the Gods provide,
    I sang my songs and made glad holiday,
Now I have cast my broken toys aside
    And flung my lute away.

A singer once, I now am fain to weep.
    Within my soul I feel strange music swell,
Vast chants of tragedy too deep - too deep
    For my poor lips to tell.

WHO MADE THE LAW?

Who made the Law that men should die in meadows?
Who spake the word that blood should splash in lanes?
Who gave it forth that gardens should be bone-yards?
Who spread the hills with flesh, and blood, and brains?
    Who made the Law?

Who made the Law that Death should stalk the village?
Who spake the word to kill among the sheaves,
Who gave it forth that death should lurk in hedgerows,
Who flung the dead among the fallen leaves?
    Who made the Law?

Those who return shall find that peace endures,
Find old things old, and know the things they knew,
Walk in the garden, slumber by the fireside,
Share the peace of dawn, and dream amid the dew -
    Those who return.

Those who return shall till the ancient pastures,
Clean-hearted men shall guide the plough-horse reins,
Some shall grow apples and flowers in the valleys,
Some shall go courting in summer down the lanes -
    THOSE WHO RETURN.

But who made the Law? the Trees shall whisper to him:
"See, see the blood - the splashes on our bark!"
Walking the meadows, he shall hear bones crackle,
And fleshless mouths shall gibber in silent lanes at dark.
    Who made the Law?

Who made the Law? At noon upon the hillside
His ears shall hear a moan, his cheeks shall feel a breath,
And all along the valleys, past gardens, croft, and
    homesteads,
HE who made the Law,
    He who made the Law,
He who made the Law shall walk along with Death.
    WHO made the Law?

– 21st - 22nd OCTOBER 1916 –

LIEUTENANT EDMUND BLUNDEN, M.C.
11th Battalion Royal Sussex Regiment

After the failed attack, and heavy casualties, of 3rd September the Battalion was billetted in Englebelmer before taking over trenches at Beaumont Hamel on the 14th. The men then marched to a camp in Martinsart Wood and after ten days were back in the Hamel trenches. They were relieved by The Royal Naval Division on 16th October and moved into assembly trenches in Authuille Wood, south of Thièpval; The Germans still held defensive positions just behind Thièpval Ridge, at Schwaben, Stuff and Zollern Redoubts and the Battalion was ordered to capture and consolidate Stuff Trench. The men, after little rest for almost five weeks, were exhausted.

Then we found ourselves filing up a valley under the noses of howitzers standing black and burnished in the open, and loosing off with deadly clamour while the bare-chested gunners bawled and blasphemed - Happy Valley or Blighty Valley, which was it? Further along stood Authuille Wood, and we went in along a tram-line and a board walk, whereon with sweating foreheads and sharp voices some Highland officers were numbering off some of the most exhausted men (just relieved) I had seen. Near here was the captured German work called Leipzig Redoubt, with its underworld comforts, from bakehouse to boudoir; the companies were accommodated there, while the battalion headquarters entered the greasy, damaged shanties of typical British sandbags and tinware in the Wood, at a spot called Tithe Barn, and the night came on...

It fell to me then to take up a party of men to the battalion's assembly position and make up a dump of tools, ammunition and other requirements for the attack. The walk to the front line lay over the most bewildering battlefield, so gouged and hummocked, so denatured and dun, so crowded with brown shrapnel-cases and German long-handled grenades, shell-holes, rifles, water-bottles; a billowing desert; and yet there was not much opportunity or reason for contemplating this satire in iron brown and field grey, for the staff-supplied motive of "offensive operations" was not yet weakening, and a rough road was being made here, and limbers were tipping and clattering ahead there, and guns being hauled forward, and signallers running out their lines and burying their cables, and little strings of burdened soldiers like mine trickling onward until they passed tragi-comically among those black accidents and emanations on the skyline.

The front trench, shallow and narrow, clean-cut by good craftsmen, soft and heavy with the night's downpour, was on the hither side of a ridge, nor could the enemy's present position be seen from it. The brown plain all round lay without landmark or distinction. Thièpval was vaguely gestured at on our left. Pozières had once been a village on our right. We got out on top, and dug a square recess to receive the picks and shovels, the small arms ammunition, the bombs, the water-cans and flares and what else we had carried up; and then the loud whirring of an aeroplane sounded just over our heads. British! - not so: flying perhaps thirty yards above the trench was a plane with the formidable Prussian cross as bold as the observer looking down; the machine-gun bullets thumped the soft soil, and missed us. The sarcastic visitors flew on at their ease along the trench, but our hearts sank at the knowledge that they knew about to-morrow.

That night, our attacking companies went forward and lay in a ditch with a few "baby elephant" shelters in it, and much water, a little way behind their assembly positions. There was a white frost. Behind them, a few field-guns, covered only with netting dressed up as withered foliage, were waiting too. I went to see them on the morning of the attack, and I remember chiefly the voice of F. Salter, as he emerged from a rough shelter, stretching his stiff arms and trying to move his eyebrows like a man awake, cursing the frost; I remember the familiar song of my old companion Doogan, now for the last time, "Everybody's doing the Charlie Chaplin walk." He broke off, and without self-pity and almost casually he said, "It's the third time. They've sent me over, this is the third time. They'll get me this time." Nor would it have availed to use in reply one's familiar trench tags, nor to speak out the admiring friendship which never fully found words; Doogan seemed to know; and he was tired.

The clear autumn day was a mixed blessing for Harrison, who, in his determination to send over the companies to take Stuff Trench after as much "rest" as could be found in that Golgotha, had arranged that they should advance from the reserve trench direct to the assault. And by way of novelty the assault was ordered to be made a few minutes after noon; the men would therefore have to move forward in broad day and over a sufficiently long approach - liable to the air's jealous eyes. Watches were synchronized and reconsigned to the officers, the watch hands slipped round as they do at a dance or a prize distribution; then all the anxiety came to a height and piercing extreme, and the companies moving in "artillery formation" - groups presenting a kind of diamond diagram - passed by Harrison's headquarters in foul Zollern Trench. I watched him as he stood on the mound roof of his dugout, that simple and martial figure, calling out to those as they went in terms of faith and love.

Lapworth, who had just joined us, went by at the head of his platoon, a youth with curling golden hair and drawing-room manners, sweetly swinging his most subalternish cane from its leather thong; and he was the last officer to go by.

Orders had been admirably obeyed; the waves extended, the artillery gave tongue at the exact moment. The barrage was heavy, but in uproar was diffused in this open region. Harrison had nothing to do but wait, and I with him, for I was acting as his right-hand man in this operation. News of the attack always seems to take years in reaching headquarters, and it almost always gets worse as it is supplemented. At last some messages, wildly scribbled, as may be imagined, but with a clearness of expression that may not be so readily imagined, came to Zollern Trench. One was from Doogan: Stuff Trench was taken, there were few men left, and he had "established bombing blocks". G. Salter had sent back some forty prisoners. A message was brought with some profanity by my old friend C.S.M. Lee, whose ripped shirt was bloody, and who could not frankly recommend Stuff Trench. The concrete emplacement halfway thither, looking so dangerous on the maps, had not been found dangerous, and the gunners' preparation there had been adequate; but, he said, we were being blown out of Stuff Trench. Should we be able to hold it? We was 'olding it when I got THIS; and so departed Lee, tall, blasphemous, and brave.

Looking about in the now hazier October light, I saw some German prisoners drifting along, and I stopped them. One elderly gentleman had a jaw which seemed insecurely suspended; which I bound up with more will than skill, and obtained the deep reward of a look so fatherly and hopeful as seldom comes again; others, not wounded, sourly observed my directions down the communication trench. As they went, heavy German shells were searching thoroughly there, and I do not think they ever got through. Their countrymen lay thick in these parts. Even the great shell-hole which we hazardously used as a latrine was overlooked by the sprawling corpses of two of them, and others lay about it.

Our regimental sergeant-major was by this time in disgrace. This fine man, so swift in spirit and in intelligence, had lifted his water-bottle too often in the backbreaking business of getting the battalion into action; and he had not unreasonably filled the bottle with rum. In the horrid candle-light of the deep dugout he had endeavoured to keep going and with piteous resolution answered what he thought the substance of his Colonel's questions; but it would not do, and Sergeant

Ashford, the bright and clever signaller, took his place. Again the night came on; and in the captured trench the remnant who had primed themselves with the spirituous hope of being relieved had to hear that no relief was yet forthcoming. The sharpness of their experience was to be gauged from the fact that even the company held in support in our original front line, employed on incidental tasks, was reported to be exhausted, and its commander appealed to Harrison for relief in ultimatory terms.

Another day arrived, and the men in Stuff Trench had to eat their "iron rations", for we could not supply them. We had also lost touch with our battalion doctor, who was somewhere towards Thièpval, that slight protuberance on rising ground westward; the bearers of the wounded had to find another way out; yet we were in possession of Stuff Trench, and the Australians southward held its continuation, Regina. That evening, gloomy and vast, lit up with savage glares all round, a relieving battalion arrived, one disposed to quarrel with us as readily as with the Germans. "Take the companies over to Stuff Trench," said Harrison to me, "and see them settled in there." Cassels came with me. We were lucky, the night being black, to find our way through that unholy Schwaben Redoubt, but by this stage our polarity-sense was awakened and we knew how little to expect of local identifications. At last, after many doubts, we had passed (in the darkness) a fragment of road metalling which assured me that all was right; the grumbling relief followed our slow steps, which we could not hasten, even though one of many shells crashing into our neighbourhood caught a section of the incomers and the moaning cries might have distracted more seasoned tacticians.

It was Geoffrey Salter speaking out firmly in the darkness. Stuff Trench - this was Stuff Trench; three feet deep, corpses under foot, corpses on the parapet. He told us, while still shell after shell slipped in crescendo wailing into the vibrating ground, that his brother had been killed, and he had buried him; Doogan had been wounded, gone downstairs into one of the dugout shafts after hours of sweat, and a shell had come downstairs to finish him; "and", says he, "you can get a marvellous view of Grandcourt from this trench. We've been looking at it all day. Where's these men? Let me put 'em into the posts. No, you wait a bit, I'll see to it. That the sergeant-major?"

Moving along as he spoke with quick emotion and a new power (for hitherto his force of character had not appeared in the less exacting sort of war), he began to order the newcomers into sentry-groups; and stooping down to find what it was snuffing at my boots I found it was a dog. He was seemingly trying to keep me from treading on a body. I caught sight of him by some one's torch or flare; he was black and white; and I spoke to him, and at the end of a few moments he allowed me to carry him off. Cassells and myself had finished, and returned by ourselves by the shortest way; now the strain told, our feet weighed like lead, and our hope was out of action. I put down the dog, who came limpingly round the shadowy shell-holes, stopped, whined, came on again; what was the use? he perhaps thought; that way, too, there is this maniacal sport of high explosive, and the mud is evidently the same all over the world; I shall stay here. Warmly I wished to adopt this dog, but now I could scarcely stoop, and I reflected that the mud and shell zone extended a long way on; so there he stayed; feebly I passed along...

The action at Stuff Trench on October 21 and 22 had been the first in which our battalion had seized and held any of the German area, and the cost had been enormous; not intemperate pride glowed among the survivors, but that natural vanity was held in check by the fact that we were not yet off the battlefield...

– 23rd - 24th OCTOBER 1916 –

PRIVATE FRANK RICHARDS, D.C.M., M.M.
2nd Battalion Royal Welch Fusiliers

Sometime during September 'an old regular officer' joined the Battalion and was put in charge of the signallers. A strict disciplinarian, with an autocratic manner, he was nicknamed 'The Peer'. Although by now there was a 'better spirit of comradeship between officers and men', the signallers soon found out that 'The Peer' had not lost his 'pre-War ways' by insisting on the enforcement of petty regulations. On 24th October the Battalion took over trenches at Lesboeufs, facing the enemy in front of Le Transloy.

Our trenches were shell holes linked up, with gaps here and there; on our right were the French. There was also a gap between us and them. About sixty yards behind the front line was a small trench which was used as an advanced signal station. Messages were brought by runners who made use of an old German communication trench to this station: they were then transmitted back to Battalion Headquarters which was in a sunken road about five hundred yards behind. I and three young signallers were posted to the advanced signal-station and we decided to go along the line in turns to repair any breaks, and also made arrangements with Battalion Headquarters for them to keep one half of the line in repair, and we would keep the other half. In standing trenches Battalion Headquarters always appointed linesmen to look after the lines running to the front line, company signallers repairing their own between companies, but in a case like this every N.C.O. and man, with the exception of the signalling-sergeant, took their turns along the lines to repair the breaks.

It had been raining for days, and the ground was nothing but a sea of mud. On the second night the enemy, who had been sending over an occasional shell, began a heavy bombardment and we were continually repairing the lines. One of our young signallers had taken his turn and as he was a long time coming back, and we were still out of communication, I went along the line to look for him; about fifty yards from the trench I came across his body: he had been killed in the act of repairing a break. I repaired the break myself and walked back further along the line and found another break about halfway. I saw a man approaching me, who turned out to be an old signaller from Battalion Headquarters out on the line. I told him about the young signaller being killed, and he said he was sorry to hear it, as he was a damned good kid. He then began to swear, and when he cooled down a bit said: "It's rotten, Dick, how the good ones are popped over so quick and the rotten ones simply get nice blighty wounds..."

A few hours before we were relieved, the following night, The Peer who was back at Battalion Headquarters paid us a visit. It was pretty quiet at the time, only an occasional shell coming over. Just after he arrived the enemy opened out again and put up a barrage from our front line to about fifty yards in the rear of us. There were about a dozen men in the little trench and they tried to get into the signallers' dug-out, but there wasn't room for them. I was speaking to The Peer when the barrage started, and was wondering whether Old Jerrie was about to make an attack when the shelling finished. We were in the trench at the time, and The Peer made no effort to get into the dug-out. He showed he had guts and went up twenty holes in my estimation. If a large shell burst on the dug-out the men in it would be finished with, and if one pitched anywhere on our part of the trench we would be the same. It was heavy stuff they were sending over, with an occasional salvo of whizzbangs. I expect The Peer did more ducking that night than ever he had during the whole of his life before. The barrage lasted about an hour and then suddenly stopped. He asked me if I had ever been under a worse barrage and when I told him it was a popcorn barrage compared to some I had been under, he thought I was romancing. I then told him that the enemy might make an attack and some of them rush through the gaps in our front line, and be on us in no time. He lined every man in the trench, and looking over the parapet we saw a party of men crossing our front. We challenged them sharply, but they turned out to be some French troops who had been relieved and making their way back had hopelessly lost themselves. They had been wandering about for some time. The Peer gave the officer along with them his bearings and they went on their way. It was a very dark night and raining very heavily. The enemy made no attack, but just before we were relieved began shelling again...

The little experience that The Peer had just gone through did him and us a lot of good; he dropped his pre-War ways and started to act like a sensible human being...

– 28th OCTOBER 1916 –

PRIVATE FREDERIC MANNING (19022)
7th Battalion King's Shropshire Light Infantry

After training north of Arras for most of September, the Battalion arrived in Mailly-Maillet on 8th October and ten days later moved back into a camp at Bus-lès-Artois. On 28th October the Battalion took over the trenches in the Serre sector; after they were relieved on 1st November the men marched to billets in Courcelles and four days later went to Louvencourt where they remained preparing for the attack on Serre, part of the Battle of the Ancre, later that month. During October Frederic Manning was attached to the signal section of the Battalion, as a relay runner between the trenches and brigade headquarters.

TRANSPORT

The moon swims in milkiness,
The road glimmers curving down into the wooded valley
And with a clashing and creaking of tackle and axles
The train of limbers passes me, and the mules
Splash me with mud, thrusting me from the road into puddles,
Straining at the tackle with a bitter patience,
Passing me...
And into a patch of moonlight,
With beautiful curved necks and manes,
Heads reined back, and nostrils dilated,
Impatient of restraint,
Pass two gray stallions,
Such as Oenetia bred;
Beautiful as the horses of Hippolytus
Carven on some antique frieze.
And my heart rejoices seeing their strength in play,
The mere animal life of them,
Lusting,
As a thing passionate and proud.

Then again the limbers and grotesque mules.

GROTESQUE

These are the damned circles Dante trod,
Terrible in hopelessness,
But even skulls have their humour,
An eyeless and sardonic mockery:
And we,
Sitting with streaming eyes in the acrid smoke,
That murks our foul, damp billet,
Chant bitterly, with raucous voices
As a choir of frogs
In hideous irony, our patriotic songs.

THE TRENCHES

Endless lanes sunken in the clay,
Bays, and traverses, fringed with wasted herbage,
Seed-pods of blue scabious, and some lingering blooms;
And the sky, seen as from a well,
Brilliant with frosty stars.
We stumble, cursing, on the slippery duck-boards,
Goaded like the damned by some invisible wrath,
A will stronger than weariness, stronger than animal fear,
Implacable and monotonous.

Here a shaft, slanting, and below
A dusty and flickering light from one feeble candle
And prone figures sleeping uneasily,
Murmuring,
And men who cannot sleep,
With faces impassive as masks,
Bright, feverish eyes, and drawn lips,
Sad, pitiless, terrible faces,
Each an incarnate curse.

Here in a bay, a helmeted sentry
Silent and motionless, watching while two sleep,
And he sees before him
With indifferent eyes the blasted and torn land
Peopled with stiff prone forms, stupidly rigid,
As tho' they had not been men.

Dead are the lips where love laughed or sang,
The hands of youth eager to lay hold of life,
Eyes that have laughed to eyes,
And these were begotten,
O love, and lived lightly, and burnt
With the lust of a man's first strength: ere they were rent,
Almost at unawares, savagely; and strewn
In bloody fragments, to be the carrion
Of rats and crows.

And the sentry moves not, searching
Night for menace with weary eyes.

A SHELL

Here we are all, naked as Greeks,
Killing the lice in our shirts:
Suddenly the air is torn asunder,
Ripped as coarse silk,
Then a dull thud...
We are all squatting.

RELIEVED

We are weary and silent,
There is only the rhythm of marching feet;
Tho' we move tranced, we keep it
As clock-work toys.

But each man is alone in this multitude;
We know not the world in which we move,
Seeing not the dawn, earth pale and shadowy,
Level lands of tenuous grays and greens;
For our eye-balls have been seared with fire.

Only we have our secret thoughts,
Our sense floats out from us, delicately apprehensive,
To the very fringes of our being,
Where light drowns.

– 28th - 30th OCTOBER 1916 –

SECOND-LIEUTENANT MAX PLOWMAN
'C' Company 10th Battalion West Yorkshire Regiment

At the end of October, the Battalion marched from Trones Wood through Guillemont and Ginchy to Zenith and Spectrum Trenches north of Lesboeufs. The weather conditions were appalling and men in the front trenches had to stand in at least two feet of mud, and several who became stuck were unable to move until they were dug out. Shelling continued and caused considerable casualties.

On the eastern side of the tiny village of Ginchy we are suddenly confronted with a wide, rolling, open plain over which there is no road but only a single "duck-walk" track. Slowly the battalion stretches itself out in single file along this track, and one by one the men follow each other, till the trail extends like the vertebrae of an endless snake. On either side lies the open plain. Not a sign of life is anywhere to be seen, but instead there appear, in countless succession, stretching as far as the eye can pierce the gloom, shell-holes filled with water. The sense of desolation these innumerable, silent, circular pools produce is horrible. So vividly do they remind me of a certain illustration by Doré to Dante's *Inferno*, that I begin to wonder whether I have not stepped out of life and entered one of the circles of the damned; and as I look upon these evil pools I half expect to see a head appearing from each one. Here and there the succession of pools is broken by what appear in the fading light to be deep yawning graves, and over these our duck-walk makes a frail and slippery bridge.

On and on we go. Jog, jog, jog behind one another, till slowly the merciful darkness shuts out all sight of this awful land of foreboding. But now the difficulty of our march increases, for many of the laths of these duck-boards are broken, and in the darkness a man trips and falls, pitching his sand-bag of rations or box of bombs into the mud that lies deep on either side of the track. Whenever this happens, the rest of the battalion behind him has to halt while he picks himself up, recovers his load and steadies himself on the track again before trying to make good the gap between himself and the man in front. Despite the cautions passed along the file a hundred times: "Look out" - "Mind the gap" - "Hole there," these mishaps constantly occur, till we in the rear wonder why in the name of Heaven long halts should be needed when those in front must still be miles from the trenches. At last the men in front move, and on we go again. On and on, till it seems we must be seeking the very end of nowhere, for still the Verey lights, which will show us the line of the trenches, do not appear. Every now and then shells drop, sometimes near enough to spatter us with mud and make us shudder to think what kind of death we should meet if one dropped near enough to lift us into the watery, muddy depths of a shell-hole. But even the shells seem to be wandering, for they come fitfully, as if they were fired from nowhere and had lost their way.

On and on we go. It is getting towards midnight now. The duck-walk ceases and we come out on high grass-land, where the going is good so long as we keep to the crest of the hill and pick a careful way between the shell-holes. Now we are turning and gently descending the hill. The waspish flight of whiz-bangs is heard quite close. We must be near the line at last, though it is still out of sight. Now we drop into mud ankle-deep. A man shouts it is up to the knees where he stands. New voices are heard. The company is no longer extended. There is Rowley. We have arrived. Across twenty yards of quagmire rough trenches are dimly visible. They are the reserve trenches - ours. The men clamber into them and wrap themselves in their ground-sheets. We have reached the mud...

Here, by daylight, outside the dug-out, there is nothing within sight to give an inkling of where we are. The front line is said to be over the crest of the sloping ground on our right, about a thousand yards from this spot, but nothing of it is to be seen, and on all sides nothing but open rolling downs. A map is the only guide, and that instructs us we are between Gueudecourt and Lesboeufs, rather nearer Lesboeufs than Gueudecourt, though both villages are out of sight. The map declares a windmill once stood here. There is not a trace of it now. Facing the line, H.Q. dug-out is forward on our left, hidden in a sunken road, and the second line runs somewhere just beyond it. The trenches our men occupy are negligible hastily-thrown-up dykes, and as we are practically unsighted there is no harm in moving about on top - indeed there is no alternative. Ploughing through the mud I find many bodies lying about still unburied. How unreal they look! They merely remind me of the gruesome newspaper pictures of the dead on battlefields. Yet looking on them now I reflect how each one had his own life, his individual hopes and fears. Individually each one was born; dead, they come back to individuality.

THE DEAD SOLDIERS

I

Spectrum Trench. Autumn. Nineteen-Sixteen.
And Zenith. (The Border Regiment will remember.)
A little north of where Lesboeufs had been.
(The Australians took it over in December.)
Just as the scythe had caught them, there they lay,
A sheaf for Death, ungarnered and untied:
A crescent moon of men who showed the way
When first the Tanks crept out, till they too died:
Guardsmen, I think, but one could hardly tell,
It was a forward slope, beyond the crest,
Muddier than any place in Dante's hell,
Where sniping gave us very little rest.
At night one stumbled over them and swore;
Each day the rain hid them a little more.

II

Fantastic forms, in posturing attitudes,
Twisted and bent, or lying deathly prone;
Their individual hopes my thought eludes,
But each man had a hope to call his own.
Much else? - God knows. But not for me the thought,
'Your mothers made your bodies: God your souls,
And, for because you dutifully fought,
God will go mad and make of half-lives, wholes.'
No. God in every one of you was slain;
For killing men is always killing God,
Though life destroyed shall come to life again
And loveliness rise from the sodden sod.
But if of life we do destroy the best,
God wanders wide, and weeps in his unrest.

November
1916

– 3rd NOVEMBER 1916 –

LIEUTENANT EDMUND BLUNDEN, M.C.
11th Battalion Royal Sussex Regiment

The Battalion suffered over two hundred and seventy casualties during the attack on Stuff Trench on 21st and 22nd October. It was relieved at midnight on 22nd October and had a three day rest at Aveluy before it was sent to hold the line again at Thièpval Wood, 'digging and carrying and being shelled'. On 30th October the Battalion was deep in mud in the trenches at the Schwaben Redoubt; it was systematically bombarded which resulted in thirty-two casualties in the three days until 1st November, when it was relieved and sent to rest at Senlis.

We were merry when at length the relief was sent in and we went along the road in pale daylight to Senlis, a village six or seven miles behind the line. The road wound and twisted, but we liked it well, and as at one point the still lofty stump of Mesnil Church tower showed above the dingy trampled fields it was hard not to shout aloud. "Not gone yet," signalled the tower. We heard the church bell ring in Senlis, we bought beer and chocolate, and we admired with determination the girls who sold them; so great was the hour of relaxation, so kindly was the stone of the road and the straw of the barn. We envied the troops employed as road-sweepers and ditchers in their drains and puddles. But, prime gift of eccentric heaven, there was the evening when Harrison took all the battalion to the divisional concert-party performing in the town. The roof ought indeed to have floated away in the paeans and warblings that rose from us, as the pierrots chirruped and gambolled there. In sweet music is such art - and never was music sweeter than the ragtime then obtaining, if appreciation indexes merit.

AT SENLIS ONCE

O how comely it was and how reviving,
When with clay and with death no longer striving
Down firm roads we came to houses
With women chattering and green grass thriving.

Now though rains in a cataract descended,
We could glow, with our tribulation ended -
   Count not days, the present only
   Was thought of, how could it ever be expended?

Clad so cleanly, this remnant of poor wretches
Picked up life like the hens in orchard ditches,
   Gazed on the mill-sails, heard the church-bell,
   Found an honest glass all manner of riches.

How they crowded the barn with lusty laughter,
Hailed the pierrots and shook each shadowy rafter,
   Even could ridicule their own sufferings,
   Sang as though nothing but joy came after!

– 4th NOVEMBER 1916 –

PRIVATE FRANK RICHARDS, D.C.M., M.M.
2nd Battalion Royal Welch Fusiliers

After the Battalion had been relieved from the Lesboeufs trenches on 28th October it went back to a sunken road on the edge of Trones Wood and then to bivouacs at the Briqueterie at Montauban. On 4th November the Battalion returned to the Lesboeufs trenches.

Paddy took his turn with B Echelon, which consisted of the transport and a small number of officers and men who were left out of the line when the Battalion went in. Some time later Minimum Reserve was introduced and a certain number of officers and men of each battalion were left out, so in case of a battalion being wiped out there was something left to make a new one with. We were only going in for forty-eight hours, and it was decided not to send the mail up for that period. I instructed Paddy that if anything happened to me he was to do what he liked with a parcel I was expecting, and to give the tobacco away to a pipe smoker. About an hour before we moved off, one of our planes brought a German plane crashing to the ground about half a mile in front of us and on the edge of a sunken road which we knew we would have to pass. I had seen it happen once or twice that when a German plane had been shot down just behind our front line some time later the enemy would do their level best to blow it to pieces. This plane was about a mile behind our front. I had been posted to Battalion Headquarters and it was dark when we were passing the plane, which was now being shelled. We had a few casualties and one of the killed was the Regimental Sergeant Major's batman, who was carrying a lovely bag of rations. One of our old signallers picked it up. During the following day each one of us put on a little weight and the R.S.M. lost a little. There were more rations in that bag than what the whole of the signallers had, put together.

We stayed in an old German dug-out. Two steps below us in another dug-out stayed the Colonel and Adjutant. All communication with our front line was by runners. We had lines running back to Brigade, which were very weak and we had difficulty in receiving Morse or speaking to them. The following morning the Colonel's servant came into the dug-out and reported that the Colonel's raincoat, which was a new one, was missing. The servant had put it on the bank of the sunken road by the dug-out, along with other stuff, and no doubt someone of the troops we relieved had walked off with it. The servant seemed more cut up over the loss than what the Colonel did, who took it as the fortune of war. Sealyham now went out of the dug-out saying that he had dumped his haversack on the bank, which had two fine razors and other valuables in it; at the same moment the Adjutant got on the phone to speak to the Brigade-Major and the line being so weak he was continually asking "What's that?" Sealyham came to the mouth of the dug-out and shouted down: "The swine have pinched my haversack too." "What's that?" asked the Adjutant. "The bloody pigs have pinched my haversack with the two best razors in France in it." "What's that?" shouted the Adjutant, but this was too much for Sealyham who, being under the impression that one of us was answering him and pulling his leg, launched out with a flow of language which would have done credit to the Old Soldier. The Adjutant put the phone down and burst out laughing and told me to go outside to tell him to shut up until he had finished speaking on the phone. He had been our Adjutant for over twelve months, and was an excellent officer in every way: his name was Mr. Mann. Sealyham found his haversack a few yards away, but it was empty. Haversacks were easy to get, but razors were scarce.

We and the Public Schools Battalion on our left, with the French on our right, now had to advance and capture a position in front of us. On this part of the Front the enemy were scattered here and there in shell holes and it was quite possible that the first wave of attacking troops would miss some of the enemy, who would then be popping up and firing on them from behind. So a mopping-up party was detailed off to follow in the rear of the first wave and mop up everything they had left. I was with Headquarters so I saw none of the actual fighting. Our companies and the French reached their objectives and began consolidating the position - which meant to turn the firing positions the other way about, block communication trenches and put out a bit of barbed wire. But the troops on our left never advanced a yard. The captain of the Public Schools company on our left reported to our Colonel that they had been held up by heavy machine-gun fire - which was all bunkum: they had never made any effort to advance, and our Colonel told him so. I had never seen the Colonel in such a rage as he was that day, and he told the captain that he and his rotten men were no good as they had endangered the lives of decent soldiers. Our left flank was now up in the air, and anything might happen.

Some of the mopping-up party discovered a concealed dug-out in a large shell hole. They were just about to throw bombs into it when they heard an English voice cry out: "Don't throw bombs in here."

Inside the dug-out were six Germans, and one of our own men who was badly wounded in the legs. He told them he had been part of a strong patrol that had been sent out to reconnoitre the night before. A German shell had fallen short and caused several casualties. He had been knocked unconscious and left for dead in the confusion. When he came to his self he tried to crawl back to our lines. He had crawled some way but could not get any further. His groans had attracted these Germans, who had carried him in and dressed his wounds and attended him as if he had been one of their own men. He had heard the first wave go by and was wondering if any of the mopping-up party would discover the dug-out, and had shouted out as soon as he heard their voices.

We were relieved that evening, and the following morning I met Paddy, who was thunderstruck to see me. "Hell!" he exclaimed, "I thought you was on the way to Blighty." I enquired what was the matter, and he replied: "I am glad to see you quite safe, but I have devoured your parcel and given the tobacco away, the same as you told me." He then explained that the night we went in the line there were all manner of yarns flying around the transport about the casualties in Battalion Headquarters... My parcel had arrived the next day and he had opened it, and gave the tobacco away as I had told him to.

– 4th - 8th NOVEMBER 1916 –

CAPTAIN GRAHAM GREENWELL, M.C.
4th Battalion Oxfordshire and Buckinghamshire Light Infantry

After it was relieved at the end of August the Battalion spent the next few weeks alternating between billets at Bus and trenches at Auchonvillers opposite Beaumont Hamel. Graham Greenwell spent a few days leave in Rouen, and then went to billets at Warlincourt. Here he celebrated his promotion with a large dinner party having 'secured some chickens and plenty of champagne - Veuve Cliquot too!' On 1st November the Battalion was in bivouacs near Contalmaison where the thick mud caked men and horses from head to foot.

November 4th. Trenches behind Le Sars, Somme. We have been here for thirty-six hours now, living like dogs or rats far from any sign of civilisation. For miles behind us there are nothing but ruined villages on which to pitch wretched little camps in the slush for rest billets. The trenches are absolutely impassable, sometimes waist-deep in liquid mud. Everything has to be carried for miles across country and at night. No one knows the way, all landmarks have been removed by shells and mud; and not for a single moment are the guns silent. Such food as we can get is gritty with mud, our clothes are caked with it; we think mud, dream mud, and eat mud. Last winter I thought was bad, but this winter in the Battle Area is quite unimaginable.

How long we shall remain here we cannot tell, but I suppose for three weeks at least, unless we do an attack.

Your beef rolls arrived on the very eve of leaving for this swamp, and provided us with a last good meal, for which I was awfully grateful. But I think you should use tins as far as possible when sending parcels now as the posts are rather uncertain.

Please don't think from this letter that I am at all depressed: thank Heaven I have got four young fellows with me and we are quite cheery, even playing vingt-et-un yesterday with matches and an old dirty pack of cards. Besides which everything sooner or later has an end and I hope this may mean that we shall be out of the trenches at Christmas time.

November 6th. Writing in dark to say "Fit as a Flea" but fagged out and absolutely filthy.

Having a very rough time this go, but ought to be out of it to-morrow. Haven't had clothes off or proper sleep for three days.

November 7th. Got out of it last night all right but had a good many casualties through shelling.

Back in a support trench or rather mud ditch. Heavy rain. Everything caked in mud.

Spirits: High.

C.O. very sporting - sent us a bottle of whisky last night on arrival; mud pouring in, and here are five of us sitting down here, simply a flight of narrow steps.

Carew Hunt, whom I left behind at Albert, has sent us up plenty of food, thank Heaven, and the other night a bottle of fizz actually reached us at 2 a.m. after twenty-four hours in the front trenches: we were simply done and soaked through. It saved our lives. The very best too, Heidsieck '06: can't think where he got it from.

Great difficulties in getting food and water up, but still it's a wonderful war.

Guns never cease.

This is our fifth day up. Hope to get back to a bivouac to-morrow night and then a night's sleep...

November 8th. Reserve Trenches, Martinpuich, Somme. Yesterday was a typical Somme day, it poured with rain and the remainder of our trenches got filled in. Perfectly hopeless.

I was relieved at about nine o'clock and came back through the most appalling mud and slush I have ever seen. We went back to some old German dug-outs here. It is the largest village captured in the Big Push with the exception of Combles, but it is nothing but a mass of ruins with its streets knee-deep in mud. However, I got into a warm dug-out belonging to an artillery headquarters and managed to get my first uninterrupted sleep for four nights, soaked through as I was.

Fortunately the Huns had installed an oven, so I roasted in front of that for some time and then wrapped my feet in sand-bags. I am quite used to sleeping in my clothes now with only a light Burberry as a cover, my British Warm being an impossible garment to carry round in these desolate regions.

We have, I believe, to spend two days here, which will make seven days without a wash or a change of clothes. Then we shall go back to a bivouac or camp...

Two nights ago three Germans gave themselves up, to everyone's joy, as Brigade headquarters were very keen on finding out the identity of the Germans opposite. They were Prussian Guardsmen! I was in support and was standing outside my headquarters dug-out about eight o'clock on a moonlight night when I saw three quaint-looking figures with long overcoats and funny-shaped helmets moving aimlessly about accompanied by a youthful Tommy with a fixed bayonet and almost in tears. I gave them a hail and brought them back. The boy then told me that he had had the three Boches entrusted to him and to a pal, but that his pal had been wounded by a piece of shell and he had therefore been left alone; now he couldn't find Battalion headquarters. I asked the Bosche if they spoke English, beamed on them and gave them a guide to take them along. They were very cheery and quite resigned to being the victims of British stupidity before profiting by their generosity.

My legs are wrapped in two sand-bags to keep them warm while my boots get dry and I haven't been out all day, so I am feeling a bit muzzy; that's the worst of this trench life. At any rate we are warm and dry here which we haven't been for four days. How I long to go back to billets again, we have been spoilt for the last two months...

– 7th - 13th NOVEMBER 1916 –

LIEUTENANT SIDNEY ROGERSON
2nd Battalion West Yorkshire Regiment

On 7th November the Battalion was at Citadel Camp 'a dreary collection of bell-tents pitched insecurely on the hillside near the one-time village of Fricourt'; that evening the Battalion received orders to relieve the 2nd Devons in the front line, the sector between the ruined villages of Lesboeufs and Le Transloy. The following day, in torrential rain, the Battalion marched to Camp 34 between Bernafay and Trones Woods, where it found a few groups of tarpaulin-sheet shelters and one or two bell-tents. The Battalion's Commanding Officer, Lieutenant Colonel James Lochhead Jack, D.S.O., noted the conditions at the camp in his war diary:

...we found the nearly officerless remnant of the 5/Cameronians, who had just suffered heavily, still in possession of our bivouac; they obstinately refused to budge from this wretched spot to billets in rear before the appointed time. We were, therefore, forced to sit in the rain for an hour until these perverse Scots had vacated their scraps of shelter and several bell tents. Battalion Headquarters are well housed in an old German trench blocked at one end by a door, roofed with some sheets of corrugated iron, and with sandbags filling the cracks... To my joy there is also a stove, rescued in the nick of time from the clutch of Rogerson's enterprising servant Purkiss, who was purloining it for his master...

On the 9th November the four Company Commanders were briefed by Colonel Jack and were told that the Devons' positions were 'sketchy', and that after much fierce fighting over the ground trenches were virtually non-existent. At 5.30 a.m. on the 10th the Company Commanders set out ahead of their men; 'A' Company commanded by Arthur Skett, a young subaltern; 'B' Company commanded by Sidney Rogerson; Captain Hawley in command of 'C'; and a Canadian, Lieutenant Sankey, in command of 'D'. They reached the Devons' headquarters in the sunken road on the left of Lesboeufs Wood just before dawn.

Each of us got a Devon guide and set off with all haste to reach the comparative safety of our respective destinations before the mist lifted and the early aeroplanes flew over as heralds of the day's shelling. The front line, our guide told us, lay over the low ridge which formed the skyline half a mile ahead, and had only been dug last night...

We crossed a low valley where the shell-ploughed ground was carpeted with dead, the khaki out-numbering the field-grey by three to one. There must have been two or three hundred bodies lying in an area of a few hundred yards around Dewdrop Trench - once a substantial German reserve line, but now a shambles of corpses, smashed dug-outs, twisted iron and wire. This was the position which C and D Companies were to take over, and whither Hawley and Sankey made their way with some misgivings.

Skett and I walked on together until we reached the slope, when he veered off to the left and I to the right. The sun was now up and the protective mist had cleared, so that I was glad when I slithered into the shallow trench half-way up the ridge where B Company of the Devons had established their headquarters by the simple expedient of roofing in the trench with two stretchers - which might have kept off a little gentle rain but nothing more substantial! Tea was being made for breakfast, and though I accepted an offer of refreshment which was very welcome, I turned away retching after the first gulp. It tasted vilely of petrol. For miles in the rear there was no water either fit or safe to drink, and all supplies had therefore to be carried up to the front in petrol tins, a system which was all right only so long as the tins had been burnt out to remove the fumes of the spirit. When they had not, as all too often happened, every mouthful of food and drink was nausea. It was only with the greatest difficulty that men could be restrained from using water from the shell-holes to make their tea or bully-stew, although this was expressly forbidden, as in addition to the danger of gas-poisoning, none knew what horror lay hidden under the turbid water...

The two companies were both posted on the ridge which had been but newly captured, and though their fronts were touching, their flanks were both entirely in the air. The only approximation to a trench was the one in which we were sitting, already christened Autumn Trench, which was merely a narrow, unrevetted channel, without shelter, or fire-steps, and in which A Company also had its headquarters some 150 yards to the left. From this line a shallow trench, nowhere more than three feet deep, had been scooped out over the ridge, joining on the far side the real front line, which had only been established the night before by linking up shell-hole to shell-hole. This sketchy line had been made to gain a sight into the valley at the other side of the ridge, and had naturally been dug under cover of darkness, but daylight showed, so I was told, that the ground fell away so steeply in front of it that complete observation was still impossible.

That was all Hill [the Devons' B Company commander] had to tell me about our own defence system, but admitted that the enemy was in little better straits. In fact, the Hun was not known to be holding any fixed line nearer than the Transloy-Bapaume road, some thousand yards away, though the area between that line and ours crawled with Germans who hung on in isolated bits of trench or in fortified shell-holes, the where-abouts of which were extremely difficult to detect.

In short, the position was as obscure as it was precarious. The two companies were virtually isolated on their ridge without knowledge of the exact dispositions of the enemy in front, and behind them, no trench, just mile after mile of battered country under its pall of mud...

The front certainly was quiet, save for the occasional sharp whip-crack of an enemy sniper and the drone of aircraft high up in a sky which was very bright and blue for November. It had been strangely peaceful sitting, smoking, and chatting in the sun, but I had not gone twenty yards before I encountered the mud, mud which was unique even for the Somme. It was like walking through caramel. At every step the foot stuck fast, and was only wrenched out by a determined effort, bringing away with it several pounds of earth till legs ached in every muscle.

No one could struggle through that mud for more than a few yards without rest. Terrible in its clinging consistency, it was the arbiter of destiny, the supreme enemy, paralysing and mocking English and German alike. Distances were measured not in yards but in mud...

I had only to struggle some fifty yards before I came to the communication trench over the ridge, along which, crouching double or on all fours, we went for a further fifty yards before finding ourselves in the front line, christened by us, and thereafter known as Fall Trench. This I found to be better than I expected, already fairly deep and reasonably dry. I found that there was a detachment of brigade machine-gunners there as a welcome addition to the trench garrison, and floundered along towards the left till I met Skett, with whom I compared notes and discussed a working programme for the night. We eventually agreed that we must at all costs deepen and consolidate Fall Trench, and run a couple of saps out from it, so as to command a full view of the valley in front. Secondly, to protect our flanks, Skett agreed to put a subaltern into an isolated post on his left, and I to make a T-head for a Lewis gun-post opening out on the right of the so-called communication trench to cover that flank. Leaving Skett, I returned by the way I had come to find that the round of a few hundred yards had taken over two hours of strenuous walking!

The impression left on my mind was that we were as much at the mercy of the elements as of the enemy. Of the ordinary amenities of trench life there were none. The two stretchers at Company Headquarters formed the only roof in the sector. There was not even a hole into which men could crawl to be under shelter. They slept as they sat, huddled into themselves, in positions reminiscent of prehistoric burial. As cooking was out of the question, there was no apology for a cook-house. The one latrine yet made was a hole dug into the side of the support trench. In short, there was as much to be done to make the place habitable as defendable...

Although Company Headquarters were less than 100 yards from Fall Trench, the distance measured in terms of mud was so great that I could not be sure of maintaining any effective touch from the support line. I told Mac, [Lieutenant Mathew McConville] therefore, that he would have to take charge of the front-line trench...

But by far the most important task was somehow or other to put the rudimentary trenches into something approaching a defensive system before daylight. Accordingly I told Mac that his first job must be to see that a sap was dug out so as to secure a view into the dead ground in front. Lastly, but not least, I impressed upon him - and indeed upon every man I passed - that as there were no dug-outs our safety depended upon our energy in digging, as a deep, narrow trench was as safe from shell-fire as anything but a tunnel or mined dug-out; further, that since we did not know where the Germans were, it was unlikely that they were any the wiser as to our whereabouts. The order, therefore, was "dig like blazes all night and lie doggo all day" - hard orders to have to give to men, many of them strangers to the regiment, whose period of rest had been exhausting discomfort, and who were now utterly weary after their seven hours' tramp through mud and debris in the dark...

A prompt start had been made on digging out the two saps, and to protect those engaged on the task Skett had sent out a covering party under a 2nd Lieutenant named Pym, just as I had sent out one under Mac. Pym, who was yet another importation from the ranks of the Canadian forces, had barely got his party out in front when a German machine-gun opened fire. Every man threw himself flat, but it was only a random burst. Although from some shell-hole close to them in the darkness Pym ordered his men back to the trench, he himself did not return with them. Neither did he follow them in. He was a wild individual, so that at first his absence was not out of the ordinary. Then Skett called out to him by name. There was no reply. Alarmed, Skett, having no other officer with him except the other subaltern in charge of the isolated post on the left, sent out a first and then a second patrol in charge of a non-commissioned officer. These scoured the inky waste, crawling from shell-hole to shell-hole, calling the missing officer's name. All in vain. Poor Skett was at his wits' end. The first time he had been in charge of a company in the front line, and here was one of his officers missing. Pym might have been captured, possibly killed, but he might equally well be lying wounded or dying in No-Man's-Land.

Getting together a larger patrol, Skett sent them out in charge of a trusted sergeant, and stumbled along Fall Trench to explain the situation to Mac. The two agreed that if this last patrol met with no success it was essential that an officer's party should go out. Skett had no officer to send, while orders were insistent and explicit that Company Commanders were not to leave the line themselves. Mac immediately volunteered to go himself as soon as he could get permission from me to leave his sap, and sent off a note to me.

The messenger plodded down the communication trench to Company Headquarters where, after sending my report to the Adjutant, I was trying to get a little sleep on the floor of the trench. "Work on sap going well," I read. "Can I go to A Company and have a look for Pym?" "Have a look for Pym?" I thought. "What the devil does he want to do that for?" I knew they were friends and that it was their habit to forgather for a talk and a smoke when work was slack. "Blast Mac!" I said to myself. "Can't he understand that we have *got* to get these trenches a decent depth before daylight?" and promptly wrote a reply to the effect that this was "no time for demonstrations of affection", and that he was to carry on with the sap till it was finished before indulging in any informal trench conference.

In other words, even at such a short distance from the scene no word had reached me, nor had Mac, thinking I already knew, made it clear that any untoward incident had occurred. Of course, as soon as he got my reply, Mac realised what had happened, hastily wrote another note, and went back to his sap to wait for the few minutes it would take me to come up as soon as I knew the situation.

Meanwhile, Skett returning to his own company, had found that the third patrol had just crawled in to report that they had found no trace of Pym. Desperate, as time was of the utmost importance, Skett determined to go himself, against orders though this was. He conceived it to be his personal responsibility to leave no stone unturned to find Pym. Some premonition must have come to him, for as he collected a few reliable men together to go with him, he turned to his servant, and handing him the valuables and documents out of his pockets said, "Here are the wages I owe you. You'd better take them while you can get them," and without more ado scrambled out of the trench.

Hardly had he put a foot in No-Man's-Land than he fell back dead, his head split open by a random bullet. Who shall say that he did not know his fate was upon him? Those who had been with him from the morning have little doubt about it.

This was the news that greeted me as I reached Mac in response to his second note. A Company being now without an officer, I took over the company and at once sent out patrols under both Mac and George. All night these two scoured the ground in front, but no trace was found, nor has word ever since been heard of Pym.

The mud had swallowed him up as completely as it had, by delaying communication between Mac and myself, killed poor Skett. Him we buried before daylight as reverently as we could in the circumstances, digging a grave between bursts of machine-gun fire in the parados of Fall Trench.

Dawn on the 11th found us all feeling the effects of our labours and the lack of sleep. Legs were attacked by acute shooting pains due to the strain of constant movement in the mud. Eyes smarted with tiredness. Faces and fingernails were caked with mud...

The day again turned out bright and sunny, and the craving for sleep passed off. This was just as well, for Cropper, the additional subaltern reported for duty and had to be taken round to A Company and duly installed... [Rogerson remained in command of A and B Company].

Wandering round our little sector, talking here with some Yorkshire corporal, here with some of the new draft, the morning passed easily and pleasantly, to be rounded off with the midday meal, chiefly bully and a little whisky diluted with the precious pure water in my water-bottle.

Shortly afterwards a very hot and breathless artillery officer and his orderly fell into our headquarters trench, dragging their telephone wire with them. They were representatives of a 6-inch gun battery which was proposing that afternoon to shell a piece of trench which was said to lie opposite the front of A Company, and to be still manned by the enemy. This fragment was all that remained of Zenith Trench which, with the help of the mud, had resisted the "full dress" attack which had cost us so heavily last time we had been in the line, and the officer's attitude suggested that he was apologising on behalf of the Royal Regiment for having been so remiss as to leave even so short a length of enemy trench undemolished. I was not disposed very charitably towards him, as so far we had gone almost unmolested, and experience had taught us that any form of artillery offensiveness promptly evoked retaliation, which as often as not fell on the P.B.I. Still, I extended to him the ordinary courtesies of the trenches in the shape of a cigarette and whisky and water in a tin cup, and then escorted him to A Company's front line, where Cropper joined us. By careful scrutiny of No-Man's-Land we managed to identify something which we took to be the surviving stretch of trench, though we were by no means certain until the battery started firing. Then as our Forward Observing Officer corrected the range, and the shells started falling all round the spot, first one and then another German, ludicrous in their coal-scuttle helmets, long coats and boots, emerged and floundered wildly into the nearest deep shell-hole. Cropper, seizing a rifle, at once opened fire and continued firing, with a man loading a spare rifle for him.

There must have been twenty or thirty Germans who bolted, but Cropper's fire was not accurate enough to account for more than four or five at most, though we could not really tell which were hit or which had merely stumbled and fallen. Still, it was some consolation to know that those who were not casualties must have been severely frightened! Their "shoot" over, our gunner guests took a speedy departure, while we waited apprehensively for the retaliation which, for some unaccountable reason, came not...

During the day the platoon had been resting, and mention of sleep reminded me that I had had none for a very strenuous forty-eight hours, and I promised myself that I would "get down to it" as soon as I got back to Company Headquarters and had got off my night's report.

It was quite dark by the time I did get back, and Robinson [a New Zealand Corporal, known as 'Buggy'] came up and asked me in a confidentail undertone if he might go and "hunt for souvenirs" behind the line. He was an incorrigible "scrounger", for ever collecting the flotsam of battle - shell nose-caps, German grenades, cap rosettes, weapons, even gloves and boots - which he would take back and sell to the Army Service Corps, and I recognised his request as a polite way of saying that he wished to go out and loot the enemy dead lying between us and Dewdrop Trench. He and his platoon had done such excellent work and he was such a law unto himself that I had no heart to refuse him, although I could not give him permission to leave the trench. I compromised by saying that I should know nothing about it. If he went and returned without being found by any one in authority or hit by the enemy, all would be well. If he were caught, then he'd have to stand the racket! I further told him that he must search every British corpse and bring me back the paybooks, after which what he did with the Germans was no concern of mine.

He hopped over the parados without more ado and was lost in the gloom. Not long afterwards the ration party arrived panting and sweating with their heavy loads of sand-bags full of bread, bully, jam, and biscuits, and petrol-tins of water. They reported two of their number hit on the way from Battalion Headquarters and their loads lost in the darkness. Luckily that most precious item of the day's rations - the half-jar of rum - had not been lost!...

With the day's duties successfully accomplished and the enemy contenting himself with shelling of a desultory nature and mostly directed far away in rear, I curled myself up on the trench floor and was soon off to sleep. Hardly had my senses left me than I was up and on edge in a second! Shells had begun to fall more quickly all around us! Then, with a whoosh of metal overhead, down came the barrage! Explosions whirled, stamped, and pounded the tortured ground; the splitting hiss and bang of the field guns screaming above the deep, earth-shaking thud! thud! of the heavies until they blended into the one steady pandemonium of drumfire. The trenches rocked and trembled, while their garrisons, blinded by the flashes, choked by the acrid fumes, pressed themselves tight to the sodden walls as the avalanche of metal roared above and around them.

Out of the smoke along the trench emerged a runner, crouching low. "Front line - Verey lights - urgent!" he croaked, his tongue parched with the biting smoke. "Verey lights!" I yelled, "Where are they?" They should have come up with the rations, but none had arrived. "There are some Boche ones here, sir," shouted a voice I recognised as belonging to Purkiss, the company cook. "Are you sure they are white ones?" I roared back across the din. "Yes, sir," was the assurance, "Parkin fired one off in the latrine this morning and it burnt white all right!" Seizing the rotting box marked "Signal Patronen," Mac's messenger departed again into the smoke. By now the explosions around us were fewer, but the curtain of fire, leaping and crashing, hung relentlessly in the valley, which raged and seethed, an inferno of smoke and destruction.

So the Boche had done what we feared! He had dropped his barrage in rear of us to cut off supports while he came across and "snaffled" my two companies! This was the conviction which possessed me.

"Stand-to, No. 7!" I shouted, at the same time sending off one runner to order A Company to do the same, and another to Mac for news. While behind us the barrage flared and thundered, in front all was quiet. As we stood, tense and alert, peering over the parapet, all we could see was the black crest of the ridge some fifteen yards in front over which rose, wavered, and fell the enemy Verey lights, some burning white and steady, others soaring up in a fountain of golden sparks. Over our heads the rush of shells continued, but from in front there came no rattle of small arms. Clearly the enemy had not yet attacked.

Suddenly, from about the position of Fall Trench, over the brow there was a hiss, and up flew a rocket. Horror of horrors! It burst with a rosy glow and hung, a ball of claret light, over our line! Before it had died out a second went up, bursting this time into golden rain. That German box of lights had been a mixed lot for signal purposes! But what had we done? Whatever request to the enemy had we in our extremity sent up? For a few breathless minutes we waited, momentarily expecting the barrage to be shortened and fall on our unlucky heads.

Instead, just as a thunder-shower abruptly ends, so the shelling on the instant died away, as suddenly as it had begun, and only a few random shells, like scattered raindrops, burst sporadically in rear before silence, heavy and oppressive, succeeded strife.

All danger of an attack over, I stood the men down and hurried off to the front line where Mac laughingly described what a shock he had got when he sent up the two German lights. We thought over what signals they might be, and, after much fruitless conjecture over the first claret affair, we decided that the golden rain rocket must mean "Lengthen range: we are here," as whenever the enemy started shelling a forest of golden rockets would rise from the shell-holes in front. That we were right was soon confirmed, and the Divisional Intelligence Report next day contained the reassuring information that "hostile signal golden rocket bursting into golden rain means lengthen range instead of barrage." Much more important from our point of view was the fact that never again until we were relieved did a German shell fall on our company front! Even more wonderful to relate, neither A nor B Company had a single man hit during the enemy's shelling, which we could only put down to a belated retaliation for our "shoot" of the afternoon.

My return to Company Headquarters coincided with the reappearance of Robinson. One look at his drawn and ashen face showed me that, tough old hand as he was, he had had a fright, realising which, I forbore to curse him as I meant to, and merely asked him what had happened. His reply was that after he left the support line he turned down towards Dewdrop Trench, and that as he was examining some very promising bodies he had been caught by the barrage and forced to spend a very unpleasant and smelly half-hour in the same shell-hole with "two dead Jerries". Then he had tried to get back to the trench, but losing his way had roamed and groped about in the filth and darkness until he had been challenged by Mac's men in Fall Trench! In other words, he had passed through the big gap on our right flank and had had a very narrow escape from walking unwittingly into the German lines. It was a very chastened "Buggy" that rejoined his platoon.

As for me, I had had about enough, and I lay down once again at the bottom of the narrow trench, where there was just room for my body, and slept the sleep of exhaustion till aroused, numb and cramped, for stand-to four hours later. This was the first proper rest I had had since I left Camp 34...

13th November
Our relief by the 1st Battalion of the Worcester Regiment was confirmed in Battalion orders...

I had to make a final last trip round the sector, noting with a certain pride the improvements that the kindness of the elements had allowed us to make. Not only had we temporarily subjugated the mud, but we had added another brand-new piece to the great jig-saw puzzle of the trench system of the Western Front. There were also arrangements to be made with Mac about moving the company out. We had been ordered to salvage as much derelict equipment and stores as possible, and that meant putting further burdens in the shape of waterproof capes, sheets, or great-coats on to already tired and overladen men. But there was another point, and one which served to show me how very easy it is to write orders which were capable of more than one interpretation. I, for some incomprehensible reason, had read the command about Company Commanders reporting "relief complete" at Battalion Headquarters, to mean that I, at the head of my straggling followers, was to flounder through the mud to that death-trap the Sunken Road, and, while they awaited almost certain destruction, inform the Adjutant that we had handed over properly and without incident. I waxed righteously indignant. Whatever was the Colonel thinking about, I asked Mac, giving orders so unlike him in their disregard of the men's safety! Anyway, I would do nothing of the sort. If I had to report personally I would report alone, and Mac should take the company out by the quickest and easiest way he could find. I would meet him at Ginchy cross-roads...

As soon as the last man was clear of the trenches, I started out for Battalion Headquarters in the Sunken Road, so confident in my ability to find it that I took no orderly with me. Alas for such presumption! I had gone no more than a few dozen paces when I began to have misgivings. Surely, I should have passed Dewdrop Trench by now. I paused to take what bearings I could, but the night was black as pitch. Landmarks there were none. A shell burst here and there, and I remember thinking what a wrong impression the ordinary war pictures gave. They always showed shells exploding with a vivid flash, but all that now happened was a scream, a thud, and a little shower of red sparks as from a blacksmith's anvil. There was not the faintest glimmer to light me on my way. I stumbled on. Doubts became anxiety. I was lost! No matter that I ought to know I could not be far away from some one; I was afraid. Throughout the war this was my worst nightmare - to be alone, and lost and in danger. Worse than all the anticipation of battle, all the fear of mind, raid, or capture, was this dread of being struck down somewhere where there was no one to find me, and where I should lie till I rotted back slowly into the mud. I had seen those to whom it had happened.

So now anxiety passed almost at once into panic. I went forward more quickly first at a sharper walk, then at a desperate blundering trot. Was it imagination? Or were more shells really beginning to fall, rushing down to sink into the soft earth and burst with smothered thuds? Yes! Little showers of red sparks were all around me. I struggled on, fell once, again, many times, tore my coat on barbed wire, cut my hand. When would a bullet from those chattering machine-guns strike me in the head or back? The nape of my neck ran cold at the thought. My heart thumped louder than ever, both from terror and effort. I was getting blown. I could go no further. Then I stumbled, pitched forward, slithered down several feet, caught my kit on some signal wires, sank up to my elbows in wet mud. I had reached the Sunken Road!

Breathless and shaken, I struggled to my feet. A head peered at me out of a sand-bagged dug-out entrance. I asked the owner the whereabouts of the West Yorkshire headquarters. He thought there were some infantry battalion headquarters a little farther up the road on the opposite side, but whose he did not know. He was a signaller, he confessed, as if to excuse his lack of information. There was nothing for it but to find out for myself.

What a cess-pit that Sunken Road was! Over ankle-deep in slime, it was strewn with the bodies of horses and mules in varying stages of decay. Yet its battered banks afforded the only convenient cover for a wide area around, so into them had been driven dug-outs, British and German, into which were crammed all those whose duties kept them in the forward zone without taking them into the trenches. There were the headquarters of two or three battalions, the forward posts of batteries, both field and heavy, signallers, sappers, and odd details of all arms. I made shouted inquiries down two or three shafts before I pulled aside the tattered sandbag cover which hung before the right dug-out, and entered a tiny candle-lit burrow. In it were installed the Worcesters. My own regiment had gone!

This was the crowning blow. With apologies for my intrusion, I set out again into the darkness, feeling more wretched and hopeless than ever after the brief vision of light and warmth. But this time luck was with me, and hardly had I scrambled up the bank than some one said, "Who's there?" and I recognised Hawley's voice. He was making for Ginchy with an orderly who knew the way, so we set off together. With company the whole atmosphere seemed to change. The danger remained the same, yet the presence of others banished at once the terror that had assailed me. In a few minutes we were passing battery positions and were dazzled by the stabbing, lemon flashes of the guns as they fired towards us. Then we struck the duck-board track which, rickety and shell-smashed though it was, lead us steadily towards Ginchy. Lights again began to appear in dug-out doors and gun-positions, now far enough away from the enemy to disregard the risk of detection, and at last we were able to make out groups of men in the darkness. We had made Ginchy cross-roads, and the men were B Company in artillery formation, into which Mac had put them to lessen the danger from any chance shell. Thanks to his guidance in avoiding the bad places, they had got out without loss.

Without wasting time in marvelling at this miracle, the Company fell in and moved off. That march was a nightmare. Not till then did I realise how tired I was, nor how done the men. I had snatched less sleep than they - my total for the three days was no more than six hours - and had been more continuously "on the go". They, on the other hand, were overloaded with sodden kit. We had not gone far before requests were made for a halt. I turned a deaf ear. Men so weary, I argued, would only fall asleep the moment they broke rank. It would be the harder to get them on the move again. Besides, we were still in the shelled area. Requests turned to protests. Some of the younger men could hardly walk. Officers and the fresher N.C.O.s took over rifles and packs from the most fatigued but without avail. The querulous, half-mutinous demands for rest grew more insistent. They were the cries of semiconscious minds tortured by over-exertion and lack of sleep. Still I took no notice, vowing that not until we were in the haven of our own camp would I call a halt. "I won't stop! I won't stop! I won't stop!" I repeated to myself with each agonising step. My ears, deaf to all else, sung the refrain. But to no purpose. Will said, "I won't stop"; Body argued, "I can't go on." And so it was. After what seemed hours of tramping I could go no farther. All my determination was thrown to the winds. "Halt!" I could do no more than speak the command. It was enough. The word was scarce uttered before every one, myself included, had thrown himself down on to the bricks and rubbish at the roadside. There we lay, silent, exhausted. Will began to reassert itself. This was no good. The longer we stayed the more difficult it would be to go on. Somehow, how I do not know, we stirred and prodded the men into movement again. Cursing and grunting, they shambled forward with the unsteady steps of sleep-walkers. I tried to square my shoulders for the long march that I felt must lie ahead. Irony of ironies! We had not moved more than a few score paces before the gruff voice of Company Sergeant-Major Scott was heard shouting "This way, B Company." We had fallen out less than a hundred yards from camp!

But what miles we must have marched! How many was it? The distance from Ginchy cross-roads to La Briqueterie camp was no more than three and a half miles! The front line was under five miles away. There is no doubt the Somme taught us that distance is a relative term, not to be measured in yards and feet...

– 13th NOVEMBER 1916 –

LIEUTENANT EDMUND BLUNDEN, M.C.

11th Battalion Royal Sussex Regiment

By 10th November the Battalion had left Senlis and returned to 'that death-trap known as the Schwaben Redoubt... an almost obliterated cocoon of trenches in which mud, and death, and life were much the same thing'. Colonel Harrison made his headquarters at the Thièpval end of St. Martin's Lane trench. 'Bodies, bodies, and their useless gear heaped the gross waste ground' round the 'filthy, mortifying, and most lonely acre' where once the village of Thièpval had stood. On 11th a patrol was sent out to raid a German stronghold some distance ahead of the Schwaben Redoubt; it was unsuccessful but returned with some prisoners which included 'a milkman and an elementary schoolmaster - most welcome guests'. Early on 13th November the fierce assault was launched northward towards Grandcourt and Beaumont Hamel.

That was a feat of arms vieing with any recorded. The enemy was surprised and beaten. From Thièpval Wood battalions of our own division sprang out, passed our old dead, mud-craters and wire and took the tiny village of St. Pierre Divion with its enormous labyrinth, and almost 2,000 Germans in the galleries there. Beyond the curving Ancre, the Highlanders and the Royal Naval Division overran Beaucourt and Beaumont, 'strongholds of the finest' and as this news came in fragments and rumours to us in Thièpval, we felt as if we were being left behind. Towards four o'clock orders came that we were to supply 300 men that night, to carry up wiring materials to positions in advance of those newly captured, those positions to be reconnoitred immediately. This meant me.

A runner called Johnson, a red-cheeked silent youth, was the only man available, and we set off at once, seeing that there was a heavy barrage eastward, but knowing that it was best not to think about it. What light the drudging day had permitted was now almost extinct, and the mist had changed into a drizzle; we passed the site of Thièpval Crucifix, and the junction of Fiennes Trench and St. Martin's Lane (a wide pond of greyness), then the scrawled Schwaben - few people about, white lights whirling up north of the Ancre, and the shouldering hills north and east gathering inimical mass in their wan illusion. Crossing scarcely discernible remains of redoubts and communications, I saw an officer peering from a little length of trench ahead, and went to him. "Is this our front line?" "Dunno: you get down off there, you'll be hit." He shivered in his mackintosh sheet. His chin quivered; this night's echoing blackness was coming down cruelly fast. "Get down." He spoke with a sort of anger. By some curious inward concentration on the matter of finding the way, I had not much noticed the furious dance of high explosive now almost around us. At this minute, a man, or a ghost, went by, and I tried to follow his course down the next slope and along a desperate valley; then I said to Johnson, "The front line must be ahead here still; come on." We were now in the dark and, before we realised it, inside a barrage; never had shells seemed so torrentially swift, so murderous; they seemed to swoop over one's shoulder. We ran, we tore ourselves out of the clay to run, and lived. The shells at last skidded and spatttered behind us, and now where were we? We went on.

Monstrously black a hill rose up before us; we crossed; then I thought I knew where we were. These heavy timber shelters with the great openings were evidently German howitzer positions, and they had not been long evacuated, I thought, stooping hurriedly over those dead men in field grey overcoats at the entrances, and others flung down by their last "foxholes" near by. The lights flying up northward, where the most deafening noise was roaring along the river valley, showed these things in their unnatural glimmer; and the men's coats were yet comparatively clean, and their attitudes most life like. Again we went on, and climbed the false immensity of another ridge, when several rifles and a maxim opened upon us, and very close they were. We retreated aslant down the slope, and as we did so I saw the wide lagoons of the Ancre silvering in the Beaucourt lights, and decided our course. Now running, crouching, we worked along the valley, then sharply turning, through crumpled pits and over mounds and heaps, came along high ground above what had been St. Pierre Divion, expecting to be caught at every second; then we plunged through that waterfall of shells, the British and German barrages alike, now slackening; and were challenged at last, in English. We had come back from an accidental tour into enemy country, and blessed with silent gladness the shell-hole in which, blowing their own trumpets in the spirit of their morning's success, were members of four or five different units of our division. We lay down in the mud a moment or two, and recovered our senses.

The way to Thièpval was simpler. At the edge of the wood a couple of great shells burst almost on top of us; thence we had no opposition, and, finding a duckboard track, returned to the battalion headquarters. Johnson slipped down the greasy stairway, and turned very white down below. We were received as Lazarus was. The shelling of the

Schwaben had been "a blaze of light," and our deaths had been taken for granted. Harrison was speaking over the telephone to Hornby, and I just had vitality enough to hear him say, "They have come back, and report an extraordinary barrage; say it would be disaster to attempt to send up that party. Certain disaster. Yes, they say so, and from their appearance one can see that they have been through terrific shelling..."

– 13th NOVEMBER 1916 –

LIEUTENANT EWART ALAN MACKINTOSH, M.C.
5th Battalion Seaforth Highlanders

The Battalion took part in the successful assault on the fortress village of Beaumont Hamel, thought by the Germans to be impregnable, and suffered nearly two hundred casualties. The objective was a line about 200 yards east of the village, and the line of advance just south of the Auchonvillers-Beaumont Hamel road. While he was in hospital recovering from the wound he had received at High Wood, Alan Mackintosh wrote poems mourning those in his Battalion who had been killed.

FROM HOME
To the Men who Fell at Beaumont-Hamel
November 13th, 1916

The pale sun woke in the eastern sky
And a veil of mist was drawn
Over the faces of death and fame
When you went up in the dawn.
With never a thought of fame or death,
Only the work to do,
When you went over the top, my friends,
And I not there with you.

The veil is rent with a rifle-flash
And shows me plain to see
Battle and bodies of men that lived
And fought along with me.
Oh God! it would not have been so hard
If I'd been in it too,
But you are lying stiff, my friends,
And I not there with you.

So here I sit in a pleasant room
By a comfortable fire,
With every thing that a man could want,
But not the heart's desire.
So I sit thinking and dreaming still,
A dream that won't come true,
Of you in the German trench, my friends,
And I not there with you.

BEAUMONT-HAMEL

1

Dead men at Beaumont
In the mud and rain,
You that were so warm once,
Flesh and blood and brain,
You've made an end of dying,
Hurts and cold and crying,
And all but quiet lying
Easeful after pain.

2

Dead men at Beaumont,
Do you dream at all
When the leaves of summer
Ripen to their fall?
Will you walk the heather,
Feel the Northern weather,
Wind and sun together,
Hear the grouse-cock call?

3

Maybe in the night-time
A shepherd boy will see
Dead men, and ghastly,
Kilted to the knee,
Fresh from new blood-shedding,
With airy footsteps treading,
Hill and field and steading,
Where they used to be.

4

Nay, not so I see you,
Dead friends of mine;
But like a dying pibroch
From the battle-line
I hear your laughter ringing,
And the sweet songs you're singing,
And the keen words winging
Across the smoke and wine.

5

So we still shall see you,
Be it peace or war,
Still in all adventures
You shall go before,
And our children dreaming,
Shall see your bayonets gleaming,
Scotland's warriors streaming
Forward evermore.

BEAUMONT-HAMEL, November 13th, 1916

But the North shall arise
Yet again in its strength;
Blood calling for blood
Shall be feasted at length.
For the dead men that lie
Underneath the hard skies,
For battle, for vengeance
The North shall arise.

In the cold of the morning
A grey mist was drawn
Over the waves
That went up in the dawn,
Went up like the waves
Of the wild Northern sea;
For the North has arisen,
The North has broke free.

Ghosts of the heroes
That died in the wood,
Looked on the killing
And saw it was good.
Far over the hillsides
They saw in their dream
The kilted men charging,
The bayonets gleam.

By the cries we had heard,
By the things we had seen,

By the vengeance we took
In the bloody ravine,
By the men that we slew
In the mud and the rain,
The pride of the North
Has arisen again.

– 13th - 15th NOVEMBER 1916 –

CAPTAIN DAVID RORIE, D.S.O.

Royal Army Medical Corps
(Attached 51st Highland Division)

The Division took over the line opposite Beaumont Hamel in the middle of October 1916, but by then the various medical posts were inadequate for the forthcoming assault on the village. A Relay Bearer Post had to be enlarged at Tenderloin in White City and two new ones made in Second Avenue Trench and at Uxbridge Road; an Advanced Dressing Station in the cellars of a brasserie at Mailly-Maillet had to be repaired. Supplies of stretchers, blankets, splints, dressings, medical stores, rations and water in petrol tins were gathered at the first Field Ambulance Post, which was also the Collecting Post, in the stable of a farmyard at Auchonvillers where Captain Rorie was in charge. Here too the Scottish Churches Tent provided nourishment for the wounded, stretcher bearers and prisoners.

At 5.30 on 13th November our furious barrage started, and by 7 a.m. a steady stream of wounded was flowing in, which lasted all day; but evacuation went on well and steadily with no congestion at the various posts. At 11 a.m. and 2.45 p.m. Auchonvillers was vigorously shelled; and we had, for the time being, to carry all the cases lying in the farmyard, awaiting dressing or removal, inside our already crowded Dressing Room. By the middle of the forenoon German prisoners began passing in large numbers; and a hundred fit men were held up to help to clear the field of their own wounded. These men were fed and treated like our own bearers and worked willingly and well, being docile to a degree; any number up to fifteen at a time going off in charge of one R.A.M.C. man.

Corporal Charlie, one of the best known characters in our unit, had general charge of the Hun auxiliaries, and his management of them and of the language difficulty was admirable. Ordered in the evening to detail twelve men for wheeled stretcher work, in answer to a call for more bearers to go to Thurles Dump, he went to the ruined shed where his command lay; most of them smoking cigarettes supplied by their friendly enemies. It was dark by then, and I happened to cross the yard as he began operations. Holding on high a hurricane lamp he shouted:-

"Noo, then, you Fritzes! A dizzen o' ye! Compree?"

"Nein!" said a puzzled voice from amongst the huddle of Huns in the shed.

"Nine, ye gommeral? It's nae nine; it's twal' o' ye! C'wa' noo! Look slippy! *You*, Nosey!" (indicating a gentleman well endowed in this way by nature). "An *you*, Breeks!" (to another, the seat of whose trousers was severely damaged by barbed wire).

He then most appropriately fitted Nosey between the front handles of a wheeled streetcher with Breeks at the tail end, and with a deft shove sent them and their apparatus out of the way; while, again applying his personal method, he rapidly picked out another two. When the tally was complete he turned to the orderly in charge with:-

"Noo, laddie, there's your Fritzes! See ye dinna loss ony o' them!" - and calmly made off in quest of another job.

As a practical linguist he was unique: his French being quite as good as his German. An equal adept was he with penny whistle or mouth organ, or as Rabelaisian raconteur in chief. He was a man of never-failing cheerfulness, and much legendary lore deservedly circulated round him.

Later, going round a dark corner of the farmyard, I collided violently with someone coming from the opposite direction. After tersely commenting on the situation I flashed on a torch light and discovered the corporal, with both arms crossed, like a tombstone saint, over a mass of bulging material inside his tunic.

"What on earth have you got there?" I asked.

"Booms!" came the laconic reply.

"Bombs! What are *you* doing with bombs?"

"Pittin' them in a holie roond at the back."

He had collected about forty bombs from the wounded who had come in, and I was rather glad our collision had not been more violent than it was...

All day the run of cases continued and all night of 13th-14th. In spite of the shelling of the evacuation routes there had so far been no casualties amongst our personnel. Morning saw things rather quieter; but in the forenoon, near White City, an M.O. [Captain H. Begg], of the 2/1st Field Ambulance, one of the most efficient and gallant R.A.M.C. officers in the Division, was killed by a shell, as later was a private [Blair] of our unit along with two Boche bearers. The good old motor transport, with their usual sang-froid, were now steadily running cars down to Tenderloin Post in White City by the much battered Auchonvillers-Beaumont Hamel road, the route being risky...; it was necessary at all costs to ease off the strain on the now thoroughly exhausted bearers, many of whom had their shoulders absolutely raw with the constant friction and pressure of the stretcher slings. Evacuation went on steadily all day and night of 14th-15th.

On the evening of the 14th a batch of some half dozen Boche officers was temporarily left in our charge until an A.P.M.'s guard was available to remove them back. We stuck them under a guard of our own in the much battered part of our building which faced the enemy lines. Shortly afterwards I got a message asking for an interview. On entering their quarters there was much heel-clicking and saluting; and a fat, walrus-faced fellow who spoke semblable English asked:-

"Are you aware, sir, that we are German officers?"

I murmured politely that the fact was obvious.

"Are you aware, sir, that this room is not suitable accommodation for German officers?"

By good luck I remembered what Sam Weller, as boots of "The White Hart," had said to Mr. Perker when the little lawyer remarked: "This is a curious old house of yours." So I gave Sam's reply to the indignant Hun:-

"If you'd sent word you were coming, we'd have had it repaired."

The effect was magical! Walrus-face beamed and translated the remark to his brethren, who all saluted with pleased smiles, while their interpreter observed in the most amiable manner:-

"Do not further apologise!"

I replied that I would not; and, looking in later, found them in very audible enjoyment of some liquid nourishment from the soup kitchen. The incident was happily closed.

And now came the inevitable stage of clearing up the battlefield and searching all possible places where wounded, whether British or Boche, who had not been picked up in the actual battle, might have sought shelter. At daybreak an M.O. and a party were sent to work from Y Ravine towards White City; while another party, including two Jocks with rifles (as the dug-outs with which Beaumont Hamel was tunnelled were not yet clear of whole-skinned Huns), worked across to meet him, an officer of the 6th Seaforths acting as guide. A further object was to search for a wonderful legendary under-ground Hun dressing station of the Arabian Nights variety which, incidentally, we failed to locate.

It was drizzling wet and vilely cold, the trenches in places thigh deep in clay and an awful mess of smashed barbed wire, mud, disintegrated German dead and debris of all sorts. In one trench our occupation for half an hour was hauling each other out of the tenacious and blood-stained mud; and during our mutual salvage operations we had evidently made ourselves too visible, as the enemy started shelling. There was nothing for it but to take to the open and make for another trench, which we promptly did; doing a hundred yards in rather good time.

Now, the Jocks and I were of the Julius Ceasar, Napoleon and Lord Roberts type of physique, while our guide was a tall man, whose greatcoat - which for some obscure reason he had put on before starting - blew out as he led us, doubled up on account of the *phut-phut* of bullets, across the open; and it struck me with a great feeling of irritation as we ran that we must be providing excellent comic effect for any of the enemy observing us through glasses, by suggesting an alarmed hen and three chickens on the run... In the next trench we again set about searching the dug-outs and placarding them, to catch the eye of the stretcher-bearers who would follow, as containing so many wounded for removal; but again the Hun gunners got on to us in an exposed place and we had a second sprint across the open for another trench, where we had to stay below in a *sous-terrain* for an hour till things got quieter.

This dug-out was typical of the many with which Beaumont Hamel was honeycombed. On descending about forty steps one was in a large floored and timbered chamber some fifty feet long; and at the further end a second set of steps led to a similar chamber, one side of each being lined with a double layer of bunks filled with dead and wounded Germans, the majority of whom had become casualties early on the morning of the 13th.

The place was in utter darkness; and, when we flashed our lights on and the wounded saw our escort with rifles ready, there was an outbreak of "Kamarad!" while a big bevy of rats squeaked and scuttled away from their feast on the dead bodies on the floor. The stench was indescribably abominable: for many of the cases were gas-gangrenous. Any food or drink they had possessed was used up, and our water bottles were soon emptied amongst them. After we had gone over the upper chamber and separated the living from the dead, we went to the lower one where the gas curtain was let down and fastened. Tearing it aside and going through with a light, I got a momentary jump when I caught a glimpse in the upper bunk of a man, naked to the waist, and with his right hand raised above his head. But the poor beggar was far past mischief - stark and stiff with a smashed pelvis. Some twenty other dead Germans lay about at the disposal of the rat hordes. The romance of war had worn somewhat thin here.

When the shelling had eased up and we quitted the place, the wounded firmly believed they were being left for good; although we had repeatedly assured them that in a short time they would all be taken to hospital. But to the end of the campaign the wounded Boche could never understand that he was not going to be treated with the same brutality he had meted out to others at the outset of war; so it was amidst a chorus of shrieks, wails and supplications that we made for the welcome open air, ticketed the dug-out as containing fourteen wounded for removal, and renewed our search in similar surroundings for fresh casualties.

– 13th NOVEMBER 1916 –

LIEUTENANT ALAN PATRICK HERBERT

Hawke Battalion, Royal Naval Division

On the 13th November the Royal Naval Division took part in the successful but costly attack on Beaucourt; Hawke Battalion went into action with 20 officers and 415 other ranks. The Battalion Diary recorded:
'... The Hawke Battalion after the first few minutes of the attack no longer existed as a unit... The Battalion suffered grievous losses...' Alan Herbert was one of two officers who came out unscathed. He later wrote a poem 'Beaucourt Revisited'.

Five days before the attack Sub-Lieutenant Edwin Leopold Arthur Dyett, of the Nelson Battalion, applied to be transferred to duties at sea on the grounds that his nerves were unable to stand the strain of trench warfare. The prosecution at Dyett's subsequent court-martial gave the details of the incident which led to his arrest. On the 13th November Dyett was in reserve when the attack on Beaucourt was launched at dawn and at mid-day he and another officer were sent forward as reinforcements. After failing to locate their unit in the mud and chaos the two men went their separate ways. Dyett wrote 'I rambled about and lost touch with everybody, and my nerves, not being strong, were completely strung up.' Dyett soon joined a fellow officer, Sub-Lieutenant Fernie, who was organising the return of stragglers from various units of the Royal Naval Division. Although of the same rank, Fernie ordered Dyett to take charge of the men and guide them back to the line; Dyett was to follow the party to make sure nobody dropped out. Dyett refused preferring to return to Headquarters for fresh orders and Fernie reported him for refusing to obey an order. In the confusion of the battlefield Dyett became lost a second time and took refuge in a dug-out.
Sub-Lieutenant Dyett's General Court Martial was held on 26th December 1916. The prosecution case depended crucially on the evidence of a fellow officer who was said to bear Dyett a grudge. Dyett declined to give evidence and no defence witnesses were called. Seemingly, the only defence was the suggestion that the defendant was neurotic and unfit for active service. Dyett was found guilty of desertion and sentenced to death. The Court recommended mercy on the grounds of his youth and because the prevailing conditions at the time were likely to have a detrimental effect on any young officer 'unless he had a strong character'. Major-General C.D. Shute, the Divisional Commander, recommended that the sentence be commuted; but Lieutenant General Fanshawe, commanding V Corps and General Gough, the Army Commander, considered that the sentence should be carried out. Edwin Dyett was shot at dawn on 5th January 1917.

Alan Herbert and Edwin Dyett served in different Battalions of the Royal Naval Division but both were in the attack on Beaucourt on 13th November 1916. Herbert was deeply concerned with the injustice of Dyett's court-martial and conviction, and in 1919 published his novel, 'The Secret Battle', in which he brought out the horrendous conditions suffered by men in action; the inadequate presentation for the defence; the bias towards the prosecution in courts-martial; and the lack of compassion shown to men whose nerves were shattered.

The novel relates the fictitious Harry Penrose's secret battle within himself. In Gallipoli, and then in the trenches in France, Penrose is tried beyond endurance. He faces a court-martial for desertion and is found guilty but is recommended to mercy. 'The Secret Battle' concludes:

'But he got no mercy. The sentence was confirmed by the higher authorities. I heard afterwards that the officers of the Court Martial were amazed and horrified to hear it...

The thing was done seven mornings later, in a little orchard behind the Casquettes' farm.

The Padré told me he stood up to them bravely and quietly. Only he whispered to him, 'For God's sake make them be quick.' That is the worst torment of the soldier from beginning to end - the waiting.

He was shot by his own men...'

BEAUCOURT REVISITED

I wandered up to Beaucourt; I took the river track,
And saw the lines we lived in before the Boche went back;
But Peace was now in Pottage, the front was far ahead,
The front had journeyed Eastward, and only left the dead.

And I thought, how long we lay there, and watched across the wire,
While the guns roared round the valley, and set the skies afire!
But now there are homes in HAMEL and tents in the Vale of Hell,
And a camp at Suicide Corner, where half a regiment fell.

The new troops follow after, and tread the land we won,
To them 'tis so much hill-side re-wrested from the Hun;
We only walk with reverence this sullen mile of mud;
The shell-holes hold our history, and half of them our blood.

Here, at the head of Peche Street, 'twas death to show your face;
To me it seemed like magic to linger in the place;
For me how many spirits hung round the Kentish Caves,
But the new men see no spirits - they only see the graves.

I found the half-dug ditches we fashioned for the fight,
We lost a score of men there - young James was killed that night;
I saw the star shells staring, I heard the bullets hail,
But the new troops pass unheeding - they never heard the tale.

I crossed the blood-red ribbon, that once was No-Man's Land,
I saw a misty daybreak and a creeping minute-hand;
And here the lads went over, and there was Harmsworth shot,
And here was William lying - but the new men know them not.

And I said, "There is still the river, and still the stiff, stark trees,
To treasure here our story, but there are only these";
But under the white wood crosses the dead men answered low,
"The new men know not BEAUCOURT, but we are here - we know."

AFTERMATH

Have you forgotten yet?...
For the world's events have rumbled on since those gagged days,
Like traffic checked while at the crossing of city-ways:
And the haunted gap in your mind has filled with thoughts that flow
Like clouds in the lit heaven of life; and you're a man reprieved to go,
Taking your peaceful share of Time, with joy to spare.
But the past is just the same - and War's a bloody game...
Have you forgotten yet?...
Look down, and swear by the slain of the War that you'll never forget.

Do you remember the dark months you held the sector at Mametz -
The nights you watched and wired and dug and piled sandbags on
    parapets?
Do you remember the rats; and the stench
Of corpses rotting in front of the front-line trench -
And dawn coming, dirty-white, and chill with a hopeless rain?
Do you ever stop and ask, 'Is it all going to happen again?'

Do you remember that hour of din before the attack -
And the anger, the blind compassion that seized and shook you then
As you peered at the doomed and haggard faces of your men?
Do you remember the stretcher-cases lurching back
With dying eyes and lolling heads - those ashen-grey
Masks of the lads who once were keen and kind and gay?

Have you forgotten yet?...
Look up, and swear by the green of the spring that you'll never forget.

Siegfried Sassoon, March 1919

Appendix A

Notes on Part 7 from 'In Parenthesis' by David Jones

17. *chalk predella... his wire.* The approach to the German trenches here rose slightly, in low chalk ridges.

21. *tripod's clank.* The movement of a German machine gun was often recognisable by the clank of chain or of some metal on metal.

40. *golden vanities make about.* Cf. song, *The Golden Vanity.*

45. *Cook's tourist to Devastated Areas... for the bearers.* This may appear to be an anachronism, but I remember in 1917 discussing with a friend the possibilities of tourist activity if peace ever came. I remember we went into details and wondered if the unexploded projectile lying near us would go up under a holiday-maker, and how people would stand to be photographed on our parapets. I recall feeling very angry about this, as you do if you think of strangers ever occupying a house you live in, and which has, for you, particular associations.

Appendix B

THE BATTLE OF THE SOMME – 1916
CHRONOLOGY OF EVENTS

1 - 13 July	-	Battle of Albert
14 - 17 July	-	Battle of Bazentin Ridge
15 July - 3 September	-	Battle for Delville Wood
23 July - 3 September	-	Battle of Pozières Ridge
3 - 6 September	-	Battle of Guillemont
9 September	-	Battle of Ginchy
15 - 22 September	-	Battle of Flers-Courcelette
25 - 28 September	-	Battle of Morval
26 - 30 September	-	Battle of Thièpval Ridge
1 - 18 October	-	Battle of Transloy Ridges
1 October - 11 November	-	Battle of the Ancre Heights
13 - 18 November	-	Battle of the Ancre

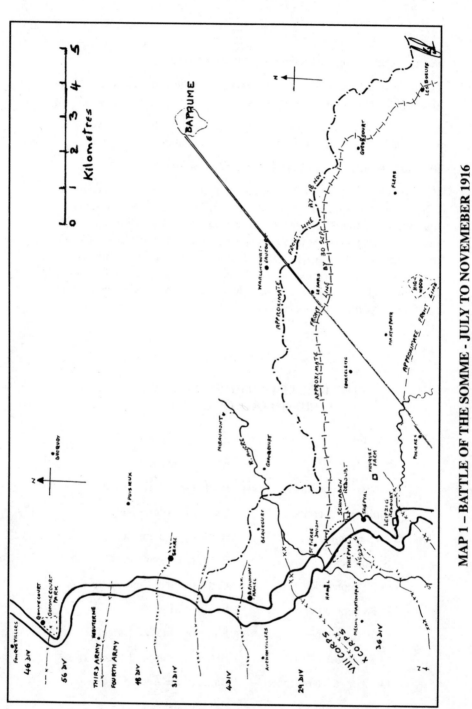

MAP 1 – BATTLE OF THE SOMME - JULY TO NOVEMEBER 1916
NORTH AREA

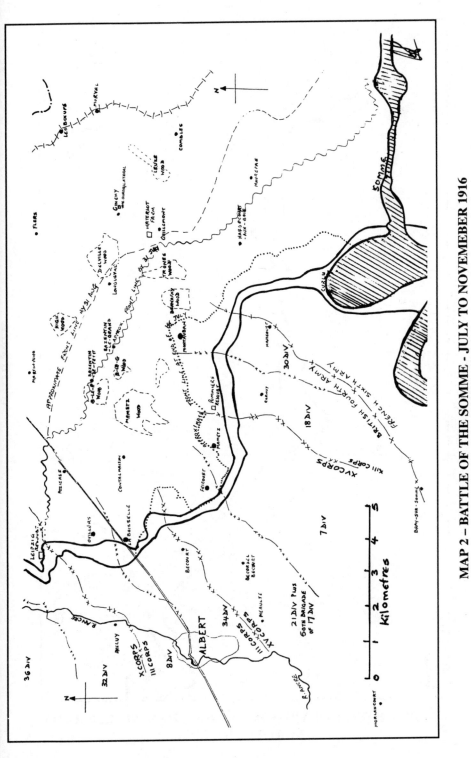

MAP 2 – BATTLE OF THE SOMME - JULY TO NOVEMEBER 1916
SOUTH AREA

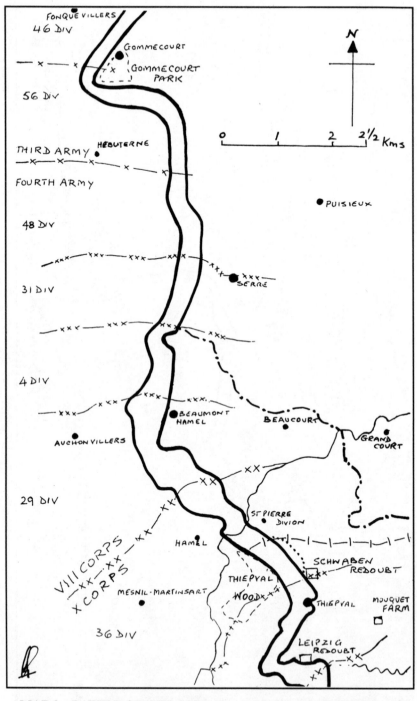

**MAP 3 – BATTLE OF THE SOMME - JULY TO NOVEMEBER 1916
NORTH WEST AREA**

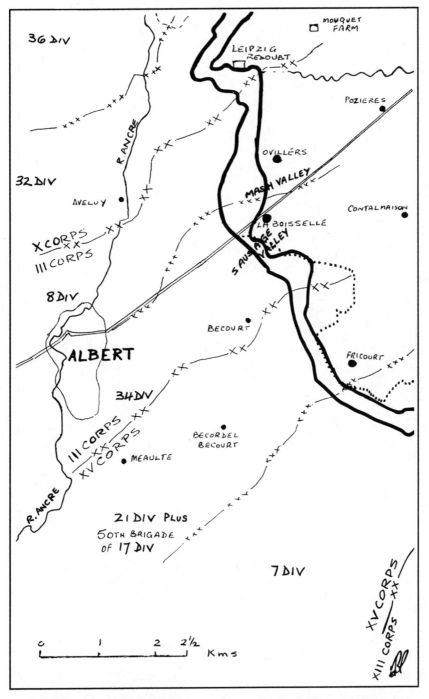

**MAP 4 – BATTLE OF THE SOMME - JULY TO NOVEMEBER 1916
SOUTH WEST AREA**

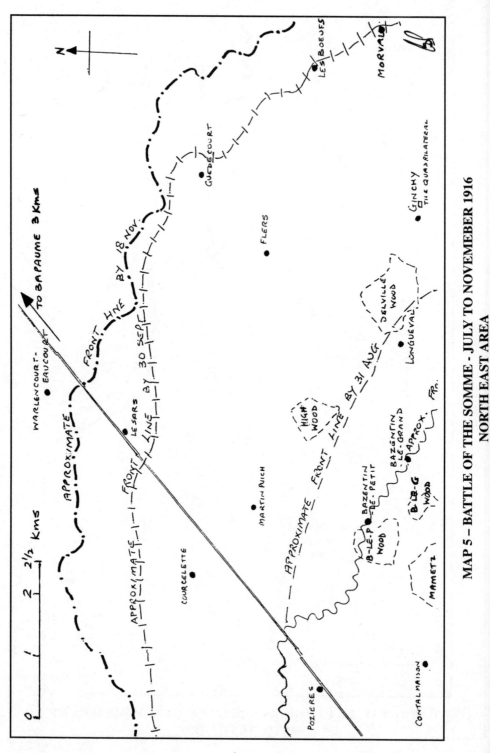

MAP 5 – BATTLE OF THE SOMME - JULY TO NOVEMEBER 1916
NORTH EAST AREA

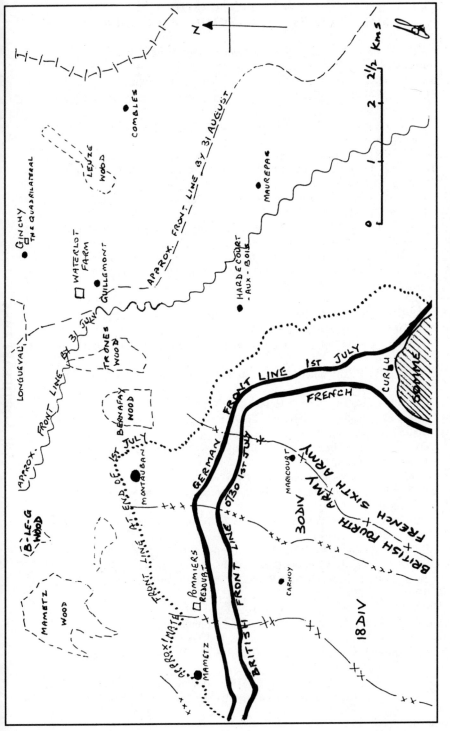

**MAP 6 – BATTLE OF THE SOMME - JULY TO NOVEMEBER 1916
SOUTH EAST AREA**

SELECT BIBLIOGRAPHY
MAIN SOURCES AND RECOMMENDED READING

AITKEN, Alexander. Gallipoli to the Somme: Recollections of a New Zealand Infantryman. Oxford University Press, 1963.

ASQUITH, Raymond. Life and Letters by John Jolliffe. Collins, 1980.

BLUNDEN, Edmund. Undertones of War. Cobden-Sanderson, 1928 and Collins, 1965.

BLUNDEN, Edmund. The Poems of Edmund Blunden: 1914-1930. Cobden-Sanderson, 1930.

BLUNDEN, Edmund. The Mind's Eye: Essays. Cape, 1934.

BLUNDEN Edmund. Edmund Blunden: A Biography by Barry Webb. Yale University Press, 1990.

BRENAN, Gerald. A Life of One's Own: Childhood and Youth. Hamish Hamilton, 1962.

BRENAN, Gerald. The Interior Castle: A Life of Gerald Brenan by Jonathan Gathorne-Hardy. Sinclair-Stevenson, 1992.

CARRINGTON, Charles [Under his pseudonym Charles Edmonds]. A Subaltern's War. Peter Davies, 1930 and Anthony Mott Limited, 1984.

CARRINGTON, Charles. Soldier from the Wars Returning. Hutchinson, 1965.

COOMBS, Rose E.B. Before Endeavours Fade: A guide to the Battlefields of the First World War. After the Battle Publication, 1990.

COULSON, Leslie. From an Outpost and other Poems. Erskine Macdonald, 1917.

CROZIER, F. P., Brigadier-General. A Brass Hat in No Man's Land. Cape, 1930.

DEARMER, Geoffrey. Poems. Heinemann, 1918.

DEARMER, Geoffrey. A Pilgrim's Song: Selected Poems to mark the Poet's 100th Birthday. Murray, 1993.

DOYLE, Father William, S. J. A Biography by Alfred O'Rahilly. Longmans, Green and Co., 1922.

EDMONDS, Charles. (See under CARRINGTON).

EYRE, Giles. Somme Harvest: Memories of a PBI in the Summer of 1916. Jarrold, 1938.

FEILDING, Rowland. War Letters to a Wife: France and Flanders, 1915-1919. The Medici Society, 1929.

GILBERT, Martin. First World War. Weidenfeld and Nicolson, 1994.

GLIDDON, Gerald. When the Barrage Lifts: A Topographical History of the Battle of the Somme. Gliddon Books, 1987; Leo Cooper, 1990; Alan Sutton, 1994.

GRAVES, Robert. Good-bye To All That. Cape, 1929.

GRAVES, Robert. But it still goes on: An Accumulation. Cape, 1930.

GRAVES, Robert. Poems about War. Cassell, 1988.

GRAVES, Robert. Robert Graves: His Life and Works by Martin Seymour-Smith. Hutchinson, 1982.

GRAVES, Robert. Robert Graves: The Assault Heroic, 1895-1926. A Biography by Richard Perceval Graves. Weidenfeld and Nicolson, 1986.

GRAVES, Robert. Robert Graves: Life on the Edge. A Biography by Miranda Seymour. Doubleday, 1995.

GREENWELL, Graham, H. An Infant in Arms: War Letters of a Company Officer, 1914-1918. Lovat Dickson & Thompson Ltd., 1935., and Allen Lane, 1972.

GRIFFITH, Llewelyn Wyn. Up to Mametz. Faber & Faber, 1931.

GRIFFITH, Llewelyn Wyn. The Barren Tree and other Poems. Penmark Press, Cardiff, 1947.

HERBERT, A. P. The Bomber Gypsy. Methuen, 1919.

HERBERT, A. P. The Secret Battle. Methuen, 1919 and Oxford University Press paperback 1982.

HERBERT, Alan. A. P. H.: His Life and Times [Autobiography]. Heinemann, 1970.

HERBERT, Sir Alan. A. P. Herbert: A Biography by Reginald Pound. Joseph, 1976.

HITCHCOCK, Captain F. C. "Stand To": A Diary of the Trenches, 1915-1918. Hurst & Blackett, 1937 and Gliddon Books, 1988.

HODGSON, William Noel ['Edward Melbourne']. Verse and Prose in Peace and War. Smith, Elder & Co., 1916.

HODGSON, William Noel. The Gentle Poet. A Biography by Jack Medomsley. Mel Publications, Durham, 1989.

HUEFFER [FORD], Ford Madox. On Heaven and Poems Written on Active Service. John Lane, The Bodley Head, 1918.

HUTCHISON, Graham Seton (Lt-Col), Warrior. Hutchinson, 1932.

HUTCHISON, Graham Seton (Lt-Col). Footslogger. An Autobiography. Hutchinson, 1931.

JONES, David. In Parenthesis. Faber & Faber, 1937 and paperback edition Faber & Faber 1963.

JONES, David. David Jones: A Fusilier at the Front. His Record of the Great War in word and image selected by Anthony Hyne. Seren, 1995.

KETTLE, T. M. Poems & Parodies. Duckworth & Co., 1916.

KETTLE, T. M. The Ways of War: With a Memoir by his wife, Mary S. Kettle. Talbot Press, Dublin, 1917.

KETTLE, T. M. The Enigma of Tom Kettle: Irish Patriot, Essayist, Poet, British Soldier 1880-1916 by J. B. Lyons. Glendale Press, Dublin, 1983.

LEWIS, Cecil. Sagittarius Rising. Peter Davies, 1936 and Greenhill Books, 1993.

LEWIS, Cecil. All My Yesterdays: An Autobiography. Element Books Ltd., 1993.

LIVEING, Edward G. D. Attack: An Infantry Subaltern's Impressions of July 1st 1916. Heinemann 1918, and SPA Books in association with Tom Donovan Military Books, 1986.

MACKINTOSH, E. A. A Highland Regiment. John Lane, The Bodley Head, 1917.

MACKINTOSH, E. A. War, The Liberator and other Pieces. With a Memoir by John Murray. John Lane, The Bodley Head, 1918.

MANNING, Frederic. Eidola. John Murray, 1917.

MANNING, Frederic. (Under his pseudonym Private 19022). Her Privates We. Peter Davies, 1930.

MANNING, Frederic. An Unfinished Life: A Biography by Jonathan Marwic. Duke University Press, North Carolina, 1988.

MIDDLEBROOK, Martin. The First Day on the Somme: 1st July 1916. Allen Lane The Penguin Press, 1971.

MIDDLEBROOK, Martin & Mary. The Somme Battlefields: A Comprehensive Guide From Crecy to the Two World Wars. Viking, 1991.

MILNE, A. A. It's Too Late Now: The Autobiography of a Writer. Methuen, 1939.

MILNE, A. A. A. A. Milne: His Life. A Biography by Ann Thwaite. Faber and Faber, 1990.

PENROSE, Claude L. Poems. Harrison and Sons, 1919.

PLOWMAN, Max. [Under the pseudonym Mark VII]. A Subaltern on the Somme in 1916. J. M. Dent & Sons Ltd., 1927.

PLOWMAN, Max. A Lap full of Seed [Poems]. Blackwells, 1917.

PLOWMAN, Max. Bridge into the Future: Letters of Max Plowman. Andrew Dakers, 1944.

POWELL, Anne (Editor). A Deep Cry: A Literary Pilgrimage to the Battlefields and Cemeteries of First World War British Soldier-Poets Killed in Northern France and Flanders. Palladour Books, 1993.

PUTKOWSKI, Julian and Julian Sykes. Shot at Dawn: Executions in World War One by authority of the British Army Act. Wharncliffe Publishing Limited, 1989.

RICHARDS, Frank. Old Soldiers Never Die. Faber & Faber, 1933 and Philip Austen, 1994.

ROGERSON, Sidney. Twelve Days: The Somme November 1916. Arthur Barker, 1930 and Gliddon Books, 1988.

RORIE, David. A Medico's Luck in the War: Being Reminiscenses of RAMC Work with the 51st (Highland) Division. Milne and Hutchison, Aberdeen, 1929.

SASSOON, Siegfried. Memoirs of a Fox-Hunting Man. Faber & Gwyer, 1928.

SASSOON, Siegfried. Memoirs of an Infantry Officer. Faber & Faber, 1930.

SASSOON, Siegfried. Sherston's Progress. Faber & Faber, 1936.

SASSOON, Siegfried. Siegfried's Journey, 1916-1920. Faber & Faber, 1945.

SASSOON, Siegfried. Diaries: 1915-1918. Edited and introduced by Rupert Hart-Davis. Faber & Faber, 1983.

SASSOON, Siegfried. The War Poems. Arranged and introduced by Rupert Hart-Davis. Faber & Faber, 1983.

SASSOON, Siegfried. Siegfried Sassoon: The making of a War Poet. A Biography by Jean Moorcroft Wilson (To be published 1996).

STEPHEN, Adrian Consett. An Australian in the R.F.A. Penfold, Sydney, 1918.

STEWART, J. E. Grapes of Thorns [Poems]. Erskine Macdonald, 1917.

TENNANT, Edward Wyndham. A Memoir by his Mother, Pamela Glenconner. John Lane, The Bodley Head, 1920.

TENNANT, Edward Wyndham. Bim: A Tribute to Lieutenant, The Honourable Edward Wyndham Tennant by Anne Powell. Palladour Books, 1990.

TERRAINE, John. (Editor). General Jack's Diary 1914-1918: The Trench Diary of Brigadier-General J. L. Jack, D.S.O. Foreword by Sidney Rogerson. Eyre & Spottiswoode, 1964.

VERNEDE, R. E. War Poems and Other Verses. Heinemann, 1917.
VERNEDE, R. E. Letters to his Wife. Collins, 1917.
WEST, Arthur Graeme. The Diary of a Dead Officer: Being the Posthumous Papers of Arthur Graeme West. Allen & Unwin [1918] and Imperial War Museum (Arts and Literature Series Number 3), 1991.
WINTERBOTHAM, Cyril William. Poems. Privately Printed [1917].

ANTHOLOGIES

For Remembrance: Soldier Poets Who Have Fallen In The War. By A. St. John Adcock. Revised and Enlarged edition. Hodder and Stoughton [1920].
Lads: Love Poetry of the Trenches. Edited by Martin Taylor. Constable, 1989.
Never Such Innocence: A New Anthology of Great War Verse. Edited and introduced by Martin Stephen. Buchan & Enright, 1988.
Poetry of the Great War: An Anthology. Edited by Dominic Hibberd and John Onions. With an Introduction, Notes and Biographical Outlines. Macmillan 1986.
Promise of Greatness: The 1914-18 War: A Memorial Volume for the Fiftieth Anniversary of the Armistice. Foreword by Sir Herbert Read. Edited by George A. Panichas. Cassell 1968.
The Lost Voices of World War I. An International Anthology of Writers, Poets and Playwrights. Edited by Tim Cross. Bloomsbury, 1988.
The Penguin Book of First World War Poetry. Edited by Jon Silkin. Penguin Books, 1979.
The Penguin Book of First World War Prose. Edited by Jon Glover & Jon Silkin. Viking, 1989.
Up the Line to Death: The War Poets 1914-1918. An Anthology selected and arranged with an introduction and notes by Brian Gardner. Foreword by Edmund Blunden. Methuen & Co., 1964.
Vain Glory: A miscellany of the Great War 1914-1918 written by those who fought in it on each side and on all fronts. Edited with an introduction by Guy Chapman, OBE., MC. Cassell, 1937.
Wales on the Western Front. Edited by John Richards. University of Wales Press, Cardiff, 1994.
War Letters of Fallen Englishmen. Edited by Laurence Housman. Gollancz, 1930.

I have also consulted the appropriate Battalion Diaries at the Public Records Office and various relevant Regimental and Divisional histories.

FURTHER RECOMMENDED READING

BARING, M. R.F.C. H.Q. 1914-1918. Bell and Sons, 1920.
BUCHAN, John. The Battle of the Somme. Nelson, 1916.
BLAKER, Richard. Medal Without Bar. [A Novel]. Hodder and Stoughton, 1930.
CECIL, Hugh. The Flower of Battle: British Fiction Writers of the First World War. Secker & Warburg, 1995.

CHARLTON, Peter. Australians on the Somme, Pozières 1916. Leo Cooper, 1986.

CRUTCHLEY, C. E. (Compiler and Editor). Machine-Gunner 1914-1918: personal Experiences of the Machine Gun Corps. Bailey Brothers and Swinfen, 1975.

DAWSON, Captain A. J. Somme Battle Stories. Illustrated by Captain Bruce Bairnsfather. Hodder and Stoughton, 1916.

DUGMORE, A. R. When the Somme Ran Red. Doran, New York, 1918.

DUNN, Captain J. C. The War the Infantry Knew 1914-1919: A Chronicle of Service in France and Belgium. New Introduction by Keith Simpson. Jane's Publishing Company, 1987.

EDMUNDS, G. B. Somme memories: memoirs of an Australian artillery driver, 1916-1919. Stockwell, 1955.

FARRAR-HOCKLEY, A. The Somme. Batsford 1964.

FORD MADOX FORD. Some Do Not. [A Novel]. The first in the 'Tietjens' saga. Duckworth, 1924.

FORD MADOX FORD. No More Parades. [A Novel]. the second in the 'Tietjens' saga. Duckworth, 1925.

FORD MADOX FORD. A Man Could Stand Up. [A Novel]. The third in the 'Tietjens' saga. Duckworth, 1926.

FORD MADOX FORD. Last Post. [A Novel]. The fourth in the 'Tietjens' saga. Duckworth, 1928.

FORD MADOX FORD. Parade's End. (Combined edition of the four 'Tietjens' novels). Penguin Modern Classics, 1982.

FORD MADOX FORD. A Biography by Alan Judd. Collins, 1990.

FRANKAU, Gilbert. Peter Jackson Cigar Merchant: A Romance of Married Life [A Novel]. Hutchinson, 1920.

GARDNER, Brian. The Big Push: A Portrait of the Battle of the Somme. Cassell, 1961.

GIBBS, Philip. The Battles of the Somme. Heinemann, 1917.

GILES, John. The Somme Then and Now. Bailey Brothers and Swinfen, 1977.

GIRARD, G. La Bataille de la Somme. Paris, 1937.

GLADDEN, E. N. The Somme, 1916: A Personal Account. Kimber, 1974.

GLIDDON, Gerald. VCs of the First World War: The Somme. Gliddon Books, 1991; Alan Sutton Publishing, 1994.

GRISTWOOD, A. D. The Somme: Including also The Coward. Cape, 1927.

HAIG, Sir Douglas. Sir Douglas Haig's Great Push: The Battle of the Somme. Hutchinson, 1916.

HAIG, Sir Douglas. Sir Douglas Haig's Despatches: December 1915-1919. Dent, 1919.

HAIG, Douglas. Douglas Haig: The educated soldier. A biography by John Terraine. Hutchinson, 1963.

HAIG, Douglas. Haig's Command: A Reassessment by Denis Winter. Viking, 1991.

HARRIS, John. Covenant with Death. [A Novel]. Hutchinson, 1961.

HARRIS, John. The Somme: Death of a Generation. Hodder & Stoughton, 1966.

HENDERSON, Keith. Letters to Helen: Impressions of an Artist on the Western front. Chatto & Windus, 1917.

HUGHES, C. Mametz: Lloyd George's 'Welsh Army' at the Battle of the Somme. Orion Press, 1982.

JOFFRE, Marshal. The Memoirs of Marshal Joffre. Geoffrey Bles, 1932.

JÜNGER, Ernst. The Storm of Steel: From the diary of a German Storm-Troop Officer on the Western Front. Chatto & Windus, 1929.

KABISCHE, E. Somme 1916. Berlin, 1937.

LEWIS, G. H. Wings over the Somme, 1916-1918. Kimber, 1976.

LUDENDORFF, General von. My War Memories 1914-1918. (2 Volumes). Hutchinson, 1919.

MACDONAGH, M. The Irish at the Front. Hodder & Stoughton, 1916.

MACDONAGH, M. The Irish on the Somme: being the second series of 'The Irish at the Front'. Hodder & Stoughton, 1917.

MACDONALD, Lyn. Somme. Michael Joseph, 1983.

MARTIN, C. Battle of the Somme. Wayland, 1973.

MASEFIELD, John. The Old Front Line: Or the beginning of the Battle of the Somme. Heinemann, 1917.

MASEFIELD, John. The Battle of the Somme. Heinemann, 1919.

MAZE, Paul. A Frenchman in Khaki, Heinemann, 1934.

NICHOLSON, G. W. L. The Fighting Newfoundlanders. Government of Newfoundland, 1964.

NORMAN, Terry. The Hell They Called High Wood: The Somme 1916. Kimber, 1984.

ONIONS, John, English Fiction and Drama of The Great War, 1918-39. Macmillan, 1990.

PALMER, F. With the New Army on the Somme: My second year of the War. Murray, 1917.

QUINN, Patrick J. The Great War and the Missing Muse: The early Writings of Robert Graves and Siegfried Sassoon. Associated University Presses, 1994.

ROBINSON, H. P. The Turning Point: The Battle of the Somme. Heinemann, 1917.

TALBOT KELLY, R. B. A Subaltern's Odyssey: memoirs of the Great War 1915-1917. Edited by R. G. Loosmore. Kimber, 1980.

THOMAS, W. Beach. With the British on the Somme. Methuen, 1917.

TILSLEY, W. V. Other Ranks. [A Novel]. With an Introduction by Edmund Blunden. Cobden-Sanderson, 1931.

UYS, I. Delville Wood. Uys, South Africa, 1983.

WILLIAMSON, Henry. The Golden Virgin [A Novel]. Macdonald, 1957.

BIOGRAPHICAL NOTES ON THE AUTHORS

AITKEN, Alexander Craig (1895-1967)

Born in Dunedin, New Zealand. Educated at Otago Boys High School and Otago University. Enlisted in the New Zealand Expeditionary Force in April 1915. Gallipoli with the 6th Infantry Reinforcements November 1915. Commissioned in the 1st Otago Battalion in France in August 1916. Hospital in London recovering from the wound received in September 1916 and invalided home to New Zealand early 1917. Between 1920-1923 taught French and Latin at Otago Boys High School. 1923 Edinburgh University; DSc in 1925. Appointed Professor of Mathematics at Edinburgh University in 1946. Gifted with a phenomenal memory and widely known for his ability at mental calculations; also a linguist, composer, violinist and athlete. Published over 70 papers and 4 books.

ASQUITH, Raymond (1878-1916)

Born in Hampstead, London. Eldest son of H.H. Asquith. Educated at Winchester and Balliol College, Oxford, where he was considered 'the most remarkable figure of his Oxford generation'. First in Classical Moderations, Greats and Law and elected a Fellow of All Souls in 1902. Became a Barrister. International Court at the Hague arbitrating in a Newfoundland fisheries dispute in 1910. Adopted as prospective Liberal candidate for Derby in 1913. Appointed a Junior Counsel to the Inland Revenue in 1914. Joined the Queen's Westminster Rifles in December 1914. Transferred to the 3rd Battalion Grenadier Guards in July 1915. Ypres Salient between October 1915-July 1916 except for four months as Intelligence Officer at General Headquarters at Montreuil. Arrived on the Somme front with his Battalion at beginning of August 1916. Killed at Lesboeufs on 15th September 1916. Buried in Guillemont Road Cemetery, France.

BLUNDEN, Edmund Charles (1896-1974)

Born in London. Educated Christ's Hospital and Queen's College, Oxford (after the War). Commissioned in 11th Royal Sussex Regiment August 1915. Served at Festubert, Cuinchy and Richebourg between May and July 1916. Somme front between August and November 1916. Awarded M.C. 'for conspicuous gallantry in action' in November 1916. Ypres and Passchendaele from December 1916 to December 1917. Professor of English Literature at the Imperial University of Tokyo 1924-1927. Appointed Literary and Assistant Editor of *The Nation* in 1930. Fellow and Tutor in English at Merton College, Oxford between 1931-1942. Professor of English at the University of Hong Kong from 1953 until 1964. A distinguished poet; wrote over 170 books and pamphlets, and made prolific contributions to periodicals, newspapers and books. Created a Companion of Literature in 1962. Professor of Poetry at Oxford between 1966-1968.

BRENAN, Gerald (1894-1987)

Born in Sliema, Malta. Educated at Radley. Commissioned in the 5th Gloucestershire Regiment at the beginning of the War. Seconded to the 48th Divisional Cyclists Company which later merged with VIII Corps Cyclists

Battalion. Served on the Somme front and at Ypres. Wounded at Ypres. Awarded M.C. and Croix de Guerre in 1918. After the War he lived alone in the Alpujarra mountains of southern Spain for four years. Wrote books mostly on Spain, articles and reviews. Appointed CBE in 1982. Lived in England and Spain and died in Malaga.

CARRINGTON, Charles (1897-1990)
Born in West Bromwich, Staffordshire. Went to New Zealand with family as a small child. Educated at Christ's College, New Zealand and Christ Church, Oxford, after the War. Enlisted in 1914. Commissioned in 1/5th Royal Warwickshire Regiment in 1915. Served on the Somme front from July 1916 until May 1917. Awarded M.C. at Passchendaele in 1917. History master at Haileybury from 1921-1924. On staff of Cambridge University Press from 1929-1954, except for the four years of the Second World War, when he served as a Staff Officer liaising between the Army and the RAF. Professor of British Commonwealth Relations at Chatham House between 1954-1962. Broadcast, lectured and wrote on Commonwealth affairs. Amongst other publications "*Rudyard Kipling: His Life and Work*".

COULSON, Frederick Leslie A (1889-1916)
Born at Hendon. Became a journalist and was working as a Reuters' correspondent when war broke out. Refused to apply for a commission as preferred to take his place in the ranks. Enlisted in September 1914 in the 2nd Battalion the London Regiment (Royal Fusiliers). Between December 1914 and April 1916 served in Malta, Gallipoli and Egypt. [qv Geoffrey Dearmer]. Sergeant attached to 12th Battalion on the Somme front from June 1916. Killed during attack on Lesboeufs on 8th October 1916. Buried in Grove Town Cemetery, Méaulte, France.

CROZIER, Frank Percy (1879-1937)
Educated at Wellington College. Served in Boer War and Zulu Rebellions; Canadian Forces 1908-1912. Joined 9th Battalion Royal Irish Rifles as Captain in 1914; Brigadier-General commanding 119th Infantry Brigade November 1916. D.S.O.,(1917), C.M.G., C.B., Croix de Guerre with palme, mentioned in despatches seven times. Commanded 3rd Battalion Welch Regiment 1919. G.O.C. 40th Division (France) March-April 1919. Received further decorations. Served with Lithuanian Army 1919-1920 and later Military Adviser to the Lithuanian Government. Published six books.

DEARMER, Geoffrey (1893)
Born in Lambeth. His father, Percy, was a well-known hymn writer and his mother, Mabel was a novelist, childrens' writer and illustrator. Educated at Westminster and Christ's College, Oxford. Commissioned in September 1914 in 2/2nd Battalion London Regiment (Royal Fusiliers). Served in Malta, Gallipoli and Egypt from December 1914 - April 1916 [qv Leslie Coulson]. Attached to 1/2nd Battalion on Somme front. Transferred to Royal Army Service Corps in August 1916. Mentioned by Secretary of State for valuable war services in August 1919. After the war wrote poetry, plays and novels. Member of the Incorporated Stage Society which was responsible for the first production of R.C. Sherriff's '*Journey's End*' in

1928. Examiner of Plays to the Lord Chamberlain from 1936-1958. Editor of B.B.C's Children's Hour between 1939-1959 and loved by millions of children as 'Uncle Geoffrey'.

DOYLE, Father William Joseph Gabriel, S.J.(1873-1917)
Born at Melrose, Dalkey, Co. Dublin. Educated at Ratcliffe College, Leicestershire. Became a Jesuit Novitiate in 1891. Taught at Clongowes Wood College 1894-1898 and 1901-1903. Studied Philosophy at Enghien, near Brussels and Saint Mary's Hall, Stonyhurst. Teaching and Mission staff of Belvedere College, Dublin 1910-1915. Appointed Chaplain to the 16th Division in November 1915. Arras area February 1916. Somme front August 1916. Awarded M.C. Attached 8th Royal Dublin Fusiliers from December 1916. Battle of Messines and Ypres, 1917. Preached his last Sermon at St. Omer Cathedral to a congregation of 2,500 on 21st July 1917, shortly before the start of the Third Battle of Ypres. Killed, as he gave Absolution to the dying in a battlefield of mud, on 16th August 1917. Dedicated to a life of penance and sacrifice, his sense of humour and compassion gained the love and respect of soldiers of all denominations and ranks. Commemorated on Tyne Cot Memorial to the Missing, Passchendaele, Belgium.

FEILDING, Rowland Charles(1871-1945)
Grandson on 7th Earl of Denbigh. Educated Haileybury and Royal School of Mines. Went to South Africa 1894; Served in Gifford's Horse during the Matabele Rebellion in 1896 and was wounded. Captain in City of London Yeomanry 1914; 1st Battalion Coldstream Guards 1915; arrived in Loos area May 1915; Battle of Loos September 1915; Somme front July-November 1916; Messines area 1917. Member of the Institution of Mining and Metallurgy. Practised as mining engineer in New Zealand, Canada, Ceylon, India, Africa, South America, Russia, Siberia, Scandinavia, Spain, Italy, etc.

GRAVES, Robert von Ranke (1895-1985)
Born in Wimbledon, London. Father, Alfred Perceval, Irish poet and folklorist; maternal grandfather distinguished German doctor; also connected to the German historian Leopold von Ranke. Educated at Charterhouse and St. John's College, Oxford (after the War). Commissioned in the 3rd Battalion Royal Welch Fusiliers in August 1914. Arrived in Northern France in May 1915. Front line trenches at Cuinchy and Laventie; fought during first ten days of Battle of Loos. 2nd Battalion R.W.F., wounded at High Wood in July 1916 and reported dead; after convalescing in England he returned to France in January 1917 but invalided home the following month. Went to live in the village of Deyá in Majorca in 1929 where he wrote poetry and historical novels. Left Majorca at the outbreak of the Spanish Civil War in 1936 and lived in Rennes. Spent the Second World War years in England; his eldest son killed in action in 1943. Returned to Deyá in 1946 with his second wife and continued his prolific literary output. Professor of Poetry at Oxford between 1961-1966; awarded the Queen's Gold Medal for Poetry in 1968; became an Honorary Fellow of St. John's College in 1971. He died in Deyá.

GREENWELL, Graham Hamilton (1896-1988)
Educated at Winchester. Gained a place at Christ Church, Oxford for October 1914 but at the outbreak of the war joined the 4th Battalion Oxfordshire and Buckinghamshire Light Infantry. Ypres sector May 1915; Somme front August 1915-June 1917; Ypres August 1917; Italian front November 1917-November 1918. Oxfordshire and Buckinghamshire Light Infantry 1939-1945; Member of the London Stock Exchange. Deputy Lieutenant of Oxfordshire 1952.

GRIFFITH, Llewelyn Wyn (1890-1977)
Born in Llandrillo-y-Rhos, near Colwyn Bay on the coast of North Wales. Educated at Blaenan Ffestiniog County School and Dolgellau Grammar School where his father was Headmaster. Worked before and after the War in the Inland Revenue. Commissioned in the 15th Battalion Royal Welch Fusiliers; later held various staff posts. Mentioned in despatches for his part in the action at Mametz Wood and later awarded the Croix de Guerre and OBE. His eldest son was killed in action in 1942. Distinguished man of letters and broadcaster. Chairman of the Welsh Arts Council and Vice Chairman of the Arts Council. Honorary doctor in the Universtity of Wales; appointed CBE in 1961.

HERBERT, Alan Patrick (1890-1971)
Born at Elstead, Surrey. Educated at Winchester and New College, Oxford. Gained a First in Jurisprudence in 1914. Sub-Lieutenant in the Hawke Battalion, Royal Naval Division. Gallipoli May 1915. Mentioned in despatches. Imbros January-May 1916. France June 1916. Wounded in France in April 1917 and invalided home. Served on staff of H.M.S. President. Called to the Bar 1918. Staff of *Punch* from 1924. Independent Member of Parliament for Oxford University between 1935-1950. During Second World War served as Petty Officer in the River Emergency Service on the Thames and the Naval Auxiliary Patrol. A champion of minority causes and energetic campaigner who hated injustice and cant. His grim, realistic novel '*The Secret Battle*', led to some improvement in court-martial procedure. Also a humourist and satirist and writer of novels, light verse, musical plays and reviews. Knighted in 1945; Companion of Honour in 1970.

HITCHCOCK, Francis Clere (1896-1972)
Born in Dublin. Educated at Campbell College and Sandhurst Royal Military College. Commissioned in 2nd Battalion Leinster Regiment in 1915. Won M.C. at Battle of Loos. Served in 1st Battalion Leinster Regiment in the Moplar Rebellion, Malabar, India in 1921. 1939-1945 War Office and Military Secretary to G.O.C. Northern Ireland Command and later to G.O.C. Eastern Command. Invalided out of Army in 1947. Appointed a Military Knight of Windsor in 1954; also awarded an O.B.E. Wrote and illustrated books on horses.

HODGSON, William Noel (1893-1916)
Born in Thornbury, Gloucestershire. Father later became the first Bishop of St.Edmondsbury and Ipswich. Educated at Durham School and Christ

Church, Oxford. Gained a First in Classical Moderations in 1913. Commissioned in the 9th Battalion Devonshire Regiment in September 1914. Trenches at Festubert in July 1915. Awarded M.C. during Battle of Loos. Front line trenches at Fricourt and Mametz during Spring 1916. Under the pseudonym 'Edward Melbourne', wrote regular articles on all aspects of life in the trenches for *The Spectator, Saturday Review* and *Yorkshire Post.* Killed on 1st July 1916 in the attack on the village of Mametz. Buried in the Devonshire Cemetery, Mansel Copse, Mametz, France.

HUEFFER, Ford Madox (1873-1939)
Born at Merton, Surrey. Father, a musicologist, a German immigrant. Maternal Grandfather the Pre-Raphaelite painter, Ford Madox Brown. Educated Praetorius School, Folkestone and University College School, London. First book, a fairy story, published at age of eighteen. Editor of *The English Review* 1908-1909. A well-known and established writer with over 40 published books when he was commissioned in the 9th Battalion Welch Regiment in July 1915 at the age of forty-one. Blown up and concussed in August 1916; invalided home March 1917. Changed surname from Hueffer to Ford in 1919. Editor of *Transatlantic Review* 1924-1925. Lived in France and the United States of America from 1922. Died at Deauville in June 1939.

HUTCHISON, Graham Seton (1890-1946)
Born at Inverness, Scotland. Educated at Bradfield and Royal Military College, Woolwich. King's Own Scottish Borderers 1909; served in Egypt, Sudan and India; Staff Officer to Durbar Committee, 1911; Lt. 3rd Battalion Argyll and Sutherland Highlanders 1913. Wounded three times between 1914-1918, awarded M.C., later D.S.O., and mentioned in despatches four times. First Chairman Old Contemptibles Association 1919; A.D.C. and Secretary to British Commissioner, Upper Silesian Commission 1920-1921; arranged Armistice between Korfanty's Polish Insurgents and German Defence Corps, 1921. Liberal candidate for Uxbridge Division 1923; First Principal Shri Shivaji Military School, Poona, 1932; Air Ministry 1939. Landscape painter; 33 books published.

JONES, David (1895-1974)
Born in Brockley, Kent of Anglo-Welsh parents. Educated Camberwell Art School 1909-1914 and Westminster School of Art after the War. Enlisted in 15th Battalion Royal Welch Fusiliers in January 1915; front line trenches Neuve Chapelle early 1916; wounded in Mametz Wood July 1916 and invalided home. Ploegsteert Wood October 1916; Ypres early 1917 and Battle of Pilkem Ridge July 1917; Armentières sector September 1917 until invalided home again with severe trench fever February 1918. His War experiences and his Roman Catholicism influenced his writing and art. In 1927 joined Eric Gill's community at Ditchling, Sussex and later at Capel-y-ffin near Abergavenny in the Black Mountains. Poet, essayist and artist he was made an Honorary Doctor of Literature at the University of Wales; appointed a CBE; and made a Companion of Honour a few months before his death.

KETTLE, Thomas Michael (1880-1916)

Born at Artane, County Dublin. Educated Clongowes Wood College and University College, Dublin. Became a founder member and first President of the Young Ireland Branch of the United Irish League in 1903. Called to the Bar and elected the Irish Parliamentary Party's Member of Parliament for East Tyrone in 1906. A gifted and powerful orator he spoke for Home Rule, the suffragette movement, the oppressed and under privileged, and strongly criticised British imperial administration. In 1909 appointed Professor of National Economics at Dublin University. Resigned his seat at Westminster in 1910. One of the first prominent men to be identified with the Irish Volunteers on their formation in 1913, and travelled widely as recruiting spokesman. Commissioned in the Dublin Fusiliers in November 1914. He was deeply affected by the murder in custody of his brother-in-law, Francis Sheehy-Skeffington, who was involved in the Easter Rising in 1916. Kettle was sent to France three months later and was killed, commanding 'B' Company, during the attack on the village of Ginchy on 9th September 1916. Commemorated on Thièpval Memorial to the Missing, near Albert, France.

LEWIS, Cecil Arthur (1898)

Born in Birkenhead. Educated Dulwich College; University College School and Oundle. Commissioned in the Royal Flying Corps in 1915. Awarded the M.C., and twice mentioned in despatches. Flying Instructor to Chinese Government, Peking 1920-1921. One of the founder members of the B.B.C., and Chairman of B.B.C. Programme Board 1922-1926. Wrote books and radio plays and directed the first two of George Bernard Shaw's plays made into film; received an Oscar for the script of *Pygmalion*. Served in R.A.F. during Second World War. Sheep farming in South Africa 1947-1950. United Nations 1951; radio and television in United States of America and in London between 1953-1956. Staff of *Daily Mail* 1956-1966. Retired to Corfu in 1968 and continued to write books.

LIVEING, Edward G.D. (1895-1963)

Educated at Bradfield and St. John's College, Oxford. Served in France and Palestine during First World War; Assistant to the Military Censor in Egypt 1918-1919. Worked in the B.B.C. between 1924-1937. Established the B.B.C. Cairo office in 1943. A historian and contributor to various magazines.

MACKINTOSH, Ewart Alan (1893-1917)

Born in Brighton, Sussex. Educated at Brighton College, St. Paul's School, and Christ Church, Oxford. Commissioned in the 5th Battalion Seaforth Highlanders in December 1914. Front line opposite Thièpval October 1915. Won M.C. in May 1916 in raid on German trench west of Arras. Wounded and gassed at High Wood in August 1916; joined the 4th Battalion Seaforth Highlanders near Bapaume in October 1917. Killed on the second day of the Battle of Cambrai on 21st November 1917. Buried in Orival Wood Cemetery, Flesquières, France.

MANNING, Frederic (1882-1935)
Born Sydney, Australia. Son of Mayor of Sydney. Arrived in England in
1902. Educated privately. Published first book of poems in 1907. Enlisted in
7th Battalion King's Shropshire Light Infantry in 1915; Arrived on Somme
in August 1916 aged thirty-four. Commissioned in 3rd Battalion Royal Irish
Regiment in July 1917 but resigned his commission because of ill health in
November 1917. After the War lived outside Chobham, Surrey. His
autobiographical-novel *The Middle Parts of Fortune*, based on his war
experiences, was first published anonymously in 1929 in a limited edition of
520 copies; the following year the expurgated edition *Her Privates We* by
Private 19022 was published. Manning's name did not appear on the book
until eight years after his death.

MILNE, Alan Alexander (1882-1956)
Born in Hampstead, London. Educated at Westminster and Trinity College,
Cambridge. Assistant Editor of *Punch* 1906-1914. Although a Pacifist he
was commissioned in the 11th Battalion Royal Warwickshire Regiment in
1915. Joined Battalion on Somme front at end of July 1916; invalided home
with trench fever November 1916; War Office until 1919. Writer of plays,
poetry, novels, short stories, biographies and children's verse and stories.

PENROSE, Claude Quale Lewis (1893-1918)
Born in Florida. Educated at the United Services College; Royal Military
Academy Woolwich 1911-1913. Gazetted to the Royal Garrison Artillery
1913. France November 1914. Mentioned in despatches after attack at
Neuve Chapelle in March 1915. Wounded twice during Battle of the Somme
and awarded the M.C. after the attack on Combles in September 1916.
Promoted Major in October 1917; commanded the 245th Siege Battery in
the Ypres sector; mentioned in despatches in December 1917. Won a Bar to
his M.C. for 'conspicuous gallantry and devotion to duty' during the Allied
retreat in March 1918. Killed near St. Omer on 1st August 1918. Buried in
Esquelbecq Military Cemetery, France.

PLOWMAN, Mark (Max) (1883-1941)
Born at Tottenham, London. Journalist and writer. Served with 4th Field
Ambulance in 1915. Commissioned in 1916. Somme mid-July 1916-January
1917. 1934 Co-Founder with Dick Sheppard of the Peace Pledge Union;
Secretary of the Union 1937-1938. Editor of *The Adelphi Magazine* 1938-
1941.

RICHARDS, Frank (1883-1961)
Born in Monmouthshire. Enlisted in the Royal Welch Fusiliers in 1901.
Served in India and Burma. Left Army 1910 and worked as a timberman's
assistant in a colliery. Volunteered for service in the 2nd Battalion Royal
Welch Fusiliers at beginning of August 1914. Sailed with the British
Expeditionary Force on 10th August 1914. Served throughout the War, and
for his bravery was awarded the D.C.M. and M.M.

ROGERSON, Sidney (1894-1968)
Born Bury St Edmunds, Suffolk. Educated at Worksop College and Sidney
Sussex College, Cambridge. Commissioned in 3rd Battalion West Yorkshire

Regiment in August 1914. Part of reinforcements sent from England to the 2nd Battalion which had suffered very heavily on 1st July 1916. Adjutant to Lt. Col. J.L. Jack; Promoted to Captain in February 1917 and took part in the follow-up during the German retreat to the Hindenburg Line; served at Divisional Headquarters 1917-1918; returned to Battalion as Adjutant; demobbed 1919. Career in Public Relations after the War with the Federation of British Industries and later with ICI; 1952-1954 on loan to the Army Council as Publicity and Public Relations Adviser. Wrote several books.

RORIE, David (1867-1946)
Born in Edinburgh. Educated at Aberdeen Collegiate School and Aberdeen and Edinburgh Universities. Served on the Western Front from May 1915 until the end of the War. Awarded the D.S.O., 1917; Officer of the Order of St. John of Jerusalem; Chevalier de la Légion d'Honneur. Chairman Aberdeen Medical Board; President, Aberdeen Branch, B.M.A., 1932. Published books and papers on Folk Lore and Folk-Medicine.

SASSOON, Siegfried (1886-1967)
Born Weirleigh, Near Paddock Wood, Kent. Educated Marlborough and Clare College, Cambridge. Enlisted as a trooper in the Sussex Yeomanry in August 1914. Commissioned in Royal Welch Fusiliers in May 1915. Joined 1st Battalion at Béthune in November 1915. Won M.C.for action at Fricourt in May 1916. Invalided home with trench fever August 1916. Joined 2nd Battalion on Somme front March 1917 and wounded one month later. Craiglockhart War Hospital, Edinburgh, June-November 1917. July 1917 his statement against the continuation of the War read out in the House of Commons; later threw his M.C. ribbon into the River Mersey. Palestine with 25th Battalion Royal Welch Fusiliers February 1918. Abbeville area, north-west of Amiens May 1918. Wounded in head and invalided home July 1918. Retired from Army 1919. After the War became Literary Editor of *The Daily Herald*. A prolific writer of poetry; memoirs; biographies. Appointed C.B.E. in 1951. Became a Roman Catholic in 1957.

STEPHEN, Adrian Consett (1892-1918)
Born Sydney, Australia. Educated Sydney Grammar School and St. Paul's College, University of Sydney. Wrote four short plays, edited two University magazines, and was a member of the University Drama Society. Graduated in Law in 1915. Commissioned in the Royal Field Artillery in 1915. Arrived in France in August 1915. Promoted to acting Major in command of a Battery 1917. Mentioned in despatches May 1917; awarded Croix de Guerre avec palme June 1917 and M.C. four months later. Made numerous contributions to the *Sydney Morning Herald* covering all aspects of life on the Western Front. Killed near Zillebeke 14th March 1918. Buried in La Clytte Military Cemetery, Belgium.

STEWART, John Ebenezer (1889-1918)
Born at Coatbridge, near Glasgow. Educated at Glasgow University. Taught at Langloan School, Coatbridge. Enlisted in the Highland Light Infantry August 1914. Commissioned in the 8th Battalion Border Regiment October

1914. Trenches in Ypres sector October 1915-January 1916. Front line trenches south of Thièpval July 1916. Commanded 'D' Company during an attack on Regina Trench on Pozières Ridge October 1916. Ypres sector December 1916. Awarded M.C. 'for consistently good work' January 1917. Wounded during Battle of Messines June 1917. As a twenty-nine year old Lieutenant-Colonel took over command of 4th Battalion South Staffordshire Regiment in April 1918. Killed in counter-attack at Kemmel Hill on 26th April 1918. Commemorated on Tyne Cot Memorial to the Missing, Passchendaele, Belgium.

TENNANT, The Hon. Edward Wyndham (1897-1916)
Born at Stockton House, and moved to Wilsford House, Wiltshire at the age of nine. Educated at Winchester. Commissioned in 4th Battalion Grenadier Guards in August 1914. Became a Company Commander, aged eighteen, in September 1915, during the Battle of Loos. Ypres sector March 1916. Somme front August 1916. Wrote poetry from childhood and throughout the year he served in the trenches until he was killed in action on 22nd September 1916. Buried in Guillemont Road Cemetery, France.

VERNEDE, Robert Ernest (1875-1917)
Born in London of French Huguenot descent. Educated at St. Paul's School and St. John's College, Oxford. Four novels and two travel books published between 1905-1911. Enlisted aged thirty-nine in 19th Battalion Royal Fusiliers. Commissioned in the 5th Battalion in May 1915. Ypres Salient, attached to the 3rd Battalion The Rifle Brigade November 1915. Somme area August 1916 and wounded at Delville Wood one month later. Joined the 12th Battalion at Maricourt in January 1917; Died of wounds received from German machine-gun fire while on patrol in the Havrincourt Wood area on 9th April 1917. Buried in Lebucquière Communal Cemetery Extension, France.

WEST, Arthur Graeme (1891-1917)
Born in Warwickshire. Educated at Blundells and Balliol College, Oxford. Enlisted in the 16th Public Schools Battalion, Middlesex Regiment in January 1915. Trenches east of Béthune November 1915 and at Beuvry February 1916. Officers Training Camp in Scotland March-August 1916. Commissioned in the 6th Battalion Oxfordshire and Buckinghamshire Light Infantry. Joined the Battalion in billets at Corbie in September 1916 and remained on the Somme front until March 1917. A convinced Pacifist he corresponded with Bertrand Russell from the trenches and billets. Killed on 3rd April 1917 at Barastre, south-east of Bapaume, during the follow-up of the German retreat to the Hindeburg Line. Buried in the HAC Cemetery, Ecoust-St.Mein, France.

WINTERBOTHAM, Cyril William (1887-1916)
Educated at Cheltenham College and Lincoln College, Oxford. Called to the Bar in 1911. Adopted as prospective Liberal Candidate for East Gloucestershire in 1913. Commissioned in the 1st/5th Battalion Gloucestershire Regiment October 1914. Trenches at Hébuterne, north of Albert, over Christmas 1915. Killed in command of 'C' Company in an

attack on a German trench near Ovillers on 27th August 1916. Commemorated on the Thièpval Memorial to the Missing, near Albert, France.

YOUNG, Arthur Conway (1890-1917)
Educated at City of London School. On Staff of Japan Chronicle, Kobe. Commissioned in 4th Battalion Royal Irish Fusiliers. Served with 7th Battalion on the Somme. Killed in Flanders on 16th August 1917. Buried in Tyne Cot Military Cemetery, Passchendaele, Belgium.

We have been unable to trace any biographical details for Giles Eyre.

ACKNOWLEDGEMENTS

I would like to thank the following who have kindly given permission to reprint copyright material.

Mrs. Margaret Mott. For extracts from *Gallipoli to the Somme: Recollections of a New Zealand Infantryman* by her father, Alexander Aitken. Oxford University Press, 1963.

The Hon. John Jolliffe. For extracts from *Raymond Asquith: Life and Letters*, Collins 1980.

Mrs. Claire Blunden and Harper Collins Publishers Ltd. For prose extracts and the poems *Escape, Preparations for Victory, At Senlis Once*, and *The Ancre at Hamel: Afterwards*, from *Undertones of War* by Edmund Blunden, Collins 1965; *Thièpval Wood* and *Premature Rejoicing* from *The Poems of Edmund Blunden: 1914-1930*, Cobden-Sanderson 1930.

Penguin Books Ltd. For extracts from *A Life of One's Own: Childhood and Youth* by Gerald Brenan. Hamish Hamilton, 1962.

Mr. Geoffrey Dearmer. For his two poems *Gommecourt* and *The Somme*, from *Poems* by Geoffrey Dearmer, Heinemann, 1918.

The Medici Society Limited, London. For extracts from *War Letters to a Wife: France and Flanders, 1915-1919* by Rowland Feilding, The Medici Society Ltd., 1929.

Mr. William Graves and Carcanet Press Limited. For extracts from *Good-bye To All That* by Robert Graves, Cape 1931; and for two poems *A Dead Boche* and *Bazentin 1916*, from *Poems About War* by Robert Graves, edited by William Graves, Cassell 1988.

Penguin Books Ltd. For extracts from *An Infant in Arms: War Letters of a Company Officer, 1914-1918* by Graham H. Greenwell, Lovat Dickson, 1935. Reprinted with an Introduction and Note by John Terraine, Allen Lane, The Penguin Press 1972.

Mr. E.A. Creighton Griffiths. For the poem *The Song is Theirs* from *The Barren Tree and other Poems* by Llewelyn Wyn Griffith, Penmark Press, Cardiff, 1947.

A.P. Watt Ltd. on behalf of Crystal Hale and Jocelyn Herbert. For the poem *Beaucourt Revisited* from *The Bomber Gypsy and other Poems* by A.P. Herbert, Methuen 1919; and for an extract from *The Secret Battle* by A.P. Herbert, Methuen 1919.

David Higham Associates. For the poem *The Iron Music* from *On Heaven and Poems written on Active Service* by Ford Madox Hueffer, John Lane, The Bodley Head, 1918.

Faber and Faber Limited. For extracts from *In Parenthesis* by David Jones, Faber & Faber, 1937.

Mr. Cecil Lewis and Greenhill Books, Lionel Leventhal Limited. For extracts from *Sagittarius Rising* by Cecil Lewis, Greenhill Books, 1993.

John Murray (Publishers) Ltd. For the poems *The Face, Transport, Grotesque, The Trenches, A Shell* and *Relieved* from *Eidola* by Frederic Manning, John Murray 1917.

Excerpts from *It's Too Late Now: The Autobiography of a Writer* copyright 1939 A.A. Milne, copyright renewal 1967 by Daphne Milne, reproduced by permission of Curtis Brown, London.

ACKNOWLEDGEMENTS

Mrs. Greta Plowman. For two poems *Going into the Line* and *The Dead Soldiers* from *A Lap Full of Seed* by Max Plowman, Blackwells 1917.

The Orion Publishing Group Ltd. For extracts from *A Subaltern on the Somme in 1916* by Mark VII (Max Plowman), J.M. Dent, 1927.

Mr. George Sassoon. For permission to quote four poems *At Carnoy, A Night Attack, To his Dead Body* and *Aftermath* from *The War Poems of Siegfried Sassoon.* Arranged and introduced by Rupert Hart-Davis, Faber and Faber, 1983.

Faber and Faber Limited. For extracts from *Memoirs of an Infantry Officer* by Siegfried Sassoon, Faber & Faber 1930; and *Siegfried Sassoon: Diaries 1915-1918* edited by Rupert Hart-Davis, Faber and Faber, 1983.

Arthur Conway Young's letter to his Aunt was first published in *War Letters of Fallen Englishmen.* Edited by Laurence Housman, Gollancz 1930.

Every effort has been made to trace all copyright holders and we apologise to anyone who inadvertently has not been acknowledged.

I am very grateful to the following for their help in numerous ways:

Mr. Philip Austen; Mr. Trevor Craker; Mr. Stephen Clarke, Clearwater Books; Captain Garth de Courcy-Ireland, R.N. (Rtd)., Mr. Tom Donovan; The Dowager Countess of Denbigh; The Hon. Mrs. Basil Feilding; Mr. Gerald Gliddon; Miss Lucy Homfray; the staff of the Imperial War Museum, particularly from the Printed Books and Documents Departments, and the Photographic Department; Mr. and Mrs. Anthony Laurence; Major (Rtd) J.N. McConnell, Curator, The Royal Irish Fusiliers Regimental Museum; Liz Powell, Editor, University of Wales Press; the staff of the Public Records Office, Kew; Professor Patrick Quinn; Professor Elmer Rees, Department of Mathematics and Statistics, Edinburgh University; Mr. Robin Reeves, Editor, The New Welsh Review; Lt. Colonel R.J.M. Sinnett; Dr. David Sutton, Writers and Their Copyright Holders (WATCH), University of Reading; Mr. Martin Taylor; Paula Thomson, The Haileybury Society; Mr. Nick Wetton; Dr. Jean Moorcroft Wilson; Mr. Paul Woolhouse, Commonwealth War Graves Commission; and the ladies of Aberporth and Cardigan Women's Institute for sustaining us with many delicious meals.

I am especially indebted to three friends:

Gill Hiley for her patience and guidance throughout the various stages of decision-making over her cover design; Alan Jeffreys, the Department of Printed Books, Imperial War Museum, for his enthusiastic support and the valuable research he has undertaken on my behalf; and Brian Turner for much helpful information.

My final thanks are to all my lovely and ever-increasing family.

To my children and children-in-law, Jonathan and Sarah; Rupert and Clare; and Lucinda and Andrew, who have never been too busy to give me every encouragement, loving support and many hours of practical help.

As always my never-ending thanks are to Jeremy, the back-bone of Palladour Books. His quiet efficiency, sense of humour, infinite patience, comfort and love, have never failed throughout all the many phases in the preparation of *The Fierce Light*.

INDEX